HISTORY AND HOPE IN THE HEART OF DIXIE

the MODERN SOUTH

series editors
Glenn Feldman & Kari Frederickson

History and Hope in the Heart of Dixie

Scholarship, Activism, and Wayne Flynt in the Modern South

Edited by
GORDON E. HARVEY, RICHARD D. STARNES,
AND GLENN FELDMAN

THE UNIVERSITY OF ALABAMA PRESS
Tuscaloosa

Publication of *History and Hope in the Heart of Dixie* has been made possible in part by a grant from the History Department of Auburn University.

Typeface: ACaslon

Cataloging-in-Publication Data is available from the Library of Congress

ISBN-13: 978-0-8173-1507-8 (cloth)
ISBN-13: 978-0-8173-5320-9 (paper)
E-ISBN-13: 978-0-8173-8195-0 (electronic)

Contents

Editors' Introduction

"You don't love because," William Faulkner once wrote. "You love despite; not for the virtues, but despite the faults." For Wayne Flynt, an abiding love for his state and region has not prevented his recognizing the inequities and despair that define southern life for so many. As a scholar, he traced the contours of southern political history, documented the lives of poor whites, and helped to bring southern religious history to center stage. But, unlike so many historians, Flynt has not been content to confine his attentions to matters historical. For this scholar, teacher, and preacher—roles that were rarely mutually exclusive—history is a way to inform, to, in his words, "hold up a mirror" to southerners asking them to consider the past and its contemporary implications. Beyond academe, he has emerged as one of Alabama's most articulate social critics and voices of reform, a respected and often controversial leader in causes ranging from childhood poverty to public health to equitable taxation. Although once rumored to be a Cuban agent smuggled into the country to integrate the First Baptist Church of Tallahassee, Flynt spent his life in the South and most of it in his beloved Alabama.

In his 1992 presidential address to the American Historical Association, William E. Leuchtenberg explored the relationship of the historian and public engagement. He noted the tensions between scholars who become involved in public policy matters and those who choose to remain more isolated from contemporary concerns. Leuchtenberg found merit in both positions and concluded by encouraging historians to blend their scholarship and activism while at the same time cautioning them to maintain their analytical detachment.[1] Historians have long used their research as a means of trying to improve their present. From Charles Beard, Herbert Baxter Adams, John

Hope Franklin, and C. Vann Woodward to Morgan Kousser, Allan Licht-
man, and Michael Kelly, historians throughout the twentieth century have
served the dual role of historian and public advocate, whether on issues ranging from women's suffrage to economic reforms to voting rights and disfranchisement.

Wayne Flynt is a vocal advocate of such interaction between historians
and the world in which they live. From his ivory pulpit, he spoke loud and
often of the need for education reform and a revised state constitution, and
for a state to care enough about itself to make hard choices that might result
in temporary discomfort in order to establish fundamental change. To be
sure, critics of Flynt's public advocacy abound, from colleagues in the profession to the Alabama Farm Bureau Federation to members of his university's
Board of Trustees to those who believe that increased funding cannot cure all
ills. He remains eloquent and prophetic to some, wrongheaded and naive to
others, but he casts a long shadow as both a scholar and a reformer.

As a scholar, Flynt's research opened new ways of looking at the South's
past. His biographies of Florida politicians Duncan Upshaw Fletcher and
Sydney Catts, both of which were praised by reviewers for what they revealed about southern Progressives, linked politics, religion, and a southern
reform ethos. His next book explored a topic closer to heart and home—the
South's poor whites. Published in 1979, *Dixie's Forgotten People: The South's
Poor Whites* garnered praise for filling what had become a great chasm in
southern historiography. Unlike anyone since Frank L. Owsley, Wayne Flynt
moved poor whites to the center of the region's historical narrative, giving scholars a rare insight into their meager yet complicated lives. Although
criticized by Bill C. Malone for "vague terminology" and "hazy conceptualiza-
tion," Flynt's work nonetheless received praise for its sympathetic, but not
uncritical, treatment of this overlooked segment of society.[2] Flynt may have
been criticized for a not quite complete definition and portrayal of just who
was a southern poor white, but no one criticized him for his fairness. Although sympathetic to his fellow poor white, Flynt nonetheless did not hesi-
tate to provide a "cold-eyed view of their racism and their violence."[3]

In 1989, Flynt published his most important work. When a young undergraduate student with an interest in the historical profession asked Flynt
how long it took him to produce it, Flynt responded dryly, "twenty-five
years." But, in reality he had worked on *Poor but Proud: Alabama's Poor Whites*
since his childhood, steeped in the reality of growing up poor in Alabama. In
exploring the occupations, religious beliefs, and culture of Alabama's poor
whites, Flynt asserted that poverty was the most consistent theme in Ala-

bama's history. The state's poor whites were resilient, sectarian, and bitterly racist, but they maintained their dignity through decades of poverty by close familial ties and a distinct, vibrant culture. The book earned Flynt a number of awards and the praise of fellow historians for producing a sympathetic but not uncritical examination of a "forgotten" people.[4]

Following the success of *Poor but Proud,* Flynt continued his exploration of Alabama history, and with Leah Atkins, William Warren Rogers, and Robert David Ward, coauthored *Alabama: The History of a Deep South State.* The first comprehensive history of the state in sixty years, this book filled a large historical chasm in that it finally addressed equitably the story of Alabama Indians, African Americans, and women.[5]

If *Poor but Proud* was Flynt's examination of his people, *Alabama Baptists: Southern Baptists in the Heart of Dixie* was an inquiry into his faith. From the denomination's establishment to its rise as a dominant group in the state, Flynt's study reveals that as the Baptists of all races and creeds tried to shape the world in which they lived, for in the name of Christ they too were recast by such outside events as secession, Civil War, and emancipation to redemption, Progressivism, segregation, integration, and the culture wars of the modern era. Aimed at Baptists and non-Baptists alike, the book offered Flynt's fellow Baptists a fair but critical look at themselves, while providing for non-Baptists and fellow scholars a detailed study of the South's largest denomination. As he had with poor whites, Flynt tried to move southern historians toward the region's religious history as a way of better understanding the South and its people.[6]

As the last book published before his retirement, *Alabama in the Twentieth Century* might be considered his farewell address to the state. "Alabama," he wrote in the preface, "is like a disease. Once it infects a person, it is hard to cure the ailment. Every time I thought I had obtained a cure, I experienced a relapse." In an unconventional format, the book traces the state's modern era topically rather than chronologically within three large sections: political economy, society, and culture. Beginning with the infamous and much-lamented 1901 constitution and including sports as a window into Alabamians' best and worst characteristics, *Alabama in the Twentieth Century* does not seek so much to mark new historiographical ground as it does to delineate what may be the most tumultuous century in the state's history and to provide Alabamians some insight as to why their state seems to struggle with itself so much. It is history, political commentary, social critique, and prophecy, blended together in accessible style.

These essays further with original scholarship the themes and subjects

Flynt explored in his own work: religious history, southern political history, and the experience of the region's downtrodden and powerless. The authors use ideas and topics central to Wayne's work as points of departure in their essays, providing new views on important aspects of the southern historical experience. Brooks Blevins and Susan Youngblood Ashmore open the volume with considerations of the region's poor. Blevins examines race relations between Arkansas hill country whites and blacks and finds the existence of a peaceful relationship primarily because local African Americans did not challenge the area's racial mores. Ashmore provides a legislative history of one of Lyndon Johnson's main weapons in the War on Poverty, the Economic Opportunity Act of 1964, and the political tension that developed over its passage as southern politicians saw the act as a civil rights bill in disguise. Richard D. Starnes builds on Flynt's controversial ideas concerning the link between southern Protestantism and Progressive-era social reform. Examining Baptists in North Carolina, he finds that not only did these believers develop a powerful brand of social Christianity, but as a group they played an essential role in shaping North Carolina's reform ethos and reputation as the South's most progressive state. Andrew M. Manis explores the origins of interracialism in Macon, Georgia, in the 1930s and asserts its roots in religious motivations. Glenn Feldman, Gordon Harvey, and Jeff Frederick explore the dynamic nature of twentieth-century Alabama politics by drawing on themes such as interest group politics and the failure of reform. Feldman chronicles the collapse of an unsteady New Deal coalition in the South in the face of attacks from conservatives, specifically Alabama's Big Mule/Planter alliance, who argued that the New Deal was radical, even communist, in nature. Harvey analyzes the 1970 Democratic gubernatorial primary contest between Albert Brewer and George Wallace as a failure of voters to move beyond race in order to embrace progressive reforms in education, economic development, and government. Jeff Frederick traces the role of interest groups such as the Farm Bureau in stifling efforts aimed at improving the lives of those at the bottom of society.

Any attempt to assess Wayne's influence must consider his work as a social reformer. Two essays by fellow reformers trace his roles in social causes close to his heart—equity in school funding and constitutional reform—allowing an interesting, informative glimpse into both his reform efforts and, more generally, the scholar as activist. These essays depart from the standard scholarly essay and serve as reform memoirs from those Flynt worked closest with in exacting change in Alabama. In conclusion, two seasoned observers of southern history and culture—John Shelton Reed and Dan T. Carter—

provide the volume's foreword and afterword and, along the way, offer their assessments of Wayne's influence on the historical profession and the region he loves.

The irony of a work like this is that it cannot do justice to the central role in Wayne's professional career, that of professor. It is easy for scholars, particularly those at research universities, to give teaching only cursory attention as they pursue their research agendas. Wayne chose a different path. Since 1990, he has served as a Distinguished University Professor at Auburn University. Even with perquisites such as a personal travel budget and a low teaching load, Wayne chose to teach courses above and beyond those required by his rank. It was in those classes that most of his students had their first formative Flynt experience. Known for his tough professorial love, his free-flowing editorial pens, his rapier-like use of the Socratic method, and his heartfelt loyalty and support, Wayne shaped and molded large numbers of graduate students who went on to appreciate his passion for the real-life implications of the history that they wrote. It is because he was a teacher of the highest order, in his classroom and by his example, that we honor his life and work.

Notes

1. William E. Leuchtenberg, "The Historian and the Public Realm," *American Historical Review* 97, 1 (February 1992):1–18.

2. Malone criticized Flynt for myopia in defining the southern poor white. Flynt, he wrote, seemed to gravitate more toward the Appalachian poor white and away from the poor white Cajuns or Texans. And of Flynt's assertion that the South was the "most ethnically homogenous region of America," Malone responded by asking if Flynt had forgotten "blacks, Indians, Chicanos, continental Europeans, Cajuns, and assorted mixed breeds?" Bill Malone, review of *Dixie's Forgotten People: The South's Poor Whites,* by Wayne Flynt, *Journal of American History* 67, 2 (September 1980):382–83.

3. James A. Hodges, in his review of *Dixie's Forgotten People: The South's Poor Whites,* by Wayne Flynt, *Journal of Southern History* 46 (November 1980):587–88, viewed it not only as a tool to aid southern African Americans but as a means of placating white southerners.

4. Durwood Dunn, review of *Poor but Proud: Alabama's Poor Whites,* by Wayne Flynt, *American Historical Review* 96 (February 1991):267–68; Paul Mertz, review of *Poor but Proud, Journal of Southern History* 57 (May 1991):366–67; Thomas Terrill, review of *Poor but Proud, Journal of American History* 77 (December 1990):1021.

5. J. Barton Starr, review of *Alabama: The History of a Deep South State,* by Wayne Flynt, *Journal of American History* 82 (September 1995):713–14; Sarah Woolfolk Wiggins, review of *Alabama, Journal of Southern History* 62 (February 1996):189–90; Michael Fitzgerald, review of *Alabama, American Historical Review* 101 (February 1996):236–37.

6. Randy Sparks, review of *Alabama Baptists: Southern Baptists in the Heart of Dixie,* by Wayne Flynt, *Journal of American History* 86 (September 1999):747–48.

HISTORY AND HOPE IN THE HEART OF DIXIE

I

Can Any Good Thing Come from Auburn?

John Shelton Reed

A few years ago Russell Jacoby lamented what he saw as the disappearance of the sort of old-fashioned intellectual "who write[s] with vigor and clarity . . . for the general reader." In his book *The Last Intellectuals,* he argued that such folks have become "as scarce as low rents in New York or San Francisco," replaced by "high-tech intellectuals, consultants and professors— anonymous souls, who may be competent, and more than competent, but who do not enrich public life." One certainly sees his point, but one also sees (at least I do) that he wasn't looking very hard.

Jacoby should get out more. To places like Auburn, Alabama, home of a distinguished public intellectual who has certainly enriched public life in his home state. Jacoby's argument, important and provocative as it is, suffers from what might be called Manhattan myopia. For him and for many other New Yorkers, intellectuals write for "little magazines," not the *Mobile Register* and *Alabama Heritage;* they hold forth in Greenwich Village coffee houses or at the 92nd Street Y, not before the Dothan Rotary Club. These Yankees might well adapt Nathanael's question about Nazareth (John 1:46): "Can any good thing come from Auburn?" To which the answer, of course, is "Sure— and one of them is Wayne Flynt."

Not that Flynt's influence and reputation have been restricted to Alabama. He has spoken at innumerable American colleges and universities, addressed learned symposia in places like Cambridge and Prague and Vienna, and even taken his tales of the American South to audiences in India and the Far East. He has been honored by his peers (most recently with the presidency of the Southern Historical Association), and his achievements as a historian have been well assessed in the preceding introduction.

But few academics of his distinction have been as willing, or able, to engage the citizens of their home place on important issues of the day. Not just in his scholarship but in his public life, Flynt has followed the advice of another great Alabamian and cast down his bucket where he is—with remarkable results. He has been tirelessly active, addressing the meetings and sitting on the boards of groups with names like the Campaign for Alabama, the Alabama Poverty Project, Voices for Alabama's Children, the American Cancer Society's Committee for the Socioeconomically Disadvantaged, and Alabama Citizens for Constitutional Reform.

No doubt he is greatly in demand as a speaker partly because he has that "command of the vernacular" that Jacoby believes most American intellectuals have lost. Listen to him tell an interviewer about the pleasures of creek fishing: "The formula is simple: Find a small Appalachian river or creek. Seine your own bait. Walk in the creek if possible. If not, use a canoe. Never fish a lake. Never ride in a boat with a motor." Even someone who prefers high-tech bass fishing with electronic fish-finders, or who doesn't fish at all, can savor those words.

The same gift accounts for the fact that apparently every American newspaper you've ever heard of, and a good many you haven't, have called him for comment on various issues. He usually obliges with something pithy and true. (As one newspaperman I know would put it, he "gives good quote.") When Alabama repealed its antimiscegenation law, for instance, he told *USA Today* simply, "A lot of white folks want to turn the page."

But Flynt has a well-deserved reputation not just for plain speech but for hard truths. As an Auburn alumni newsletter put it, "If you want an after-dinner speaker who'll lull you into sweet dreams of the Old South, don't invite Auburn University Historian Wayne Flynt." Flynt plainly loves his state and its citizens but often with the wry realism of Zora Neale Hurston, who was known for saying with exasperation, "My people, my people." It speaks well for Alabama that the invitations to address civic clubs, public libraries, and community forums keep pouring in.

More than invitations, in fact. Flynt's career seems to contradict what Jesus had to say (Mark 6:4) about prophets' being without honor in their own country: His c.v. is littered with prizes and awards from his fellow Alabamians—from the Alabama Library Association, the Alabama Historical Association, the University of Alabama Press, the Children's Hospital of Alabama, the Alabama Arthritis Foundation—the list goes on. The *Mobile Register* named him Alabamian of the Year in 1992, and (perhaps the best indicator of the respect he commands) he was chosen by the governor and

the presiding judge for the thankless job of official "facilitator" in an intermi-
nable lawsuit over equity in the funding of public schools.

Finally, Flynt must be nearly unique among academic advocates of reform
in his willingness to put his money where his mouth is. He endowed the Mae
Ellis Moore Flynt Teaching Excellence Award of the Alabama Association
of Historians, for instance, to reward outstanding K-12 history teachers like
his mother. He has also come up with at least one radical, commonsense
proposal of the sort that I identify with another maverick Baptist, Will
Campbell. When Alabama Baptist churches helped to defeat a state lottery
in support of education, Flynt called on them to give up their tax exemptions
to support local schools—and his own church, Auburn First Baptist, did just
that. "I got tired of all the pious talking and no acting," he said. "Ours is a
traditional, mainline Baptist church with money problems like most Baptist
churches. I figured if we can do it, anybody can do it."

In 2000, Samford University, his alma mater, gave Flynt an honorary
Doctor of Humane Letters degree (along with Wendell Berry, another prophetic voice from the South). The citation described him as "a teacher,
scholar and writer whose high-wattage light has beamed into the darkness
surrounding issues of poverty, race, education and state government." Certainly he has brightened the corner where he is.

Which raises some interesting questions. How can someone, these days,
be such a successful public intellectual in Alabama (I won't say "of all
places")? Why does an accomplished historian and professor devote so much
time and energy to the unrewarding grind of trying to reform his home state?
And—perhaps even more of a puzzle—why do so many Alabamians not just
listen to him but apparently *want* to listen to him?

In part, this may be a regional thing. Jacoby is right that this sort of engagement is rare these days, but it may be less rare in the South than in other
parts of the United States. In his classic study of American race relations, *An
American Dilemma*, Gunnar Myrdal wrote that the southern social scientists
of his time compared favorably to their northern colleagues precisely in that
"statesmanship enters more naturally into [their] writings" and "the signifi-
cance for human happiness of the problems under study is always a present
thought in the South." Just so, listen to Flynt sixty-odd years later, on what
Auburn University should be: "I don't want Auburn to be the Berkeley of the
South; I want Auburn to be the Auburn of the South. I want it to find out
what it can do to make a difference in the lives of the people of this state;
stop worrying about being something we can't be and that most Alabamians
don't want us to be; begin to define who we are and what our mission ought

to be from the perspective of serving the population of this state." Even at Auburn, I'm sure, this is not a popular view among college faculty members these days, but it may get more respect in the South than elsewhere.

There is another reason, though, and a more important one, for Flynt's speaking out and for his receiving a hearing. John Andrew Rice, founder and first rector of North Carolina's Black Mountain College (also, I should note, nephew of both a South Carolina Methodist bishop and Senator Ellison D. "Cotton Ed" Smith, an evangelist of a different stripe), once observed that "If you scratch a Southern teacher, a preacher will wince." In Flynt's case, of course, this is quite literally true. And I think an important component of his visibility and influence is that his social thought comes not from Karl Marx or *The Nation* magazine but straight from the Sermon on the Mount.

When he rebuked Alabama politicians for not addressing the state's high child poverty rate, for example, he reminded them of what Jesus said about "the least of these" (Matthew 25:45). When an interviewer asked him about Alabama's problems, his immediate response was that "Christian love and a sense of justice demand that we remember where we come from and not forget the people we leave behind." (Characteristically, he preached to the unconverted as well, adding, "If we have no sense of Christian charity and no sense of justice, then we sure better do something out of a sense of our own self-interest.")

This sort of rhetoric is not uncommon in Alabama. When Governor Bob Riley—a Republican but also a longtime Sunday school teacher in Ashland's First Baptist Church—claimed that "it is immoral to charge somebody making $5,000 an income tax" and argued for tax reform by saying "We're supposed to love God, love each other and help take care of the poor," the Associated Press, mystified, called Flynt for comment. He explained patiently that Governor Riley was "locating the debate in the Bible and biblical justice to the poor," and he stopped just short of saying "It's a southern thing; you wouldn't understand."

But Flynt understands, and so do most of his fellow Alabamians. He gets a hearing in Alabama because Alabamians are used to being exhorted by preachers, and usually listen politely. Unfortunately, a cynic would say, they're also used to ignoring those exhortations. But at some level maybe they feel a little guilty about that and recognize that they are the better for it.

2

Revisiting Race Relations in an Upland South Community

LaCrosse, Arkansas

Brooks Blevins

Wayne Flynt loves a good story. Anyone who has known him for very long can testify to that. Maybe it's the Baptist preacher in him. Maybe it's the southerner in him. And maybe all southerners have a little bit of Baptist preacher in them. Having read too many lifeless histories, I'm convinced it's not the historian in him. Whatever the reason, Wayne appreciates a good tale, be it fable, anecdote, parable, or just plain yarn. His appreciation for the story has served him well over a long career, whether in the classroom, on the social crusader's trail, or holding a busy pen. In a scholarly path that has been recognized most often for its social history, Wayne's dedication to telling stories—to keeping it personal, to keeping the humanity in history—has consistently infused his narratives with life and vitality.

I feel honored to have played a role in one of Wayne's stories for several years now. It's the story of how he and I came to meet, of how a boy from the Ozarks found his way to Auburn, a place the boy only knew as Bo Jackson's university and a place that he had always thought was in Georgia, not Alabama—a popular misconception, I believe, outside the Southeast. Wayne loves this story. He's told it each time he's had the opportunity to introduce me as a speaker or to slide me into a conversation with old friends. And in that true southern storytelling tradition—in which doctoring a few of the particulars is not so much changing the story as it is making it better— Wayne tells a slightly different version each time. Here's one version of the story.

As a college junior in the spring of 1991, I had the good fortune to take a course on the civil rights movement from Elizabeth "Betsy" Jacoway, who was teaching on a one-year sabbatical replacement at Arkansas (now Lyon)

College, a little Presbyterian, liberal arts school in the foothills of the Ozarks. As a requirement for the course, I completed a research paper, a project in which Betsy had required her students to use both secondary and primary sources and one in which I had taken the interpretations of a few southern historians to task. One of these historians was J. Wayne Flynt, whose *Dixie's Forgotten People: The South's Poor Whites* happened to be on the shelves in our small library. Although I had a big time with the project, I thought little about the paper until late the following summer when I got a package in the mail from Betsy—still Dr. Jacoway to me at the time. Unknown to me, Betsy, undoubtedly amused by her student's temerity in hunting large prey, had given a copy of my paper to Wayne over the summer. (This is the point at which Wayne's story usually takes up.)

The paper itself dealt with race relations in a single Ozark community, a community that I had used as a model for race relations in the highland South in general. The seemingly tranquil race relations found in this particular community had led me to take aim at Wayne, Numan V. Bartley, and whatever other historians I could fish out of the slim stacks at the Arkansas College library who seemed to view southern whites as a monolithic bunch, at least when it came to attitudes toward blacks. Or perhaps my desire to find the antithesis to the common white-black southern story had led me to this particular community. I'll come back to this later. Probably more amused than impressed, Wayne had read the little paper and on the title page had scrawled an encouraging note urging me to explore works on Appalachia for comparison, to continue working on the subject, and to consider applying to Auburn for graduate school.

I did a better job of following Wayne's last suggestion than his first two and, having been accepted to graduate school, made my first trip to see Auburn and to meet Wayne Flynt in the summer of 1992. He didn't remember my name—it turns out that Wayne had met a few folks and read some things in the intervening year—but upon mention of the belligerent paper and Betsy Jacoway, the enthralling memories of the previous summer's preliminary tête-à-tête with the kid from Arkansas came flooding back. My drop-in must have made Wayne's day. But he was polite and engaging to this youngster—ever the southern gentleman, as Betsy had promised.

I always thought Wayne had something to do with my being awarded a graduate assistantship at Auburn, although it may have been just dumb luck on my part. It's still hard to convince me that I got in on my own slim merits. And it's harder still to believe that I never followed up on the topic that had first introduced me to Wayne Flynt, or that Wayne and I never concluded our one-sided debate. I went on to other topics and other things, and I seem to recall that Wayne did too.

Naturally, when the editors of this collection graciously asked me to contribute something, it seemed that this would be the perfect time to revisit the topic that had led me to Auburn and to Wayne in the first place. The question of whether black-white interaction differed substantially—or if white oppression of blacks occurred in differing levels of thoroughness and harshness—in the southern highlands and lowlands had, until the past two decades, gone almost completely unconsidered. Over the past decade or so a handful of prominent historians have shed considerable light on race relations in Appalachia. Yet, in the Ozarks, the subject has never received adequate analysis. This brief essay, unfortunately, will not remedy the situation. I do hope, however, to accomplish a couple of small things: to reconsider my earlier conclusions on race relations in the highland South in general and in the rural Ozarks in particular by taking into consideration other works in southern history and subsequent scholarship focusing on the Ozarks and to analyze the process of historical interpretation by reconsidering my own motives underlying those earlier conclusions.

The motivation for writing the little essay that ultimately brought me to Auburn was a conviction that white residents of the upland South were too often lumped together with lowland whites when it came to the issues of race relations and attitudes toward race. (As a native of the Ozarks, my predisposition to avoid *southern lumping* was perhaps a part of my intellectual heritage.) Like many a young idealistic student from the upland South, I was reasonably positive that race relations in the hills and mountains had been more civil and involved less violence and severe oppression than had race relations in the lowland South, or the "bottoms" as Ozarkers referred to the lowlands. This notion is a product, I believe, both of the age-old sectional debate and struggle within the South and of decades of coming to terms with a heritage that includes slavery, defeat, and racism and the guilt—both self- and superimposed—that comes with that heritage.

In the backs of our minds, upland southerners are proud that there were fewer slave owners and more antisecessionists in the highlands, that parts of East Tennessee were overrun by Unionists, that residents of portions of Appalachia and the Ozarks were among the most divided in their Civil War–era loyalties. It was the plantation owners—those fat-cat slave owners in the lowlands—who dragged the South into the war. It was the denizens of the Deep South, we say, who were to blame. Likewise, it stands to reason then— through an admittedly twisted interpretation—that the upland New South, the place where one was most likely to find scalawag Republicans and less likely to find large numbers of freedmen, would somehow have been for blacks a less dangerous and oppressive place, an eminently more livable place, than would have the lowland New South. Does it not seem that this would be true? And if it were true, would this not be a soothing psychological balm for the upland southerner? Not only were we in the upland South not responsible for the war that still haunts southern society, but we treated our black neighbors better than they did in the lowland South.

That last statement, which still carries weight within the popular if not scholarly imagination of the upland South, has roots that extend at least as far back as the middle of the nineteenth century. Traveling in the Southeast in the 1850s, Frederick Law Olmsted observed that in the mountains, "the direct moral evils of slavery . . . are less—even less proportionately to the number of slaves." Highland slaves' "habits more resemble those of ordinary free laborers," he wrote, "and both in soul and intellect they are more elevated."[1]

The most important literary foundations for the perception that race relations were more benign in the highlands focused not on the treatment of blacks by whites, however, but on the supposed absence of blacks in the region. In the late nineteenth and early twentieth centuries—the era of the "discovery" of Appalachia by missionaries, local color writers, and other newcomers—a number of writers "enshrined the stereotype of nearly all-white, antislavery Appalachia." Historians James C. Klotter and Nina Silber have both argued that it was the highland South's supposed lack of black residents that appealed to northern philanthropists, missionaries, and social workers, which in turn helped foster the "pervasive mythology" of the highlanders' "unadulterated Unionism, pure and upstanding patriotism, and undiluted racial purity." In his influential *The Southern Highlander and His Homeland,* John C. Campbell informed his mostly northern audience that "large sections of the highland South were in sympathy with the North on the Negro question." Many observers of the era shared Campbell's view that the southern mountain people had little if anything to do with slavery, implying a racial innocence on the part of mountain whites. The jump from the mountaineer's supposed innocence on the slavery question to his modern views on race proved an easy one for many of these observers. According to Silber, this leap helped pave the way for the widely held assumption that highlanders "lacked the racial anxiety that supposedly preoccupied the poor white people of the lowlands."[2]

This ingrained notion has occasionally made its way into scholarship but was often in the form of a blanket statement or offhand comment—again, reinforcing the idea that the black experience in the upland South *should* have been different, so it probably was. Ironically, the first scholar to promulgate this popular notion was pioneering African-American historian and Appalachian native Carter G. Woodson. In an essay published in the second issue of the *Journal of Negro History* in 1916, Woodson argued that southern mountaineers "have always differed from the dwellers in the district near the sea not only in their attitude toward slavery but in the policy they have followed in dealing with the blacks since the Civil War." "In Appalachian America the races still maintain a sort of social contact," he continued. "White and black men work side by side, visit each other in their homes, and often attend the same church to listen with delight to the Word spoken by either a colored or white preacher." Few scholars followed up on Woodson's observations until the late twentieth century. Appalachian scholar and native Loyal Jones observed that "Appalachians have not been saddled with the same prejudices about black people that people of the deep South have." Historian Willard B. Gatewood Jr., in a study of letters written by black Arkansans to northern newspapers in the 1890s, agreed that there existed a clear sectional divide in terms of the black experience in the South. "While the dispatches from Arkansas indicated an increase in Jim Crowism, they also suggest that the degree of discrimination varied from one locality to another in the state. Those from communities in northwestern Arkansas [the Ozarks], where the black population was relatively small, left little doubt that the color line there, especially in politics, was less rigidly drawn than in the black belt of the eastern counties." More recently, in an examination of black and white Republicans in the post–Civil War highland South, historian Gordon B. McKinney noted a "relative lack of racial hostility between mountain whites and blacks," a condition explained in part by the region's small black population.[3]

But the equation of a small black population with a comparative degree of racial harmony has not always appeared so self-evident to scholars and observers of the South. W. J. Cash provides a rare example of "those who have posited that the lack of black contact by many white mountaineers resulted in an even more intense hostility toward blacks than that felt by whites in areas with more substantial black populations." Employing an interpretation of Appalachian people that would have made Arnold J. Toynbee proud, Cash claimed that the mountaineer's depravity poisoned his outlook on race. The mountaineer, according to Cash, "had acquired a hatred and contempt for the Negro even more virulent than that of the common white of the lowlands; a dislike so rabid that it was worth a black man's life to venture into many mountain sections."[4] More often scholars dealing with the South, whether during the Jim Crow era or the civil rights movement, have simply ignored potential intraregional differences or have glossed over the potential for differences, an understandable overgeneralization given the centrality of race in many scholars' definition of southern distinctiveness. As V. O. Key Jr. noted when discussing the prominence of the black belt in southern politics, "It is in this relatively small part of the South that attitudes thought to be universal in the South occur with highest intensity."[5]

Convinced that the "attitudes thought to be universal in the South" were not in fact universal and dissatisfied with the cursory way in which intraregional differences were either written off by some scholars or taken for granted by others, I decided those years ago to remedy the situation in the best way a naive student (and many a naive historian) knows how, a case study of a particular community—a case study that I would then proceed to use as a springboard to my own bloated overgeneralization. The community I chose for this study was one with which I had a fair degree of familiarity. LaCrosse, pronounced LAY-cross in good southern fashion and located less than ten miles from my home in Izard County, Arkansas, was by the early 1990s a shell of a little community. Once a bustling crossroads farming village and home to a fine late-nineteenth-century academy, LaCrosse had become a backwater community after being bypassed by the state-constructed highway in the 1920s. The old store and post office, which I drove by on my way to and from college, closed in the 1980s, and only a few scattered houses remained. By the time of my childhood, the most locally significant thing about LaCrosse was that it had been home to the last black community in Izard County and one of the last rural black communities in the Ozarks. The last remaining member of LaCrosse's black community, whom I remembered as the old man who hung around the filling station in the little town of Franklin, had died just a few weeks before I started my project in 1991, but the community had been practically abandoned for thirty years.

Like many places in the eastern Ozarks, LaCrosse was a cotton-raising community from the post–Civil War years until the middle of the twentieth century. But this was not the reason for the small black community there. There were plenty of other cotton-raising communities in the region that had no blacks at all. The core of the LaCrosse African-American community traced its roots to the slaves brought into the area in the 1840s and 1850s by a handful of white families. At the center of the small slaveholding group in LaCrosse were three Watkins brothers from middle Tennessee who brought five slaves with them when they settled in the area in 1845. Over the next decade and a half they would be joined by a number of relatives and acquaintances from middle Tennessee, some of whom also brought slaves to La-Crosse. By the outbreak of the Civil War, the 85 slave owners in Izard County owned just over 300 slaves, but the Watkinses and their kin and neighbors were among the county's largest slaveholders.[6]

After the war these freed slaves—many of them bearing the names of their former masters—settled in an area a mile or so east of the village proper, likely on land owned, or once owned, by the Watkinses. Although the absence of county records for the two decades following the Civil War prevents a thorough examination of the developments between former masters and former slaves, community oral tradition has it that the Watkinses and other LaCrosse slave owners deeded parcels of land to their former slave families.[7] Whether accomplished by gift, purchase, or homestead, by the 1880 agricultural census at least three black families at LaCrosse owned land (ranging from Joseph Watkins's 81 acres to Baalam Watkins's 214 acres) as did a few families in a smaller black community a couple of miles away in neighboring Franklin township. By 1880 the black community at LaCrosse contained a dozen households and 76 residents, and the nearby village of LaCrosse was home to an additional 11 blacks or mulattoes who worked as servants or laborers for white families. Although tiny by the standards of most of the South at the time, in Izard County, which was home to only 220 blacks and mulattoes in 1880, the LaCrosse settlement was significant and constituted the largest concentration of blacks in the entire hill country region above Batesville. And when combined with the 30 African Americans in nearby Franklin township, this extended settlement accounted for more than half the blacks living in Izard County. The existence of black landownership (which by 1909 had extended to at least nine LaCrosse-area farmers with a median holding of 120 acres), the concentration of a comparatively large number of blacks in one area, and the availability of seasonal labor on relatively prosperous white-owned farms in the vicinity all likely contributed to the stability of the LaCrosse black community well into the twentieth century, even as black families gradually abandoned other parts of the county and region. By 1930, when the black population of most Ozark counties had dwindled to minute levels, Izard County still contained 175 blacks (including eight farm owners), and the largest concentration (67) of them lived in LaCrosse.[8]

Another factor that helped account for the stability of the LaCrosse community was the apparent absence of racial violence or brutal intimidation in the community. Again, the scarcity of records prevents any thorough analysis of the county's late-nineteenth-century history. Nevertheless, we can once again turn to the oral tradition and history of the community, and none of the six former LaCrosse residents interviewed in 1991 or in subsequent years recalled having witnessed, experienced, or heard of any kind of race-related violence or intimidation in the LaCrosse area. Of course, the mere absence of violence did not in and of itself signal some sort of racial utopia in which blacks and whites lived happily side by side. But it was LaCrosse's and Izard County's ability to avoid the violence and brutality so common throughout the South that had first led me to champion the idea of a more permissive and less oppressive highland South.

The recollections and oral traditions of the black former LaCrosse residents were consistent in painting a picture of relative racial harmony in their old community. Estelle Canada Rucker, who grew up in the community in the 1920s and 1930s, recalled, "I don't ever remember any trouble. . . . We [blacks and whites] got along together well." Lillie Mae Darty Watkins, another former LaCrosse resident and only a couple of years older than Rucker, agreed: "We got along good in Izard County. They [whites] was real good to us." The situation seems to have altered little by the middle of the twentieth century, for according to Ray Kennard, who came of age in Izard County only after World War II, "up there wasn't no problem. They [whites] were good up there. . . . As far as racial disturbances, we never had any up there."[9]

Although the majority of LaCrosse's blacks lived in a rather secluded and tight-knit community, there appears to have been none of the suspicion, belligerence, and cultural and physical isolation that characterized the Kentucky highland community of Coe Ridge. Despite their similar populations and geographical settings and the fact that both black communities were practically abandoned by the end of the 1950s, Coe Ridge and LaCrosse shared little in common. In his groundbreaking study of the Kentucky foothills settlement, William Lynwood Montell found a community of black outcasts and misfits who "lived in virtual isolation from the surrounding [white] communities." By comparison, LaCrosse was a community bustling with interracial activity. "We growed up together. We worked together, chopped cotton together. They came to our church. We went to their picnics. We lived together," recalled Estelle Canada Rucker. Thinking back on her life in LaCrosse, Lillie Mae Darty Watkins said, "See, they'd come to our church and sing, and we'd go to their church and sing. . . . We mixed. That's one thing that I can truly say . . . that the blacks and the whites did mix up there."[10]

My undergraduate attempt to explain the rather benign nature of race relations in LaCrosse and Izard County during the Jim Crow era rested on two factors at work in the community and region, factors frequently identified with interracial settlements in the highland South. In my original essay, I suggested that the small number of blacks at LaCrosse and in other highland areas posed no physical or psychological threat to the majority white population and that, therefore, the whites in these areas had little need for the violent social-control tactics found in places with larger concentrations of blacks. I also claimed that widespread poverty—among both blacks and whites—and the Ozark region's rather egalitarian economic and social system instilled a sort of mutual appreciation for the hardships of survival in the hill country.

These reasons may, in fact, have played a part in the absence of racial strife in LaCrosse. Nevertheless, they comprise an insufficient foundation for a defense of southern highland race relations in general. The common interests and struggles of impoverished blacks and whites did on occasion trump southern society's racist and separatist mores. It was more often the case, perhaps, that motives of economic competition and racist pathology soured relationships between blacks and whites and even sparked eruptions of violence. How often it happened in the upland South is still unclear. In his study of blacks in the Arkansas Ozarks, sociologist Gordon D. Morgan noted that "poverty was common to both groups [blacks and whites] and the requirements for making a living from the eroded hill soil [were] too strenuous for energy to be dissipated in useless squabbles over racial superiority." But the logic of this statement could easily be overturned by southern racial codes. In a 1923 article, NAACP field secretary and Arkansas native William Pickens leveled condemnation on the racism of his state's poor whites, especially those of the hill country, who used what little power they possessed to "keep down the rising free Negro." Being unable to compete with the large, aristocratic landowners of the South, "nothing was left for" these poor whites, he observed, "but to hunt, fish, trap, engage in the illicit manufacture of spirits, and 'hate niggers.'" Scholars as well have found the roots of racism in white poverty. Wayne Flynt suggests that "because they possessed few of the tools necessary to improve their lives," poor whites "rested at the bottom of the white social structure and were most threatened by upward black mobility."[11]

White LaCrosse resident P. O. Wren Jr. observed that "there wasn't much difference in families [black or white]. They was all so poor." But the social and economic system in LaCrosse and Izard County was not that simple. Within the white community there were distinctions between and among farm families: sharecroppers and tenant farmers, small landowning farmers, and more prosperous, large landowning families. Even such a small black population reflected subtle distinctions—between landowners and tenants and even among landowners. Most black landholding families owned something between 40 and 120 acres of land, but a few owned farms as big as or bigger than the majority of white-owned farms in the area. Estelle Canada Rucker, whose family owned more than 300 acres, found it amusing that children of a black tenant farmer called her and her siblings "rich kids."[12]

LaCrosse was not a preindustrial highland community of subsistence farmers; it was not a community devoid of class and economic divisions. Since at least the early post–Civil War era, LaCrosse and most of Izard County had been a part of the South's cotton belt—on the northwestern periphery of that belt, to be sure, but in it nonetheless. The largest landowners and most successful farmers relied on the sale of cotton as their primary source of income, and a few were prosperous enough to rent parcels of land to tenant farmers and to hire black cooks or domestics. In this respect the community was not unlike the villages and rural hamlets of the lowland South. Given this comparison to the more typical South, it is likely that paternalism played a more important role than poverty in the stability and relative racial harmony of LaCrosse and surrounding Izard County. The Watkinses and allied families who had first given or sold land to freed slaves and who developed the postwar cotton economy in the community remained as prominent residents of LaCrosse well into the twentieth century. These relatively prosperous white families, as well as others who joined them as significant landowners in subsequent decades, relied on the black community for tenant farming, for domestic help, and for a variety of day-labor services, most important of which was picking cotton at harvest time. Black families, whether landowners or not, relied on the wages from domestic labor and seasonal activities such as the cotton harvest. Although the black families of LaCrosse interacted with the area's poor white families on a daily basis, it was their economic relationship with the community's most socially and economically prominent families that provided them the resources to scratch out a living in the hill country and perhaps even fostered the paternalistic oversight that could be a requisite for racial harmony in the South.

The idea that blacks and whites—bound together by a culture of poverty and backbreaking toil—would somehow bridge the divide of race maintains its elusive and idealistic appeal but seems to promise little of substance when trying to explain the absence of racial strife in a place like LaCrosse, Arkansas. The second reason that I had originally posited to explain La-

Crosse's experience—the small concentration of blacks relative to the white population—would seem at first glance to hold more promise, however. In the Arkansas Ozarks, according to sociologist Gordon D. Morgan, blacks were "mainly ignored or forgotten by the larger society." Edward Cabbell noted a similar "black invisibility" in Appalachia. And, as observed earlier, historian Willard B. Gatewood Jr. ascribed the "less rigidly drawn" color line in northwestern Arkansas during the 1890s to the relatively small black population.[13]

In spite of a certain logic embedded in the theory that a relatively insignificant, and thus less threatening, black population would somehow tend to alleviate racial violence, scholarship over the past decade suggests that not only did small black populations not lessen the likelihood of racial violence but that the very minuteness, and thus the vulnerability, of black communities in upland South areas might actually have served as a provocation to more extreme episodes of violence. In his study of lynching in Georgia and Virginia, W. Fitzhugh Brundage found high rates of race-related violence in highland areas where "seemingly the preconditions for racial violence should have been absent." Despite the fact that the small and vulnerable black population of Appalachian Georgia posed little threat to whites, "during the late 1880s and early 1890s, racial violence in northern Georgia reached levels that equaled those elsewhere in the state." And "nowhere in Virginia was the incidence of mob violence more concentrated, both in place and time, than in the southwestern corner of the state." According to Brundage, social and economic forces were as much to blame for this racial violence as was racial fear. These highland lynchings, he argued, "reflected the desperation of whites to define the status of blacks in a region where blacks were still uncommon and furious social and economic change was taking place."[14]

Recent scholarship on racial violence in the Ozarks tends to support Brundage's findings. The years surrounding the turn of the nineteenth century appear to have been especially violent ones for some Ozark black communities. Jacqueline Froelich and David Zimmermann documented two instances of white mob violence toward the small black community in Harrison, Arkansas, in the first decade of the twentieth century. Brundage found social control to be the goal of most violent acts, but in Harrison the violence was "used to completely destroy a community." In a recent study of race riots in the Missouri Ozarks, historian Patrick Huber has analyzed riots and lynchings in no fewer than four southwestern Missouri towns between 1894 and 1906. Beginning with the lynching of a black laborer who had allegedly murdered a white railroad worker in Monett and concluding with a gruesome triple lynching in Springfield, the violent acts persuaded many blacks to flee the Ozarks permanently. Sociologist James Loewen has also analyzed the flurry of racial violence in the Ozarks and has judged the exodus of blacks from the area significant enough to label the Ozarks a "sundown town" region—an area that was and is all white by design.[15]

All of this suggests that an "unthreatening" small black community would not in and of itself allay the fears and passions that sparked episodes of racial violence and that the upland South, in spite of its sparse black population, was as prone to violence—and in some cases more so—than the lowland South. Does this recent scholarship render little LaCrosse an anomaly instead of the model for peaceful coexistence that I had labeled the community more than a dozen years ago? If so, to what then do we attribute the relative harmony between blacks and whites in LaCrosse and in Izard County, Arkansas? From the perspective of the Ozarks—given the recent findings of Froelich and Zimmermann, Huber, and Loewen—it would appear at first glance that the experiences of the races in LaCrosse were notable for their lack of violent incidence. The research on the highland South in general is too spotty and incomplete to venture any blanket statements, but Brundage's findings suggest that one might have reasonably expected to uncover evidence of racial violence in LaCrosse and Izard County. It is obviously too much of a leap, however, to argue that the experience of blacks and whites in LaCrosse was unique for the highland South or even that it was unusual. Even in the Ozarks, which experienced a relatively high rate of racial violence around the turn of the twentieth century, there are other examples of small black communities living in peace amid larger white communities. Undoubtedly, Appalachia has similar examples to offer. The scattered examples of racial violence in the highland South are more often chronicled than are the examples of peaceful coexistence—for obvious reasons. The race riots and lynchings provide real *stories*—chronologies of events complete with human drama and tragedy—that are most often absent in the histories of places like LaCrosse, an absence made painfully clear by this essay.

Even if LaCrosse is not an anomaly of racial harmony, what factors accounted for the rather peaceful and fluid interaction of the blacks and whites there and in other similarly uneventful places? Although the memories of former residents, black and white, recall a significant amount of intermingling between the races—at black church services, at picnics, in the fields, and at local stores, which blacks entered through the front doors like their white neighbors—this day-to-day physical proximity was not uncommon in the South and did not in and of itself signify a racial utopia. In fact, the

blacks of LaCrosse and of other upland South communities were daily reminded of their separate and second-class status in a segregated and white-
dominated society. Black children in LaCrosse and in neighboring Franklin
township attended school in the Sweet Home Baptist Church house, a
school that never went beyond the eighth grade, even after the establishment
of all-white high schools in neighboring communities in the 1920s and 1930s.
African-American children wanting to attend high school were forced to
move to Batesville, thirty miles away, until the establishment of a bus route
in the early 1950s that transported all black LaCrosse students to Batesville.
LaCrosse's black children learned that "you didn't call [white men] by their
name . . . you called them Uncle or Mister." They learned that "we weren't
allowed to eat with [white people]. We had to sit back until [the whites] all
ate and then we would come in and eat last."[16] They learned that their ability
to use the front doors at white-owned establishments vanished at the edge of
their community, that the county seat was full of strange white folks and back
doors for blacks. They learned that their light-skinned classmates were the
offspring of a local landlord but that a victory on the baseball field was as
serious a challenge to white manhood as was advisable.[17]

LaCrosse, then, was similar to lowland southern communities in that
blacks and whites understood the boundaries of segregated society and generally observed those boundaries. One black LaCrosse resident who moved
away during the depression recalled, "Blacks knew their place and whites
knew theirs . . . didn't have no trouble." A white resident of LaCrosse attributed the community's segregation to "tradition": "We treated them good, but
it was separate."[18] The LaCrosse area's reliance on cotton farming until the
mid-twentieth century was also indicative of the lowland South, and the economic importance—to local white landowners, anyway—of the small black
population likely figured into the peace and stability of the community. But
two other factors might also have played key roles in sparing LaCrosse from
the racial violence experienced in Harrison and other Ozark communities:
the black community's apparent observance of southern racial-sexual codes
and the relative scarcity of black newcomers to Izard County.

According to the oral history of LaCrosse, there were at least two instances in the early 1900s of black women giving birth to and raising the
children of local white fathers, and the census records for Izard County
in the late nineteenth century suggest that these twentieth-century mulattoes were not isolated incidences in the community. But it appears that the
sexual/racial double standard crafted by anxious white men—who, according
to historian Joel Williamson, projected "upon black men extravagant sexual

behavior" and "came to be obsessed by the possibility of sexual relations between black men and white women"—was upheld in LaCrosse. The oral
traditions and available records contain no memories or mentions of the
kinds of racial-sexual activities that could incite white riots and violence,
such as sexual liaisons between black men and white women or alleged sexual
assault against white women by black men—the one crime that most often
justified racial violence in the minds of whites.[19] Again, the story here is
primarily in the absence of a story.

Perhaps the key to the uneventful nature of race relations in LaCrosse and
Izard County, however, was the community's relative isolation and its subsequent immunity to settlement by transient black men. Historian Edward L.
Ayers argues that lynching was most likely to occur in areas of the South
with low rural population density and significant black population growth
in the late nineteenth century, a population growth that included many
black newcomers and transients by whom whites felt threatened. "Lynchings
tended to flourish where whites were surrounded by what they called 'strange
niggers,' blacks with no white to vouch for them, blacks with no reputation
in the neighborhood, blacks without even other blacks to aid them." Ayers
continues: "Lynching seemed both more necessary and more feasible in
places such as the Gulf Plain, the cotton uplands, and the mountains. In
those places most blacks and whites did not know one another, much less
share ties of several generations."[20] Herein lies the primary difference between LaCrosse and the upland communities cited for racial violence in the
works of Ayers, Brundage, Loewen, Huber, and Froelich and Zimmermann.
The fact that LaCrosse was something of a backwater community—no railroad, no industry, nothing to generate lots of coming and going by young
black men—meant that few new blacks ever came into the neighborhood,
and most of the ones who did were from similar black communities in north-
central Arkansas and had married into a LaCrosse family. In other words,
LaCrosse attracted few "strange niggers," such as the young, unemployed
black railroad workers who sparked the Harrison, Arkansas, riot of 1905 or
the young black laborers who were lynched or burned to death in Pierce City,
Missouri, for the alleged murder of a white woman.[21]

In the final estimation it would appear that the decisive factors underlying LaCrosse's and Izard County's combination of racial harmony and the
relatively relaxed atmosphere in which blacks and whites commingled daily
were the community's isolation-induced stability, the black population's rigid
adherence to racial-sexual mores, and the crucial economic interdependence
of prominent white farmers and blacks in the area. In other words, it was

the uncharacteristically lowland South flavor of social and economic life in LaCrosse and Izard County, combined with the upland South's characteristically tiny and unthreatening black population, that seems to have created an environment in which local blacks, while subject to the restrictions and second-class status found elsewhere in the South, felt safe and secure, at least within the confines of the broader LaCrosse community. This interpretation—that the relative harmony of LaCrosse, while not unique, is not the model for race relations in the upper South and that the community's avoidance of racial violence reflects not its difference from but rather its similarity to the lowland South—represents in some respects an ironic reversal of my original thesis, which rested on the assumption that in most ways life and historical development in the upland South had been fundamentally unlike that in the lowland South.

What implications does this turn of events have, and what, if anything, does the story of LaCrosse tell us about race relations in the highland South? For upland southerners and scholars alike who have assumed or argued that race relations were more fluid and race less of an issue in the South's highlands, the scholarship of the past decade or so cannot be reassuring. In addition to the growing body of literature detailing the upland South's quite *southern* past of racial violence, historian John C. Inscoe has in recent years taken a more direct look at the issue of the historical treatment of blacks in Appalachia and has discovered the "same prejudices and even violence that characterized the rest of the Jim Crow South." In spite of "significant demographic variables in the biracial populace of the highland and lowland South," according to Inscoe, "blacks in the mountains . . . were subject to the same sorts of exploitation, abuse, and prejudice faced by blacks throughout the nineteenth-century South."[22]

It appears quite obvious that within the upland regions thus far scrutinized, racial violence was as common, if not relatively more so, than in the lowland South. The topic of race relations—in some ways a separate issue from racial violence—is more slippery and as yet insufficiently addressed. The example of LaCrosse and Izard County does, however, offer one portrait of an upland South community in which blacks and whites coexisted without any apparent violence or overt intimidation and suggests that, given the same set of circumstances, it is not unreasonable to expect other examples of relative racial harmony in the upland South. The fact that this one upland example resembled in many ways the communities of the lowland South reminds us that the upland South was in no way monolithic, that it was almost as diverse as the South itself. And that's not good news for those who would

portray the southern highlands as a separate and fundamentally different do-
main, whether, in the terms of our argument, a region in which racial violence or "sundown towns" held sway or in which whites were more humane,
or at least more tolerant, of the small black populations in their midst. It is
clear that in LaCrosse the peace and harmony did not denote a community
free of racism, oppression, and segregation; it is unlikely that such a community existed anywhere in the South—or in the nation for that matter—
during the era of the LaCrosse black community's existence.

~

Like many tiny upland black communities, the LaCrosse black neighborhood was abandoned in the second half of the twentieth century. The factors
that effected this exodus were the same ones that revolutionized agriculture
and rural life in the South. Federal cotton acreage allotments first instituted
during the New Deal and streamlined after World War II gradually reduced
Izard County's cash crop to insignificance by the early 1960s. The black residents of LaCrosse and of most other places in Izard County had long been
intimately tied to this small-scale cotton culture—both as farm owners and
tenants and as seasonal laborers—and its demise forced them to look elsewhere for a livelihood, as it also did thousands of whites in the eastern
Ozarks. Unlike the white families who supplemented their meager farming
incomes with migrant agricultural labor in the 1940s and 1950s, most black
families owned no automobile and were thus forced to make the more permanent decision to stay or to leave their home for good. Almost all of them
eventually left. By 1950 only 47 blacks remained in Izard County, which
reflected a 73 percent decline in the black population since 1930. As usual, the
landless and the day laborers were the first to leave. Between 1930 and 1950
the number of black tenant farmers decreased from 24 to 7, and only one of
the dozen black sharecroppers living in the county in 1930 was still there 20
years later; the number of blacks who owned all or part of the land they
farmed actually increased from 8 to 12.[23] But the 1950s brought an unprecedented wave of out-migration by Izard County farm owners, black and white
alike, and by the end of the decade only two black families remained in
LaCrosse—an elderly couple who would live out their days as Izard County's
last remaining black family and their son and his family who would soon
move away to find a steady income and, probably, to escape the isolation. The
last remaining member of the LaCrosse black community, a bachelor son of
this last remaining family, died almost a decade and a half ago.

Most of the black LaCrosse out-migrants made their way to one of four
destinations: Batesville, Arkansas (just 30 miles south of LaCrosse), Okla-

homa City, Peoria, Illinois, and Beloit, Wisconsin. The scattered fragments of the community and their descendants continue to hold biannual home-comings, some still own land in LaCrosse, and the oldest are returned to the old community cemetery, just up the hill from the shell of a building that once was the Sweet Home Baptist Church, for their final resting place. The memories of the former LaCrosse residents I have interviewed are gener-ally positive ones. Like their white contemporaries, they can wax nostalgic about life on the farm, about the innocence of childhood, about a simpler time. The mere fact that they share these positive recollections suggests a certain degree of harmony between the races in LaCrosse and Izard County. But anecdotal recall can also block out the dull monotony of the more pain-ful and ever-present memory of segregation and second-class status. For a white college student from the hills whose grandparents once sharecropped on the same Izard County landlord's farm as a local black family and who picked cotton alongside that black family, the prominence of the positive memories could seem a welcomed vindication of the upland South's self-proclaimed superiority in the field of race relations. If we are fortunate, the passion to vindicate becomes a passion to explain—and the apologist be-comes historian.

Over the years Wayne Flynt has helped lead more than a few apologists and others groping around the periphery of scholarship into the well-worn path of the historian. He has done so with patience and firmness and a com-mitment to truth and justice. And he has done so without losing his appre-ciation for the centrality of the "story" in history. About a half-dozen years ago at my dissertation defense, Wayne added to the story that began this essay—or the story that was spawned by the original work from which this essay is derived—when he told me that I had converted him, that he had come to accept my undergraduate interpretation of the upland-lowland di-vide in race relations. Actually, I'm quite certain that Wayne was just being nice and that he—nor I, for that matter—could scarcely recall what my thesis had been those years before. (And, besides, anyone who has been a Southern Baptist for as long as Wayne has is probably beyond the ability to convert anyhow.) My subsequent admission that I was the one who had been wrong probably rang just as hollow at the time. After reviewing the subject and taking into account subsequent scholarship, it seems more likely that I was right about being wrong. And once again, Wayne Flynt and other scholars who had for the most part avoided interregional splitting when discussing southern race relations were, it seems, pretty close to the mark. It is too much of a stretch to present LaCrosse and Izard County, Arkansas, as a microcosm of race relations in the upland South. It is not too much to expect that the relative peace and harmony of this one place was not uncommon in the hills and mountains. At the very least, it is a story of one community that escaped the violent oppression or forced removal of a small black population, and, unfortunately, that may be as good as it got.

Notes

1. Frederick Law Olmsted, *A Journey in the Back Country* (New York: Mason Brothers, 1860), 226–27.

2. Kenneth W. Noe, "'A Source of Great Economy'? The Railroad and Slavery's Expansion in Southwest Virginia, 1850–1860," in *Appalachians and Race: The Mountain South from Slavery to Segregation*, ed. John C. Inscoe (Lexington: University Press of Kentucky, 2001), 102; James C. Klotter, "The Black South and White Appalachia," *Journal of American History* 66 (March 1980):840–42; Nina Silber, "'What Does America Need So Much as Americans?' Race and Northern Reconciliation with Southern Appalachia, 1870–1900," in *Appalachians and Race*, ed. Inscoe, 248; John C. Campbell, *The Southern Highlander and His Homeland* (1929; reprint, Lexington: University Press of Kentucky, 1969), 95; Silber, "What Does America Need," 253.

3. Carter G. Woodson, "Freedom and Slavery in Appalachian America," *Journal of Negro History* 1 (April 1916):150; Loyal Jones, "Appalachian Values," in *Voices from the Hills: Selected Readings of Southern Appalachia*, ed. Robert J. Higgs and Ambrose Manning (New York: Ungar, 1975), 512; Willard B. Gatewood Jr., "Arkansas Negroes in the 1890s: Documents," *Arkansas Historical Quarterly* 33 (Winter 1974):297; Gordon B. McKinney, "Southern Mountain Republicans and the Negro, 1865–1900," in *Appalachians and Race*, ed. Inscoe, 199, 205.

4. W. J. Cash, *The Mind of the South* (New York: Alfred A. Knopf, 1941), 219. The mention of Arnold Toynbee here is in reference to his oft-cited criticism that "the Appalachian 'Mountain People' at this day are no better than barbarians. They are the American counterparts of the latter-day White barbarians of the Old World: the Rifis and Kabyles and Tuareg, the Albanians and Caucasians, the Kurds and the Pathans and the Hairy Ainu": Toynbee, *A Study of History*, vol. 2 (London: Oxford University Press, 1939), 311.

5. V. O. Key Jr., *Southern Politics in State and Nation* (New York: Alfred A. Knopf, 1950), 666.

6. Helen C. Lindley, "The Watkins Brothers and Wild Haws," *Izard County Historian* 5 (October 1974):8; Dale Hanks, "Silent Strangers: West Africans in Izard County," *Izard County Historian* 26 (October 2001):16.

7. Interview, Estelle Canada Rucker, Batesville, Arkansas, 26 August 2003; in-

terview, Norman Byrd, May and August 1994, in *Down Memory Lane*, ed. Betty McCollum and Sue Chrisco, vol. 1 (n.p., 1999), 173.

8. Hanks, "Silent Strangers," 18, 20; U.S. Department of State, Agricultural Manuscript Census Schedules, Izard County, Arkansas, 1880; Bureau of the Census, *Fifteenth Census of the United States, 1930: Population*, vol. 3, pt. 1 (Washington, D.C.: Government Printing Office [GPO], 1932), 218–19; ibid., *Agriculture*, vol. 2, pt. 3, 1144. Although a fire in 1889 destroyed all of Izard County's records, one early-twentieth-century document suggests that the county's African-American citizens were able to avoid the political disfranchisement that swept much of the South in the 1890s and early 1900s. A 1909 roll of poll tax payers listed 18 blacks from LaCrosse township, or 90 percent of the township's black men listed in the same year's personal tax assessment book. See List of Poll Tax Payers, Izard County, 1909, Izard County Courthouse, Melbourne, Arkansas; Personal Assessment, 1909, Izard County, ibid.

9. Rucker, interview, Lillie Mae Darty Watkins, interview, and Ray Kennard, interview, all in Batesville, Arkansas, 8 May 1991.

10. William Lynwood Montell, *The Saga of Coe Ridge: A Study in Oral History* (Knoxville: University of Tennessee Press, 1970), 3, 166 (quote); Rucker, interview, May 1991; Watkins, interview, Batesville, Arkansas, 12 July 1993, Ozark Oral History Project, Ozark Cultural Resource Center, Ozark Folk Center, Mountain View, Arkansas.

11. Gordon D. Morgan, *Black Hillbillies of the Arkansas Ozarks* (Fayetteville: University of Arkansas Department of Sociology, 1973), 63; William Pickens, "Arkansas—A Study in Suppression," *The Messenger* 5 (January 1923), reprinted in *These 'Colored' United States: African American Essays from the 1920s*, ed. Tom Lutz and Susanna Ashton (New Brunswick, N.J.: Rutgers University Press, 1996), 34; Wayne Flynt, *Dixie's Forgotten People: The South's Poor Whites* (Bloomington: Indiana University Press, 1979), 116.

12. P. O. Wren Jr., interview, 10 May 1991, LaCrosse, Arkansas; Rucker, interview, May 1994; Izard County Real Estate Tax Book, 1909, Izard County Courthouse, Melbourne, Arkansas, 78.

13. Morgan, *Black Hillbillies*, 75; Edward Cabbell, "Black Invisibility and Racism in Appalachia," *Appalachian Journal* 8 (Autumn 1980):48; Cabbell, "Black Invisibility and Racism in Appalachia: An Informed Survey," in *Blacks in Appalachia*, ed. William H. Turner and Edward J. Cabbell (Lexington: University Press of Kentucky, 1985), 3; Gatewood, "Arkansas Negroes in the 1890s," 297.

14. W. Fitzhugh Brundage, *Lynching in the New South: Georgia and Virginia, 1880–1930* (Urbana: University of Illinois Press, 1993), 128, 143. See also George C. Wright, *Racial Violence in Kentucky, 1865–1940: Lynchings, Mob Rule, and 'Legal Lynchings'* (Baton Rouge: Louisiana State University Press, 1990).

15. Jacqueline Froelich and David Zimmermann, "Total Eclipse: The Destruction of the African American Community of Harrison, Arkansas, in 1905 and 1909," *Arkansas Historical Quarterly* 58 (Summer 1999):141; Patrick Huber, "Race Riots and Black Exodus in the Missouri Ozarks, 1894–1906," unpublished paper presented at the Ozark Cultural Celebration, Harrison, Arkansas, 10 September 2002, 2; James Loewen, unpublished book chapters on sundown towns, in possession of author. See also Katherine Lederer, *Many Thousand Gone: Springfield's Lost Black History* (Springfield: Missouri Committee for the Humanities and the Gannett Foundation, 1986); Tom W. Dillard, "Madness with a Past: An Overview of Race Violence in Arkansas History," Arkansas Black History Online, http://cals.lib.ar.us/butlercenter/ abho/bib/MADNESS.pdf, 2003. Among the as-yet-unexplained incidents of racial violence in the Arkansas Ozarks was a December 1906 episode in which most of the residents of a small black "colony" on the outskirts of Evening Shade (Sharp County) left their homes and the area because of intimidation by some local whites (*Sharp County Record*, 28 December 1906, 1). Journalist Elliot Jaspin is at work on a book that will examine the Evening Shade incident and other examples of "racial cleansing." A similarly unexamined incident took place a dozen years earlier in the eastern Ozarks town of Black Rock (Lawrence County), when "whitecaps" attempted to force a bed manufacturing company to fire all its black workers and expel them from company housing (*Arkansas Gazette*, 17 January 1894, 2).

16. Watkins, interview, 12 July 1993; Watkins, interview, 3 September 1997, in *Down Memory Lane*, vol. 2, 163 (first quote), 158 (second quote).

17. Rucker, interview, 26 August 2003.

18. Knoxie Canada Brown, interview, 8 May 1991, Batesville, Arkansas; Wren, interview.

19. Edward L. Ayers, *The Promise of the New South: Life after Reconstruction* (New York: Oxford University Press, 1992), 158; Joel Williamson, *The Crucible of Race: Black-White Relations in the American South Since Emancipation* (New York: Oxford University Press, 1984), 308, 309. See also Lillian Smith, *Killers of the Dream* (1949; reprint, New York: W. W. Norton & Co., 1961).

20. Ayers, *Promise of the New South*, 156, 157 (quotes).

21. Froelich and Zimmermann, "Total Eclipse," 137; Huber, "Race Riots and Black Exodus," 5.

22. John C. Inscoe, "Slavery and African Americans in the Nineteenth Century," in *High Mountains Rising: Appalachia in Time and Place*, ed. Richard A. Straw and H. Tyler Blethen (Urbana: University of Illinois Press, 2004), 40–41, 42. See also John C. Inscoe, "Olmsted in Appalachia: A Connecticut Yankee Encounters Slavery and Racism in the Southern Highlands, 1854," in *Appalachians and Race*, ed. Inscoe, 154–64, as well as Inscoe's "Introduction" in the same volume.

23. *Fifteenth Census of the United States, 1930: Population,* vol. 3, pt. 1, 218–19; Bureau of the Census, *Census of Population, 1950: Characteristics of the Population—Arkansas,* vol. 2, pt. 4 (Washington, D.C.: GPO, 1952), 79; *Fifteenth Census of the United States, 1930: Agriculture,* vol. 2, pt. 3, 1138, 1144; Bureau of the Census, *Census of Agriculture, 1950: Counties and State Economic Areas—Arkansas,* vol. 1, pt. 23 (Washington, D.C.: GPO, 1952), 69, 72.

3

Southern Accents

The Politics of Race and the Economic Opportunity Act of 1964

Susan Youngblood Ashmore

In an effort to place the modern struggle for civil rights in a wider context, some historians have referred to this crusade as the Second Reconstruction. While this may not be an accurate assessment for the entire grassroots campaign for freedom that accelerated after World War II, it is an appropriate label for the federal response to African-American demands that the nation come to terms with its racial sins. It is not surprising that the history of this change in federal initiatives has focused on the Civil Rights Act of 1964 and the Voting Rights Act of 1965 as pieces of key legislation that banned the practice of separate public accommodations and opened the voting booth to southern black people who had been disfranchised since the 1890s. Yet, if this "Second Reconstruction" classification is accurate, other facets of the federal government must be studied to understand the role Washington officials played in the changing South. One place to look is at the way the Civil Rights Act affected other pieces of President Lyndon Johnson's Great Society.

On January 8, 1964, in his first State of the Union address, Johnson laid out the future plans of his administration in the aftermath of John Kennedy's assassination. LBJ did this by making connections between civil rights for African Americans and support for broader federal programs that would become the cornerstone of his policies. This speech is remembered most for articulating his commitment to pass the stalled civil rights bill to honor the slain president. However, it is also important to realize that LBJ used this national occasion to establish his own legitimacy as president by reshaping Kennedy's New Frontier into something that could be identified more closely with the Johnson style of governing. He began his speech by inspiring

Congress to envision itself as an active body that would go down in history as completing a session that did more for civil rights, that enacted a far-reaching tax cut, and that "declared all-out war on human poverty and unemployment in these United States." Johnson used the attack on poverty as a means to understand the direction his administration would take. He did this by first linking poverty with racism: "Unfortunately, many Americans live on the outskirts of hope—some because of their poverty, and some because of their color, and all too many because of both." He then proclaimed, "This administration today, here and now, declares unconditional war on poverty in America. . . . It will not be a short or easy struggle, no single weapon or strategy will suffice, but we shall not rest until that war is won. The richest Nation on earth can afford to win it. We cannot afford to lose it."[1]

Johnson's bold support for civil rights in the State of the Union address merged into his call to end poverty. Even though both of these ideas had been initiated by a different chief executive, the speed with which his administration brought legislation forward showed the nation that the president meant to move the country at a faster pace than Kennedy had. Two key components of Johnson's Great Society—the Civil Rights Act and the Economic Opportunity Act—signaled the president's intent to use the strength of the federal government in new ways. Johnson cut his political teeth during the New Deal, and as a result of his attempt to exceed Roosevelt's legacy, LBJ's programs altered the balance of power in the federal system in a manner FDR could not have imagined. In the South, the potential to undermine the old order of Jim Crow was lodged not only in the civil rights proposal but also within the antipoverty effort. The Civil Rights Act provided mandates that would change all federal legislation after its passage in July 1964. For example, when these new directives were combined with the provisions of the Economic Opportunity Act, the traditional relationship between the federal government and the states changed. In many cases the antipoverty legislation enabled administrators within the Office of Economic Opportunity (OEO) to deal directly with citizens independent of state and local elected officials. The social and political dynamics between these officeholders and newly enfranchised black people remained unsettled following the passage of civil rights legislation. Therefore, it was federal bureaucrats—like those in OEO—who were called upon to mediate between these rival forces while, in many cases, hundreds of thousands of dollars hung in the balance. As the Johnson administration moved forward, it became evident that other Great Society initiatives like the War on Poverty had the capacity to implement some of the goals of the civil rights movement.

A focus on the legislative history and initial implementation of the Economic Opportunity Act of 1964 highlights the influence the civil rights movement had on altering the political landscape of the South. The architects of the bill believed that southern state-level politicians would not incorporate their African-American constituents into the antipoverty fight, so the draft legislation circumvented local officials in order to bring all the voices of the poor into the federal initiative. While Congress debated the legislation during the summer of 1964, the presidential campaign entered its closing stages. The Republican nominee signaled a new conservatism within the party. During the early 1960s the GOP began to split over its traditional supportive stance on civil rights. This came to the fore eleven days after Kennedy announced his plan for a federal civil rights bill. On June 22, 1963, the Republican National Committee met in Denver. The rift between the progressive northeastern branch of the party and the more conservative western and heartland branches became more apparent with the recent addition of white southern Republicans. Journalist Robert Novak reported that "What was bothering . . . a good many . . . at Denver was unmistakable signs that party leaders from outside the industrialized states of the eastern seaboard were seriously contemplating transforming the Republican Party into the White Man's Party." Southern and western GOP members made it known during this meeting that they intended to overtake the party, nominate Barry Goldwater for president, and adopt the most conservative party platform since the 1920s. As a part of the Republican strategy, this new group of leaders intended to take a neutral stand with regard to the civil rights of African Americans. They succeeded in nominating Goldwater as their presidential candidate, and he attracted supporters in the Deep South based on his commitment to states' rights and his opposition to federal civil rights laws. During the hearings on the antipoverty bill, members of the GOP raised questions about the legislation to draw attention to its ability to assist poor black southerners. Republican congressmen took this calculated stance to use race as a force to attract conservative Democrats into their party. The growing popularity of the Arizona senator among white southerners made it increasingly difficult for many Democrats in Dixie to maintain their political fidelity, especially after the passage of the Civil Rights Act in July. It is well known that presidential aide Bill Moyers remembered LBJ saying the night he had signed the landmark legislation, "I think we just delivered the South to the Republican Party for a long time to come." What is not so evident is that after July 1964, President Johnson and his staff realized they were operating in uncharted territory, and the fight to pass the Economic Opportunity

Act reveals the way they maneuvered in these new conditions trying to keep as many southern Democrats within the party's fold as possible. In the end, compromises were made to the bill in an effort to hold the party together, and these changes played a significant role in the way the War on Poverty would be fought in the South, especially in Alabama.[2]

By concentrating on the details of the antipoverty legislation and the Johnson administration's strategy to get the bill passed, one can see the new reality brought about by the civil rights movement in places that may initially appear to have nothing to do with race. In the summer of 1964, the way was not certain for many southern politicians as the political ground shifted beneath their feet. Race has always been a fault line within American society, especially in the South, and the cracks in the political surface began to show in unpredictable ways after 1964, causing politicians to reexamine their positions on the new terrain. The debate over how to wage the War on Poverty underscores the manner in which the president and his staff as well as southern federal elected officials tried to maintain control over this process in an effort to contain the tremors that warned them of the changes that lay ahead. The Democratic Party was in the process of reforming, but it remained unclear what that transformation would bring.

When the Senate concurred with the House to approve the Economic Opportunity Act on August 11, 1964, it was clear that a Second Reconstruction was under way. However, just as federal officials had done in the 1870s, the southern accents of Dixie's politicians had not been ignored. Amendments to the legislation accommodated the demands of states' rights supporters. After a summer of negotiating the bill, the Johnson administration was willing to have people believe that the racial issues initially associated with the bill had been removed. The *Atlanta Constitution* described the legislation as "primarily an education bill aimed at training people now on relief rolls and potential welfare recipients—particularly the young—for employment." While accurate only in the most limited way, this narrow assessment of the bill highlights the nature of the Second Reconstruction as the manifestation of the civil rights movement in federal public policy. In the construction of legislation, changes were made and deals were cut so the bill could pass. For decades southern white politicians altered proposals to suit their social mores and economic power, and this bill shared that tradition. Yet, even after late-night meetings and closed-door sessions, the ground had indeed shifted after the Civil Rights Act passed. On the surface the final version of the Economic Opportunity Act of 1964 may have looked as if southern politicians had had their way once again. But the heavy-handed actions of a few southern governors—especially Alabama's Governor George Wallace—led to future amendments to the legislation that ultimately strengthened federal power at the expense of local and state authority. As a result, by 1972 when the doors of the Office of Economic Opportunity had closed, it was clear that, on a fundamental level, this federal initiative against poverty had played a supporting role in the Second Reconstruction, especially in the home state of George Wallace.[3]

Why Focus on the Poor in 1964?

Johnson used Kennedy's legislative agenda for the election year but made these plans his own after occupying the Oval Office for just over six weeks. The day after the assassination, LBJ met with Walter Heller, chairman of the Council of Economic Advisers. They discussed the unfinished business of the Kennedy administration, including the proposed program to fight poverty, which was being called "Widening Participation in Prosperity." LBJ asked Heller to continue working on this, telling him, "That's my kind of program. . . . Move full speed ahead." His motivations for launching the war on poverty now become clearer. Not many people outside of the Kennedy administration knew about the plans to fight poverty. Johnson could use this issue as his way out from behind the shadow cast by the national grief over JFK's death. The fight against poverty would be the evidence he needed to prove to Americans that he deserved to be president on his own merit. This legislation would also enable him to use the power of the federal government to better people's lives, a goal that defined LBJ's liberalism. Johnson summed up his motivations in his memoirs: "I believe a program that eliminated poverty—or even reduced it—would strengthen the moral and economic fiber of the entire country. It was on that basis that I prepared to move forward and commit the resources and prestige of the new administration."[4]

In addition to these stated reasons, it also appears that Johnson planned to use the antipoverty program to address the needs of black southerners without having to acknowledge openly that it was one of his goals. LBJ's entire career in government had been geared toward pulling the South into the mainstream of American society through programs that supported modernization and economic growth. He knew that white southern racism played a leading role in the region's slow advance. Prior to becoming president, LBJ had a mixed record with regard to public support of the aspirations of African Americans. He took clandestine actions on behalf of his black constituents in the National Youth Administration in Texas during the New Deal

and in his early years in the House of Representatives. In the Senate he developed a close relationship with Richard Russell of Georgia—an unabashed
advocate of racial segregation—who used the filibuster and other Senate
rules to his advantage. As Senate majority leader, Johnson managed the passage of the Civil Rights Act of 1957, but the amendments he allowed in the
bill severely weakened its ability to increase black voting or protect other civil
rights of African Americans. Each of these actions in one way or another
confirmed his purpose of modernizing the South. In the shrewd tradition of
taking what he could get from a piece of legislation and looking for more the
next time, by 1964 the Economic Opportunity Act could be that "next time."
The civil rights bill before Congress sought to end racial segregation in the
South, a monumental achievement but one that would not address the economic woes of those who had lived under Jim Crow's boot. In May, Johnson
expressed his concern about how the Civil Rights Act would be received
across the country. "The thing we are more afraid of than anything else," he
told Hubert Humphrey, "is that we will have real revolution in the country
when this bill goes into effect. . . . It took us ten years to put this Supreme
Court decision into effect on education. . . . Unless we have the Republicans
joinin' us and helpin' put down this mutiny, we'll have mutiny in this god-
damn country. So we've got to make this an American bill and not just a
Democratic bill." Fighting poverty—which affected more white Americans
than black—could serve as another way to "Americanize" the aims of the
Civil Rights Act. The war on poverty would address some real needs in the
country—the out-of-work Appalachian coal miner, the neglected inner-city
teenager, and the displaced southern sharecropper.[5]

Johnson took his cues from Kennedy in this regard. Initially JFK based his
approach to reducing poverty on stimulating the economy. Following the
lackluster performance of the Area Redevelopment Act (ARA), the Manpower Development Training Act (MDTA), and the economy in general, the
idea for a tax cut took center stage in December 1962. Knowing that the cut
in taxes would mainly benefit people in the upper- and middle-income
brackets, Walter Heller advised the president that it might be politically prudent also to have something developed specifically for poor Americans. According to historian Carl Brauer, "Heller was concerned about protecting the
Kennedy administration's left flank."[6]

Another faction of the "left flank" led Kennedy to make more direct connections between unemployment and racism. By the summer of 1963 the
direct action campaigns for civil rights could no longer go unheeded. Many
leaders within the civil rights movement feared JFK would wait until after

the 1964 election to introduce a federal civil rights bill, so on June 9 they began to plan for a March on Washington for Jobs and Freedom to gain national support for their cause. Events in Birmingham, Alabama, ultimately seized the attention of the nation and the Kennedy administration. "For two years Robert Kennedy [as attorney general] had attempted to deal with each racial crisis on an ad hoc basis," historian Adam Fairclough explained. The brutal attack on demonstrators led by Police Commissioner Eugene "Bull" Connor "finally convinced him that crises would recur with such frequency and magnitude that the federal government, unless it adopted a more radical policy, would be overwhelmed." It is clear that there was a strong connection between demonstrations in Birmingham and the introduction of the civil rights bill.[7]

On June 19, 1963, the president committed himself to take action after two and a half years of indecision. He laid out his plans for federal civil rights legislation in a special message to Congress on civil rights and job opportunities. He wanted to provide an equal right to vote, legal remedies for the denial of certain individual rights, and legislation to improve the training, skills, and economic opportunities of the "economically distressed and discontented, white and Negro." By connecting equal rights with job opportunities, JFK revealed his understanding of the civil rights crisis. The president staked out his position clearly: "There is little value in a Negro's obtaining the right to be admitted to hotels and restaurants if he has no cash in his pocket and no job." By placing the demands of the civil rights movement within an economic framework, Kennedy disclosed how he hoped to deal with these pressing issues. He could confront the intransigent problems of racism that the civil rights movement dramatized through a program that also addressed unemployment. This would enable him to meet the needs of African Americans by focusing on the economic distress of poor people in general, which would ensure a greater probability of the legislation becoming law. That August, the dramatic display of 250,000 people calling for jobs and freedom through peaceful protest in front of the Lincoln Memorial validated the goals of the civil rights movement to many Americans for the first time as they watched the March on Washington unfold through live television coverage of the event. By forging civil rights with employment, Kennedy planned to open the door of opportunity wider to include the needs of other "forgotten" Americans. In September the White House concluded that it wanted a poverty bill in its 1964 legislative package. A Kennedy advisor rationalized that "having mounted a dramatic program for one disadvantaged group [through civil rights legislation] it was both equitable and politically attractive to launch one specifically designed to aid other disadvantaged groups."[8]

The intellectual justification for the fight against poverty could be found in the January 1964 *Economic Report of the President*. This report disclosed a strategy for reaching out to poor Americans, proposing the passage of legislation that would take the country beyond the programs created by the New Deal. Robert Lampman, a member of the Council of Economic Advisors, wrote the report's second chapter, titled "The Problems of Poverty in America." He made the case that poverty had become a national problem. He also stressed that the South stood poised as one of the prime targets for improvement. In 1960, of the 31,775,000 poor people in America, 16,305,000, or 51.31 percent, lived in the South. Dixie's politicians had been aware of their poor constituents for many decades, and the statistics in the report probably did not surprise many of them. In the 1930s, FDR declared the region "the nation's number one economic problem," and as a result the South benefitted greatly from New Deal programs. Many southern congressmen acquired liberal reputations because they supported progressive legislation such as public housing, farm subsidies, hospital construction, and rural electrification that improved the living standards for many of their constituents. Historian Wayne Flynt noted with regard to Alabama that "in the 1940s and 1950s no state congressional delegation did more to expand federal powers to assist the nation's weakest and most vulnerable people." In fact, in 1950 and in 1955, Senator John Sparkman of Alabama, the son of a tenant farmer who paid for his University of Alabama education by shoveling coal, conducted the first Senate hearings on the persistence of rural poverty for the Joint Economic Committee.[9]

When Johnson became president, one might assume that the congressional delegations from below the Mason-Dixon line would have been among the first to support his antipoverty plan. Unanimous southern support, however, did not materialize. Past events made them skeptical. At the end of the New Deal, liberalism began to be closely associated with racial equality. This view solidified further when President Truman accepted a strong civil rights platform in his 1948 presidential campaign. The Democratic Party split that year with states' rights supporters forming the Dixiecrat Party in protest. The 1954 Supreme Court decision *Brown v. Board of Education*, which declared the doctrine of separate but equal in public education to be unconstitutional, and the Civil Rights Act of 1957, which was the first federal legislation for racial justice in the twentieth century, added further fuel to the flames of southern Democratic discontent. All of these things reminded southern

Democrats to be cautious. "The one issue that threatened everything was race," LBJ aide Harry McPherson explained. "It was pervasive, insistent, and aroused unequaled passion." By the early 1960s assistance from the federal government held racial overtones—as evidenced in Lampman's chapter that linked poverty and racial discrimination—that many southern politicians found distasteful. A historian of the Dixiecrat revolt concluded that those southerners who stayed within the Democratic fold did so by "convincing the white voters that party loyalty in congressional elections was the best means by which to safeguard their economic and their racial interests." Only as loyal members of the Democratic Party could they ensure the ability to alter leg-islation that would maintain the racial status quo. Despite the fact that more poor people—black and white—resided in the South than in any other re-gion of the country, many southern members of Congress cast a dubious eye at their new president's plans for a War on Poverty. While the Johnson ad-ministration prepared for the antipoverty effort, the hearings and the floor debate on the 1964 Civil Rights bill stormed through the Capitol. For some politicians from Dixie, these fierce fights punctuated the fact that assistance to the poor could promote both racial and economic equality. First Kennedy and then Johnson had been saying as much in their speeches to gain support for civil rights legislation since 1963. As appealing as this connection might have been to many across America, it dismayed the dyed-in-the-wool racist who would now oppose federal aid under these circumstances. By 1964 the risks in publicly backing efforts against poverty became too great unless the legislation could be altered to ensure states' rights.[10]

It would be a rare occasion for LBJ to send legislation up to Capitol Hill without knowing first where he stood with the Congress. Before preparing for the Economic Opportunity bill, he recognized that southern members of Congress held the key to his success. He had been willing to take on the South to get a civil rights bill; the Economic Opportunity Act could serve as his way to offer southerners a reason to stay in the party. LBJ realized that northern Democrats would support the legislation because their urban con-stituencies would clearly benefit from it. Early on, many Republicans voiced their opposition. Senator Barry Goldwater attacked the president's motives, calling him the "Santa Claus of the free lunch." With the Congress divided between liberal northern Democrats and conservative western Republicans, the president saw that his chances to get the bill enacted rested in the votes of the southern members of his party. He hoped to court them with enough federal assistance that they might look beyond their racial anxieties and take another step toward modernity. He went South looking for supporters, hoping to find the sweet fruit of a New South and not the bitter harvest of the Old.[11]

The Development of the Economic Opportunity Act

Johnson needed a specific bill that would plan and manage this domestic war for his administration. He put this new project in the Executive Office because it became obvious that no existing organization could take the necessary time to plan the program and then get it through Congress. Some have argued that having the new organization so closely identified with the president might quell the anticipated criticism—the antipoverty fight could never be mistaken as anything other than *his* program.[12]

The president tapped R. Sargent Shriver to lead this new program. LBJ wanted Shriver for the job because he had proven abilities in creating new programs and then getting legislation through Congress. For example, Shriver's work for the Peace Corps had impressed LBJ. Shriver refined the idea for a Peace Corps by using a task force of educators, businessmen, labor leaders, church officials, and other people he knew. They developed a workable program; then he roamed the halls of Congress explaining it and lining up congressional support. President Kennedy credited the passage of the Peace Corps Act to his brother-in-law's lobbying skills. Shriver had what Johnson was looking for—experience in creating new programs, a successful record with Congress, and the know-how to work the political system.[13]

To accomplish Johnson's goal, Shriver formed the President's Task Force in the War Against Poverty. It turned out to be a fluid organization made up of a variety of people who came and went as the weeks and months passed. High-level bureaucrats, economists, and sociologists constituted the majority of task force members, and a core group of people worked steadily with Shriver throughout the planning period.[14] This task force developed what would become the Economic Opportunity Act of 1964, an omnibus bill to fight poverty. All the titles in the bill shared a common grassroots goal—expanding opportunity for the poor to enable them to change their own lives. Some have criticized the legislation because it did not redistribute wealth or offer a large jobs program. Yet, even in its less ambitious and less coherent format, the Economic Opportunity bill had enough transformational possibilities to threaten entrenched local power structures. This was especially true for the South where the welfare system had habitually excluded many of the people who needed the most assistance.[15]

The bill had seven titles. The two titles that would eventually cause southern members of Congress the most consternation were the Community Action Program (Title II) and the Rural Poverty Program (Title III). Both had the potential to move integration forward by offering assistance to people who had been ignored or oppressed by southern elites, which could ultimately upset the racially lopsided balance of southern politics. The Community Action Program offered funds to communities through local governments or private nonprofit agencies to devise projects that would alleviate poverty and required the "maximum feasible participation of the residents served" in the planning and implementing of programs. The Rural Poverty Program concentrated on the poorest farmers who lived beyond the reach of the city. Through loans, grants, landownership, and development of cooperatives, task force members from the Agriculture Department hoped to curtail the stream of rural poor migrants who flowed into the nation's larger cities where some on the task force believed "they . . . accomplished nothing but a relocation of their poverty." In each of these programs lay the chance for a reformation of the rural landscape of the South.[16]

An explanation of two of these initiatives provides some insight into the potential problems that lay in the way of getting southern Democrats to accept the legislation written by the task force. It is clear that those who worked on the body of Title II knew that the Community Action Program had the capability to spur big changes in impoverished communities. For instance, during task force discussions, participants realized that not all local governments operated the same way and that therefore the legislation needed to address that issue. A debate began over the involvement of the local government in a Community Action Agency (CAA) and whether its participation should be required in the bill. When the conversation focused on the South, some wondered how local poor black southerners could be guaranteed involvement in antipoverty programs in a segregated society. "We had a problem," William Cannon explained; "we knew we couldn't get community action agencies in the established governmental structure in the South." As a result, task force members were comfortable with the idea that some CAAs should be able to bypass the local power structure to protect the rights of poor minorities. A compromise developed that enabled the Community Action Program to offer funds either to the local government or to a nonprofit agency. This allowed the federal government to evade segregationist state and local governments to support Community Action Agencies that would benefit poor African Americans.[17]

The family farm corporations section of Title III—described as the "land reform" section—promised to establish nonprofit corporations that would buy land when it came on the market and then sell it to poor farmers in individual-sized allotments. Not planned as a central part of the Rural Poverty Program, it would have provided some people with land on which they could live more comfortably. In the South, this idea had serious ramifications. The crop-lien system had kept sharecroppers and tenants economically and politically powerless since the days of Reconstruction. Providing land, free and clear, to people who had never owned property would have offered a level of independence unthinkable even in the early 1960s. Those who opposed the Civil Rights bill, including Alabama's Governor George Wallace, feared that the transfer of land would be one repercussion of civil rights legislation. He told a crowd in Jackson, Mississippi, that the proposed civil rights measure demonstrated that the federal government was "well on its way to 'land-reform' legislation under which people will be called upon to redistribute the real estate which they have labored so hard to accumulate." Even though this part of Title III had good intentions, and had nothing to do with land redistribution, it was doubtful it would pass the scrutiny of conservative southern Democrats who had Wallace supporters as constituents.[18]

The president did not personally contribute to the drafting of the Economic Opportunity bill, other than approving the ideas that had been presented to him. Kermit Gordon and Walter Heller explained the Community Action Program to him, and Johnson remembered they "warned me of the risks—particularly the political risks—that might make the outcome uncertain. I was willing to take the chance." Johnson later claimed that he knew this program had the possibility to rattle many existing institutions, "but I decided that some shaking up might be needed to get a bold new program moving. I thought the local governments had to be challenged to be awakened."[19] Once the legislation moved out of the task force and into Congress, LBJ shifted gears, thinking less about the substance of the Economic Opportunity bill and more about the political problems of getting it approved.

The Politics of Race

Finding sponsors for the bill became the first item of business on the president's agenda. Johnson knew that the Republican opposition to the bill would be fierce, especially in the climate of election-year politics. More important, he realized that his GOP opponents had been quite successful in aligning with southern Democrats to form the powerful conservative coalition in Congress. The coalition would no doubt use the same dilatory tactics with the Economic Opportunity bill as it had against earlier civil rights legislation. The president remembered they would do so "by stirring the Southerners' fears that certain provisions would enforce integration." After discussing the realities of this issue with his chief congressional liaison, Larry O'Brien, LBJ asked Georgia Congressman Phil Landrum to manage the bill in the House and Alabama Senator Lister Hill to sponsor it in the Senate. Landrum accepted; Hill declined.[20]

Landrum was a good choice for the president's plan to attract southern Democrats to the bill. His district was located in the foothills of the Appalachian mountains in north Georgia, and he was associated with some conservative issues. His voting record consistently favored federal public works while also voting to curb some of the power of organized labor—most notably the 1959 Landrum-Griffin Act. The Ninth Congressional District had a substantial white majority, and the rural poverty found there meant that many of the congressman's constituents could benefit from the bill's proposed programs. Landrum could openly support the president's Economic Opportunity plans and not risk his House seat by managing the bill.[21]

Phil Landrum exemplified the type of southern politician Johnson favored, one who could see that the benefits of the antipoverty effort out- weighed the political liabilities he associated with race. The president's Senate choice, however, was not able to follow a similar path. Unlike north Georgia, Lister Hill's constituency would not allow him to veer off their Jim Crow route. Since the late 1940s, the political climate in Alabama hampered the support of federal legislators for any program that could infringe on a state's racist customs. It is not surprising, therefore, that the senior senator from Alabama turned down LBJ's request to manage the bill in the upper chamber. As chairman of the Senate Labor and Public Welfare Committee, and fifth in seniority in the Senate, Hill distanced himself even further from the legislation when he refused to sit on the subcommittee that conducted the hearings. The Senate Select Committee on Poverty consisted of the entire Committee on Labor and Public Welfare minus Senator Hill.[22]

A short review of Hill's retreat from publicly supporting national Democratic Party causes illustrates the southern opposition that the Johnson administration faced. Not long after Truman's ascendancy to the presidency, Hill resigned as party whip in 1947. In the Senate, Hill did not vote for any legislation that could be construed as supporting the cause of civil rights. At the Democratic Convention of 1960, both Alabama senators and the state's Democratic loyalist representatives were conspicuously absent. By 1962, racial politics put the senator's career directly on the line. During his final campaign, Hill's Republican opponent accused him of being "soft" on civil rights. The senator responded to this potential threat by playing the race card to assure Alabama's white voters that he could protect their way of life. He bragged to crowds that he had killed ten "integration" bills in his committee and warned that Republicans had elected a "Negro" legislator in Georgia. The trump worked but just barely. Hill won his last election with a one percent margin. After 1962, staff members, friends, and even a White House aide noticed that Hill seemed shaken and uncharacteristically bitter that his constituents had nearly rejected him. His position could not be easily changed by the president offering more federal assistance to Alabama's poor, not as long as the Civil Rights Act promised to alter the way that support would be administered.[23]

The committee hearings began in the lower chamber, which the administration thought harbored the most hostility toward the bill labeled H.R. 10440. Meeting over a six-week period from mid-March until the end of April, the Democrats dominated—controlling who testified, monopolizing the questions asked, and muzzling the opposition whenever possible. Committee Chairman Adam Clayton Powell gave the GOP only three days to call witnesses. Eighty-five people testified in the hearings, including twenty-nine members of the administration or original members of the task force and every member of the president's cabinet.[24]

Resistance to the antipoverty bill came exclusively from the Republican members of the committee and subcommittee and nine witnesses—from the Chamber of Commerce, a state manufacturing association delegate, the Farm Bureau Federation, and two educators. The GOP critics concentrated on six key issues of concern: the omnibus nature of the bill, which they thought should have required other committees to be involved in reviewing the legislation; the duplication of programs already in existence in other departments; the usurpation of authority of the other cabinet officers by the proposed "poverty czar"; the OEO's capability of bypassing state governments, especially in Title II; the unnecessary creation of a new layer of government; and the bill's focus on race—that it could enforce integration and was really for the primary benefit of black Americans.[25]

An intraparty debate had begun within the ranks of the GOP. After the 22 June 1963 Republican National Committee meeting in Denver, party members were not in agreement over the traditional support Republicans had given to the civil rights cause. As a result, GOP members of the House Subcommittee on the War on Poverty dealt with the issue of race in a variety of ways. The progressive wing supported the civil rights aspects of the antipoverty bill, while the conservative wing used the hearings to highlight the bill's capacity to infringe on state authority. Regardless of the rift within the ranks of the GOP, each time legislators and hearing participants brought up the subject of civil rights, it underscored the connection between fighting poverty and supporting civil rights. For example, on March 20, Congressman Charles Goodell (R-NY) wanted reassurance from Agriculture Secretary Orville Freeman that Job Corps facilities conducting conservation projects would be fully integrated. "To the extent that you use local facilities or personnel, it is not going to be trying to set up any separate but equal routine?" he asked. Freeman reassured him that would not be the case. Serving as the voice for the conservatives, Congressman Peter Frelinghuysen (R-NJ) tried to get Walter Reuther to admit that the president's program was mainly for black Americans. "You also say that the Negro's position is deteriorating even though there has been a general improvement in the situation nationwide. Is it your feeling that this Landrum bill should be aimed primarily at alleviating the problems of the Negroes?" the New Jerseyan asked, "or that this would be a primary effect in passage of the legislation of this kind?" Reuther, as the head of the United Auto Workers labor union, had been a friend to civil rights for many years making it difficult to avoid the congressman's trap. "Obviously, the fight against poverty should be colorblind," he said. "But the Negroes, because they have been denied, disadvantaged, and discriminated against more than any other group, would get a larger benefit out of this program, because they are the victims of poverty more than any other group."[26]

That same day Landrum took the GOP to task for using the predicament of poor black Americans in its effort to win southern opposition to the bill: "I want it clearly understood with reference to this bill under my name, and I am proud to have my name upon it, that any assistance it may provide toward eliminating the plight of poverty affecting Americans of all races is a source of pride for me. I am not ashamed of it." Landrum called the Republican strategy inflammatory and opportunistic: "I come from a section of the country that has been bombarded with a great deal of demagoguery. . . . I want it clearly understood that my efforts . . . are directed toward relieving poverty that affects both white and Negro Americans. I want the record made crystal clear on this point." The next day, Marjorie Hunter reported in the *New York Times* that the Georgia congressman "would not be scared off from the anti-poverty program by GOP efforts to picture it as largely of benefit to Negroes."[27]

After the hearings, the full committee met on 30 April to redraft portions of the bill. The Community Action Program dominated the deliberations. The committee revised Title II, introducing an allotment formula for allocation of funds to the states. About 60 percent of the funds would be distributed equally among the states but still channeled through OEO, and the remaining funds would be left for use at OEO's discretion. The committee also limited the Economic Opportunity bill to one year in duration. Beyond the changes to Title II, there were no casualties; even the Title III family farm development corporation passed beyond this initial stage. The committee completed the redrafting process on 26 May, but the legislation stalled when conservative Congressman Howard Smith (D-VA), chairman of the Rules Committee, held the bill hostage for the entire month of June. If the president wanted his bill passed before the Democratic National Convention in August, the Senate would have to debate the legislation first.

Hearings began in the Senate on S. 2642 on 17 June. Senator Pat McNamara of Michigan agreed to sponsor the bill after Lister Hill refused. The administration decided that the best strategy for passage of a Senate bill would be to operate with the version passed in the House. On the first day of testimony, Chairman McNamara explained that the Select Committee on Poverty would meet to question witnesses only for four days because the House conducted lengthy hearings and printed copies of that testimony were available.[28]

The Senate hearings resembled those in the House. Most of the witnesses came from the administration and the same outside interest groups. The testimony of Congressman Peter Frelinghuysen, who appeared as a witness, made the Senate hearings noteworthy to interested southern senators. He complained about Shriver's future role as "poverty czar" and the new federal powers associated with the bill. He described the Community Action Program as opening "the way for direct Federal involvement in the activities of every private organization in every community in this country without the necessity for participation or approval of either State or local government." As he finished his testimony, he wondered what would happen if a southern state would not cooperate in a community effort to desegregate its school system. McNamara replied that the War on Poverty had nothing to do with school integration. "There is nothing to say that it [does] not," the New Jerseyan replied. "I think it might well be part of the poverty war." He then concluded by linking Landrum's hometown with a fictitious Community Action Program brought about by a civil rights organization: "I think it would be very unwise to give the Federal Government the power to give to the NAACP, or a local citizens group which might not even be representative of the community, Gainesville, Georgia, wherever it is, that the Federal money to do something that the community or the State does not want." Senator McNamara responded by dismissing Frelinghuysen's fears: "I don't believe, however, that we have civil rights or integration or segregation problems involved in this bill."[29]

Once the hearings ended and the bill moved into the Rules Committee, the southern bloc had plenty of evidence to support its fears. The Senate Select Committee on Poverty made some changes to the bill after the hearings. It revised Title II requiring that Community Action Programs also use the maximum feasible participation of public agencies and private nonprofit organizations primarily concerned with the community's poverty problems. This addressed one of Frelinghuysen's concerns that any community group could receive poverty funds for an area. In a Labor and Public Welfare Committee meeting on 7 July, Senator Jacob Javits (R-NY) tried to amend the bill so that state welfare agencies would be involved in the antipoverty effort. His amendment failed, but Senator Harrison Williams (R-NJ) predicted that there would be an amendment on the floor requiring governors' approval of projects. Senator McNamara feared that if this became a part of the legislation, it would be used to prevent action instead of offering greater coordination.[30]

The floor debates began in both houses of Congress at the height of an active summer session. The Civil Rights Act had passed on 2 July, and Shriver remembered that the Task Force felt that "psychologically it would then be easier to ride [the Economic Opportunity Bill] through in the wake and on the euphoria . . . that [the civil rights legislation] produced." The press predicted it would be a close vote, especially after Barry Goldwater's nomination as the GOP presidential candidate. In late July, the *Wall Street Journal* reported that conservative southern Democrats feared "being swept out of office in November by a Goldwater vote tide throughout most of their region in these race-troubled days, and they're acting in self-defense." Opposition to the bill from southern congressmen became even more predictable as the summer dragged on. Johnson hoped that if the Senate passed the bill first, "some waverers" in the House might be influenced to lend their support.[31]

All levels of the administration got involved in the effort to pass the antipoverty bill. The president worked closely with his congressional liaison staff—telephoning members of Congress to get promised endorsements and contacting leaders in the private sector to lobby their members of Congress to vote for the bill. On the eve of the Senate vote, Shriver counted on 50

Democrats and 17 Republicans to back the Economic Opportunity bill. He might have been right in his predictions of support, but Shriver missed the key point that some southern Senators would alter the legislation in order to accept the bill on their terms.[32]

The Senate debated the bill over two days, 22 and 23 July, and considered amendments intended to curb the more provocative aspects of the legislation. Senators Winston Prouty (R-VT) and George Smathers (D-FL) offered governors' veto amendments to remedy the bypassing of the states in Title I and Title II programs. Smathers called for a governor's approval before OEO could set up Job Corps conservation camps or training centers in any states. McNamara did not want to accept Smathers's amendment but agreed only after the Democratic leadership recommended that the amendment go forward. "Of course, that had the civil rights aspects to it, too," Larry O'Brien, White House congressional liaison, later admitted. For him this was a political accommodation: "It was a way of getting around the corner . . . you have to accept it for what it was; it was a maneuver." Prouty submitted an amendment allowing governors to approve Title II programs before they could begin operating in states. Upon reconsideration the Senate rejected Prouty's version of a governors' veto.[33]

The states' rights issue did not die, however. Later in the day on 23 July, Strom Thurmond (D-SC) resurrected the issue. He warned that Community Action programs would allow the federal government to establish direct control over programs functioning on the local level. The South Carolinian picked up the anti–civil rights banner carried earlier by Congressman Frelinghuysen: "Under the innocent sounding title of 'Community Action Program,' the poverty czar would not only have the power to finance the activities of such organizations as the National Council of Churches, the NAACP, SNCC, and CORE, but also a SNOOP and a SNORE which are sure to be organized to get their part of the green gravy." Thurmond bemoaned the fact that the Economic Opportunity bill addressed issues that touched on racial discrimination: "I naively thought the Congress had finished with legislation on racial matters last month." He tried to highlight the bill's intent when he said it was "pregnant with racial overtones . . . the community action programs will be aimed at what [Mr. Shriver] considers to be America's poverty of spirit as well as economic poverty. Never has there been such arbitrary and discretionary grants of power, free of congressionally imposed guidelines, vested in a nonelective Federal official."[34]

That same day Senator John Stennis (D-MS) entered into the record a letter from a constituent who refused to take a training position at Tuskegee

Institute under the Manpower Development Training Act because it "would have been [conducted] at an all-Negro institution." "My safety would be endangered if I attended such a place of training," the young man wrote to his senator. The Mississippi conservative used this anecdote to remind his likeminded colleagues that the Economic Opportunity bill could "force" integration along the lines of the MDTA.[35]

On the heels of these complaints, Smathers crafted another version of a governors' veto amendment—this time with more precise language. Georgia's Senator Richard Russell wanted this amendment in the bill, and he let Shriver know about it. "Richard Russell was one of the behemoths, one of the giants of the Senate" Shriver recounted, "and normally wouldn't even have concerned himself with a peripheral thing like the War on Poverty." The future OEO director reasoned that Russell got involved because he wanted to maintain the traditional states' rights doctrine of the South. The new amendment called for the OEO director to establish procedures to "facilitate effective participation of the State in Community Action Programs." It authorized the director to make grants to or contract with appropriate state agencies in providing technical assistance. It also specified a direct role for governors in approving these Title II programs. It did not allow grants to be made to private institutions or nonprofit organizations within a state, "except when said institution operate[d] in conjunction with or under authority of a public agency, unless a plan setting forth the proposed program has been submitted to the Governor of the State, and he has not disapproved by thirty days of submission." Unlike Prouty's earlier offering, Smathers's amendment passed resoundingly, 80 to 7. Senator Albert Gore (D-TN) stood alone as the only southerner voting against the amendment.[36]

It appears that the White House worked out a compromise with the southern senators who wanted a governors' veto provision in the bill in order to keep the omnibus legislation intact. Adam Yarmolinsky, Shriver's deputy, remembered that the White House was "getting beat on" to include this accommodation. Task force member William Cannon shed further light on why the White House agreed to this compromise. He later said that he thought the South would be able to derail the entire antipoverty effort: "I was worried to death that we wouldn't get any program, because the South would hold us up for ransom, so I was willing to pay even more than [the governor's veto]." Shriver talked to Georgia's Senator Herman Talmadge, who told him that such an arrangement would allow southern senators to tell their constituents that they had upheld the states' rights doctrine. Shriver remembered that Talmadge also predicted that the veto would not be used;

"they're not going to disapprove of many of them," Talmadge concluded, "because the governors all want to have the money come to their states."[37]

The family farm development corporation provision of Title III became the next casualty of the Senate debates. After Senator Thurmond attacked this clause using anticommunist rhetoric, Frank Lausche (D-OH) killed the program. Finally, the Senate's last amendment replaced all grants for farmers with loans in the Rural Poverty Program.[38]

On 23 July, the Senate closed its debate and voted on the Economic Opportunity bill. It passed by a vote of 61 to 34. The southern bloc that LBJ worried about had been appeased. A look at the vote count highlights the division among Dixie's senators. Nine southern Democrats, including all four senators from North Carolina and Tennessee, supported the bill. The *Wall Street Journal* pointed out that only two of the nine southern senators faced GOP challenges in the upcoming fall elections—Gore of Tennessee and Yarborough of Texas, who both had "trodden too far down liberal paths to retreat now." Twelve southerners, including all six senators from Alabama, Mississippi, and Virginia, voted against the bill. The delegations that split their votes came from Arkansas, Florida, Georgia, Louisiana, and South Carolina. Dixie's most vocal senators during the floor debate and backroom negotiations were those who had led the fight against the earlier civil rights bill—Senators Richard Russell, John Stennis, and Strom Thurmond. That almost half of the senators from the old Confederacy voted for the bill indicated that many recognized they could support the bill in its amended form and not turn their backs on a program that could benefit many of their constituents.[39]

Debates began in the lower chamber on 5 August. The administration continued to be anxious about the chances of passing the bill. On 31 July, Larry O'Brien reported to the president that the House stood deadlocked with 30 southerners remaining undecided.[40]

The possible use of the Economic Opportunity bill to enforce the new civil rights legislation came out in the open and became a primary subject of the House debates. Congressman Howard Smith of Virginia took the position supported earlier by Senator Thurmond. On the first day of debate, Smith let his fellow southerners know where he stood: "I want to say to the members from the South who are going to vote for this bill—and I know there are a lot who are going to vote for it—that they are voting to implement the civil rights bill that they opposed and voted against." He warned that the antipoverty programs would not be "popular south of the Potomac River." Like Thurmond, Smith sought to undermine support for the bill by associating an established civil rights organization with extreme groups that OEO might finance as a result of the bill. "Can they set up a project to help the Ku Klux Klan, can they turn money over to the NAACP, can anybody find anything in this bill that would stop them from sponsoring the establishment of a nudist colony in your State or county?" he asked.[41]

To counter these charges, Landrum gave his reasons for backing the bill, voicing his support with provocative language that would confirm the opinions of many southern conservatives. To him there was "not anything but conservatism" in the program. He championed the legislation for the savings it would generate for the country instead of for the support it offered to those who lived below the poverty line. He estimated that the price tag for public assistance on the federal level was just over $4 billion, and the indirect costs stood at $25 billion. In the wake of a mid-July riot that had erupted in Harlem in response to the killing of an African-American youth by a white New York City policeman, Landrum admonished his fellow representatives to concentrate on what would happen if they did nothing about this national problem: "Does it give you any pause, that these human beings are reproducing in their own images? Are you concerned that the frustration may develop into violence and anarchy?" To move the debate along, he minimized the bill's more progressive policies. In his judgment the legislation was nothing more than an education and training bill that offered some hope in the federal effort to stem welfare expenses. The Johnson administration's willingness to accept these compromises to the bill reveals the new circumstances the Civil Rights Act had created in Congress. Elected officials were willing to use whatever means necessary to get legislation passed on their terms even if it threatened the intent and spirit of the original legislation. The Johnson administration was left to maneuver as best it could under the circumstances.[42]

In an effort to streamline the passage of the bill, Landrum offered an initial amendment to substitute the Senate version of the bill that passed on 23 July for H.R. 10440. This brought the problem of the governors' veto out onto the House floor and harvested the bitter fruit that had been planted in earlier hearings. Congressman Goodell argued that instead of a states' rights amendment, it was a segregationist amendment: "It means in effect that in any State where a program is designed to help a particular type of people the Governor can simply say, 'No, if you are going to do it that way, I veto it; I do not want that kind of program here.'" The Democratic leadership could not let it remain in that light. GOP criticisms would put the president in a bad position for accepting the veto amendment under these circumstances.[43]

Landrum came to the administration's defense by trying to blunt the effect that the Civil Rights Act would have on the antipoverty fight. Countering the Republican's assessment, he stated that the civil rights bill "is an accomplished fact" and that, as public officials, members of Congress must acknowledge "facts as facts." There was no need to further the discussion; "To do so is only to fill the RECORD with inflammatory material designed to build prejudice where tolerance would be more desirable and more constructive." It appears that the administration had spent a lot of its political capital during the debates over the Civil Rights Act and that the White House accepted the governors' veto as the middle way toward passage of the legislation. The administration must have hoped that the new civil rights law would keep governors from discriminating against their minority constituents when contemplating the veto option. The *Elberton Star,* a newspaper in Landrum's district, reported that Democrats, including southerners, gave Landrum an ovation when he finished his statement.[44]

Trying one last time to rid the bill of the governors' veto, William Ryan (D-NY) pointed out that many southern governors had used their veto pens when other federal welfare legislation had encroached into their states. He reminded his colleagues that Louisiana refused to sign an agreement with the federal government for Manpower Development Training programs and that Mississippi halted the distribution of federal surplus food in LeFlore County after a voter registration drive in Greenwood in 1963. "What reason is there to believe that there is a willingness to raise the general standard of living of the Negro population in 1964?" he asked. Such arguments could not sway the majority of House members who agreed to accept the Senate version of the bill with the governors' veto intact. Nevertheless, these disputes foreshadowed the approach that four southern governors—Haydon Burns of Florida, John Connally of Texas, Donald Russell of South Carolina, and George Wallace of Alabama—would take initially in implementing the antipoverty program in their states. As a result of their heavy-handed actions, Congress would reconsider the governors' veto in 1965, allowing the OEO director to override a governors' veto and have the final say in Community Action Program funding issues.[45]

The House ended its debate on 8 August and voted 226 to 185 in favor of the bill. The Senate concurred with the House, voting to accept the Economic Opportunity Act on 11 August. The margin of victory was wider than the Johnson administration had expected. As in the Senate, the House members from Dixie split almost equally in their support for the legislation, with 51 voting for it and 49 against. Of the 49 who did not support the bill, 12 were members of the GOP and 37 came from the Democratic Party. Mississippi stood out as the only southern state whose delegation unanimously voted against the bill. Those who supported the bill must have felt that they had managed to alter the legislation to their liking, which led them to believe the legislation could assist their impoverished constituents without threatening the racial status quo. Nevertheless, it is also important to acknowledge the manner in which the administration sought to appease conservative southern Democrats. Amending the original legislation—as a result of committee hearings or from floor debates—led many of Dixie's legislators to accept the bill without risking their seats. They had been able to bend the poverty bill to their liking, proving for themselves once again that party loyalty still mattered in the ability to alter legislation.[46]

After receiving the nomination from his party, Johnson worked on his budget for fiscal 1965, which included funding for the War on Poverty. Congress held hearings in late September and marked up the president's budget, taking out $15 million from the original $962.5 million request for the Economic Opportunity Act. Johnson signed the appropriation bill on 8 October, but he would not allow members of the newly created OEO to spend any of the allocated money until after the November election to avoid any appearance that government spending bought votes. It took almost twelve months to get the omnibus legislation drafted and passed through Congress. LBJ had achieved his first major piece of Great Society legislation but at a cost.[47]

Throughout the legislative process the South held center stage in the bill's successful passage. The civil rights movement had altered southern politics, putting many forces in play. As an element of the Second Reconstruction, the passage of the Economic Opportunity Act revealed how much had changed and how much had stayed the same. Southern politics forced Johnson to strike a bargain to enable the antipoverty program to move forward without obviously challenging Dixie's racism head-on. The addition of the governors' veto, the removal of the family farm corporation, and the replacement of grants with loans to poor farmers left some southern congressmen with the impression that they had addressed the more provocative elements of the bill. For the South's poorer citizens, these alterations diminished the hopes raised by Title II and III but did not curtail overall expectations of the Economic Opportunity Act. The appointment of Shriver to head the OEO, as well as Shriver's selection of progressive task force members and OEO staff, increased the likelihood that the South's poor—black and white—would benefit from the legislation regardless of the amendments attached to it. In spite of everything, unlike the first Reconstruction, the OEO would be armed with the mandates from the new Civil Rights Act that enabled it to enforce equal treatment, and Shriver created an Office of Civil Rights and an Office of Inspection within the agency to ensure that the needs of poor minorities would receive close attention.

The Governor's Heavy Hand: The First Year of the War on Poverty in Alabama

More than one southern accent could be heard across the region as the war on poverty got under way. After 11 August 1964, a federally funded program was now available to grassroots organizations in their efforts to change the South. The mixed signals of accommodation to the white South that had emanated from 1600 Pennsylvania Avenue throughout the bill's development and passage began to be clarified as southern governors implemented antipoverty programs. Over the course of the year it became clear that some intended to manipulate the program for their political advantage, especially Alabama's governor.

George Wallace appointed Claude Kirk to study the possible benefits of OEO programs for the state. After being convinced that the antipoverty program could be beneficial, the governor appointed Kirk (who had no experience in working with the poor or federal programs) to coordinate the statewide effort once the OEO approved a $134,000 grant to the Alabama Office of Economic Opportunity. Wallace envisioned the War on Poverty as a form of patronage for his statewide political machine, not as a program to empower the poor to change their living standards by implementing programs developed from their own ideas. His advisory committee consisted of state bureaucrats, and in his first public announcement regarding the program he specified that he wanted "no part of antipoverty funds that require race mixing." As interest in the antipoverty program grew, Wallace asked his poverty coordinator to contact only individuals friendly to his administration in order to keep the federal program in check. In his correspondence to interested parties, Kirk made it clear that Wallace planned for the federal antipoverty effort to remain in the control of the governor and local elected officials, which stood in direct conflict with the spirit of the Economic Opportunity Act. "Except in extraordinary circumstances," he relayed, "the Governor will either veto or accept the particular plan based on the advice given by said governing bodies." Wallace often wrote to Kirk telling him whom to locate and hire. In Coosa County, he directed Kirk to get in touch with Jesse and James Hamil. They agreed to form a contact group to discuss organizing a community action program in their area. As they sent out word of an upcoming organizational meeting, the Hamil brothers discovered that Judge Mac Thomas had already established a group and formed a Coosa County Advisory Committee for Economic Opportunity approved by the county commission. The Hamils suspected that "Sargent Schriver [*sic*] could be the force behind a move of this sort" and asked Wallace to intercede for them. Cecil Jackson, the governor's executive secretary, arranged a meeting with Kirk and the Coosa County delegation, telling the poverty coordinator "that we were interested in seeing that Mr. Hammel [*sic*] and his delegation received the fullest cooperation from him." Similar letters followed throughout the first year as the War on Poverty got under way in Alabama. When the Office of Economic Opportunity approved community action grants, Claude Kirk sought the governor's approval of people who had been hired as administrators for the local CAA.[48]

The interference of the governor's office did not go unnoticed. The OEO began to suspect his actions in late March, and a federal employee in Alabama alerted members of President Johnson's staff to Wallace's plans: "It appears that the poverty program in Alabama is being organized along strictly political lines with 100% Wallace forces as co-ordinators in every case, and with most executive committee members being Wallaceites," he warned. "We have been told by certain key Wallace supporters that only a co-ordinator acceptable to Wallace will be placed on the payroll." Although the governor tried to dominate the program through the statewide office, he could not control the way the OEO planned to operate in his state. In an effort to jump-start the antipoverty fight, OEO officials had made contacts with people in Birmingham before the Economic Opportunity bill had passed. The Washington administrators wanted Alabama's largest city to be prepared to launch antipoverty programs immediately after Congress enacted the legislation. The conflict over who would lead the fight against poverty in the Magic City would eventually lead to a showdown between the governor and federal officials in the Office of Economic Opportunity and Congress.[49]

The issue in Birmingham centered on the activities of C. H. Erskine Smith, who worked on the initial plans for a Community Action Program for the city. On 5 January 1965, Mayor Albert Boutwell appointed Smith chairman of the newly incorporated Birmingham Area Committee for the Development of Economic Opportunity (BACDEO). As a young lawyer, Smith had served as the Kennedy-Johnson campaign chairman for the Ninth Congressional District, which encompassed all of Jefferson County. In 1963, he joined other young lawyers in an effort to change the political structure of the city that kept Eugene "Bull" Connor in office. The group of Young Turks succeeded in getting a referendum vote in November 1962 that turned out the city commission form of government and ushered in the mayor/city council model. Smith also worked with David Vann and others in negotiating a settlement to the Southern Christian Leadership Conference's boycott and demonstrations that rocked the city in 1962 and 1963. When President Johnson announced his plans for the War on Poverty, it seemed natural that Erskine Smith would try to find a way for Birmingham to participate. In his new role as chairman of BACDEO, he took the lead in spreading the word about the antipoverty program. He went to meetings around the city explaining how the Community Action Program worked, and he gave advice to leaders in Mobile and Huntsville who were also seeking to submit grant applications to OEO. By late January 1965, the BACDEO sent an application to Washington for a $100,000 program development grant to get the War on Poverty under way in Birmingham.[50]

Smith's history of participating in progressive activities that opposed the traditional way of doing business in Alabama ran counter to Wallace's modus operandi. Predictably, the governor's office tried to outflank the BACDEO's plans for Jefferson County. Smith unwittingly played into one of Wallace's political ploys. At the urging of the OEO's Southern Regional Office and the Alabama Office of Economic Opportunity, the BACDEO sponsored a statewide workshop to explain how to utilize the War on Poverty to interested communities. Smith invited Governor Wallace to welcome the participants and placed Claude Kirk on the agenda to address the gathering on the opening day. The BACDEO chairman also asked the National Urban League to cosponsor the statewide event, calling it the Alabama State Economic Opportunity Conference. When the *Birmingham Post Herald* reported the upcoming meeting, complete with a list of sponsors and the agenda for the two-day meeting, Claude Kirk responded quickly: "I have no intention of standing by and letting you and other liberal left wingers in Alabama take over this program," he wired Smith. Despite Kirk's rebuke, the conference took place and brought information to the participants without the governor's meddling. About 400 people attended, representing 40 communities, and top OEO officials came from Washington to participate. Acknowledging that the governor could veto some of the OEO programs, the *Birmingham News* coverage of the conference highlighted the role independent groups could take in the fight against poverty. The newspaper reported that "program ideas are limited only by the imagination of the local citizens. The idea is to eliminate poverty and the government feels that local citizens know best what their needs will be." A social worker from the Birmingham suburb of Mountain Brook described to Sargent Shriver the importance of the meeting: "It was the most inspiring event in which I had ever partici- pated in my professional career," Harold J. Wershow wrote. "[I]t was a true mobilization of common people from all walks of life, gathered together to discuss what they could do about their problems, rather than wait for Social Welfare Councils and public agencies to get around to them—to the back of the line, their customary place." The information distributed at the confer- ence ran counter to the governor's plans for the War on Poverty. People who had not been informed about the program now had the material they needed to access OEO and get programs started in their communities independent of Wallace's office. Wershow understood this and relayed to the OEO direc- tor why this could cause difficulties for those in the power structure: "[H]ere is . . . the nub of the problem. . . . Neither government nor private agencies, with their lily-white boards . . . want the poor, Negro or white, to organize, to by-pass the organized social agencies (which plan to use the program to 'strengthen' their own programs), to develop group relation skills." He hoped Shriver could find a way to keep control of the war on poverty in the hands of the local committees and away from state officials and agencies.[51]

Despite the meeting's success, the two-day conference became known by some in Alabama as the "Urban League's takeover of the Economic Oppor- tunity Conference." Three days after the statewide workshop, Bessemer Mayor Jesse Lanier, also a close political ally of the governor, hosted a meet- ing of the Jefferson County municipal mayors and the county commission so that Claude Kirk could explain to them how to form a community action agency. Threatened by the BACDEO/Urban League conference, the Besse- mer mayor intended to get ahead of any other group in Jefferson County so he could wrest control of the antipoverty program from local people and put it in the hands of more "responsible" elected officials. After the mayors elected him chairman, Lanier dominated the meeting, especially when they gave him authorization to appoint the five members of the executive com- mittee. Through the organization of the county mayors, Lanier hoped to dilute the power of Birmingham operating on its own.[52]

Beyond Lanier's action, more significant waves formed in the wake of the statewide conference. Mayor Boutwell asked Smith to resign as chairman of the BACDEO. He deduced that the young attorney had acted unilaterally in bringing the Urban League in as cosponsor of the statewide workshop. Smith tendered his resignation two days later, effective 12 March. Publically, he said that he did not want to jeopardize the success of the Birmingham antipoverty program and that Boutwell's lack of confidence revealed that he must step down. Privately, Smith had harbored doubts about Boutwell from the beginning. His brother Paul explained: "I know he had some concerns about the mayor. . . . I guess that's an understatement. . . . He was one of the old guard . . . he wasn't a bad man, he just . . . didn't want change." Boutwell had been involved in state and local politics since 1946. In the 1950s he served as chairman of the Interim Legislative Committee on Segregation in the Public Schools. Alabamians also elected him lieutenant governor in 1958. In spite of his segregationist past, he was not as reactionary as George Wallace, but the mayor knew how political wheels turned in the state and what needed to be done to keep his administration on track. Smith suspected the mayor's request came by way of the governor's office and that political plums were offered in exchange for Smith's removal. He told the *New York Times* that "Governor Wallace wished to control the federal program throughout the state for his own political advantage," and Smith stood in the way of that with his own political philosophy and by bringing in black people to participate. He also thought that Wallace had threatened to withhold state and federal grants from Birmingham for a needed road-building program.[53]

The conflicts over the Birmingham poverty program came at the same time that Governor Wallace ordered the violent response to protests over voter registration in Selma. Washington was on high alert regarding anything that happened in Alabama after the "Bloody Sunday" confrontation of 7 March on the Edmund Pettus Bridge, which sparked national interest in the Selma voting rights campaign. The coverage of his resignation in national newspapers enabled Smith to voice his own fears of Wallace's manipulations, which put OEO's integrity on the line: "I am very strongly concerned that the Johnson Administration will seek its normal accommodations—the President being the great accommodator—and may just accommodate Governor Wallace to give the illusion that the program is working in Alabama," he told one reporter. Administrators in the antipoverty program could not easily ignore events in Birmingham under these circumstances.[54]

Officials at OEO responded in several ways. First, they assumed that "the request for Smith's resignation was, directly or indirectly, dictated by Wallace." Operating under that supposition, Holmes Brown of the antipoverty agency's public relations office said that the Birmingham program development grant hinged on its chairman remaining in office. CAP administrators then placed two stipulations on the city's grant in order to protect the integrity of the board from "arbitrary or pressured change of its membership or officers." OEO would have to approve any change in the directors of the

CAP board for the duration of the grant, except in the case of the majority of the board voting for the change, and within thirty days after the grant has been approved, representatives from the poverty areas of Birmingham had to be selected to serve on the board. These steps were intended to protect the Birmingham program from the encroachment of the governor without confronting Wallace directly.[55]

In light of these developments, the BACDEO asked the mayor to rescind his request for Smith's resignation. The mayor wanted OEO to fund the grant first before final decisions were made about the BACDEO chairman. Smith agreed to this approach because he thought the whole controversy drained the enthusiasm out of supporters of the program. Before the mayor and the BACDEO board could meet to decide the fate of Smith as chairman, OEO approved Birmingham's program development grant for $66,349 on April 14. The antipoverty agency purposefully waited until after the Selma-to-Montgomery march took place to announce the grant approval. OEO would not know for thirty days if the compromise over Smith's position had been smoothed over. Under the stipulations of the Economic Opportunity Act, Wallace could take that long to announce his decision.[56]

In late April, Bessemer Mayor Jesse Lanier voiced his disapproval of the federal antipoverty program, calling it a "come-on deal" and a "political football." He stated that he would prefer to drop the county's plans to form a community action agency. This may have been a message for the governor to veto Birmingham's plans as well. Wallace did just that in a letter to Shriver on 7 May. He based his decision on two issues: the BACDEO did not include the entire county, and the board of directors did not constitute a representative group from across the entire Jefferson County area. The governor took the opportunity to give his judgment of the federal effort to Shriver. After complaining that the OEO stood outside "the traditional principles of government as we have known it," he claimed that the program seemed to help "those who would direct and prepare the studies rather than the poor themselves." Of course, the OEO made its best effort to keep the program from being operated in this manner; it was Wallace who planned on using the antipoverty program under his jurisdiction in that fashion.[57]

The governor's veto of the BACDEO grant revealed his true desires for the program. He had approved applications in Huntsville, Anniston, and Tuskegee. Each of these three communities had biracial committees, so race was not necessarily the overriding factor in Wallace's disapproval of Birmingham's approach. Political control, pure and simple, was the reason he stood against Mayor Boutwell and Erskine Smith. He would play the racial card to make his point, but it was not the sole reason for his opposition to the antipoverty program.

Two of the CAPs the governor approved bear this out. Milton K. Cummings dominated Huntsville's CAA. He was the president and CEO of Brown Engineering and Senator Sparkman's brother-in-law. The CAP board had black members, but they were easily outnumbered. Dr. John Cashin, an African-American leader in the area, told OEO that "Cummings had no intention of ever letting the Huntsville program become an outlet for genuine Negro aspirations." As a wealthy man with powerful connections, Cummings dealt with Wallace, but he did not fear him. Clearly, the governor did not want to cross Cummings and felt that this program did not threaten his basic agenda. In Anniston, Dan Gray, county commissioner and head of the board of voter registrars, spearheaded the antipoverty program. Three African Americans chosen by the black community served on the board. As board members they were not afraid to voice their opinions, but they were also in a distinct minority on a board of seventeen people. Gray was also someone the governor did not want to confront, especially since he managed the voter registration office. Birmingham stood in contrast to Huntsville and Anniston. Erskine Smith, as chairman of the board, could not be put under Wallace's thumb—he had already proven that in 1963. Boutwell as mayor, however, could be brought to heel by the governor's threats, and Wallace could profit in the process of vetoing the grant.[58]

Although Wallace seemed to have his say in the case of dominating Birmingham's antipoverty program, Smith had the last word. The national attention drawn to Alabama in the aftermath of Selma, and then the governor's publicized veto of the Magic City's OEO grant, had far-reaching consequences. In Washington timing is everything, and Wallace's actions took place while Congress debated the refunding of the Economic Opportunity Act. The day after he vetoed the BACDEO grant, Rep. John Brademas (D-IN) tacked an amendment onto the bill that would enable OEO's director to override a governor's veto on Community Action Programs and the establishment of Neighborhood Youth Corps projects. In its final form the amendment restored the governor's ability to object to these two programs plus adult basic education classes, but the OEO director could overrule these vetoes if they were based on racial discrimination, political manipulation, or "some other kind of undue influence." Congress attributed the amendment against the governor's veto to Wallace's handling of the grant in Bir-

mingham, even though Texas Governor John Connally and South Carolina
Governor Donald Russel had also used their veto power against OEO programs.[59]

Although armed with the ability to override a governor's veto, OEO administrators knew that this would not end the struggle in places like Alabama. Wallace would continue to seek confrontations with the federal agency
for his own political gain. By February 1966 only twelve areas in the state had
received funding from Washington. Not surprisingly, the poorest counties
had been passed over because they were also part of the Black Belt where
African Americans outnumbered their white neighbors. Unlike Huntsville,
Anniston, and Birmingham, in these counties black people could logistically
outnumber white board members and control the policy-making aspects of
the Community Action Agency. Therefore, local government officials in the
poorest part of the state dragged their feet in seeking assistance from the
federal antipoverty program. Wallace had strong support in this region and
reassured local governments that he would not fund programs that they did
not want.

In the first year of the War on Poverty, it became clear that it would take
more than federal largesse to placate the white South. As the accommodation made to southern Democrats in Congress revealed, the culture of white
supremacy was rooted throughout the governmental structure—national,
state, and local—that represented people in the Deep South. Confronting
the disparities of racial and economic power with federal legislation, while
important, still required implementation on the local level. It was in places
like Birmingham, Mobile, and Selma that the meaning of the Second Reconstruction would be defined. Another voice from Alabama offered this
view in a letter to historian C. Vann Woodward in 1967: "I agree with you
that Civil Rights has now become deja vu but I do not agree with you that it
is over or even weaker," Virginia Durr explained from her perspective in
Montgomery. "I think the great mass demonstrations are over . . . the floods
of sympathizers and the excitement, BUT all of this has left in its wake a new
spirit and a new determination on the part of the Negroes to get their due as
Americans. It has come down to the nitty gritty, and on the local level there
are fights going on all the time. . . . I agree the wave has receded but it left a
lot of residue and I do not believe that will be swept away." Her letter underscores that the battle was joined after 1965. It would be fought among federal
officials, state bureaucrats, and local people who used federal legislation like
the Civil Rights Act, the Economic Opportunity Act, and the Voting Rights
Act to give meaning to the next phase of the civil rights struggle.[60]

Author's Note

All interview transcripts cited in the notes to this chapter may be found in the LBJ Library in Austin, Texas, unless otherwise indicated.

Notes

1. Lyndon Baines Johnson, "Annual Message to the Congress of the State of the Union," 8 January 1964, *Public Papers of the Presidents of the United States: Lyndon B. Johnson, Containing the Public Messages, Speeches, and Statements of the President 1963–1964, Book 1—November 22, 1963 to June 30, 1964* (Washington, D.C.: GPO, 1965), 112–14.

2. Robert D. Novak, *The Agony of the G.O.P., 1964* (New York: Macmillan Co., 1965), 176–79; Kevin P. Phillips, *The Emerging Republican Majority* (New York: Anchor Books, 1969), 32–33. Phillips corroborates Novak's summation when he states that "Not only had the civil rights revolution cut the South adrift from its Democratic moorings and drawn the Northeast towards the Democrats, but it has increased the Southern and Western bias of the GOP to a point—the 1964 Goldwater nomination—where the party had decided to break with its formative antecedents and make an ideological bid for the anti–civil rights South." See Charles Whalen and Barbara Whalen, *The Longest Debate: A Legislative History of the 1964 Civil Rights Act* (Cabin John, Md.: Seven Locks Press, 1985), 40, 212–13, 215; Robert Dallek, *Flawed Giant: Lyndon Johnson and His Times, 1961–1973* (New York: Oxford University Press, 1998), 120.

3. *Congressional Record,* 88th Cong., 2d sess., 1964, 110, pt. 14:18634, 19023. Mississippi was the only southern state whose delegation voted unanimously against the bill. All the other southern delegations split their support. See Lyndon Baines Johnson, *The Vantage Point: Perspectives of the Presidency, 1963–1969* (New York: Holt, Rinehart and Winston, 1971), 81; *Atlanta Constitution,* 8 August 1964.

4. Richard N. Goodwin, *Remembering America: A Voice from the Sixties,* (Boston: Little, Brown and Company, 1988), 258, 260–70; William H. Chafe, *The Unfinished Journey: America Since World War II,* 2d ed. (New York: Oxford University Press, 1991), 237; Irwin Unger, *The Best of Intentions: The Triumph and Failure of the Great Society Under Kennedy, Johnson, and Nixon* (New York: Doubleday Press, 1996), 76; James T. Patterson, *Grand Expectations: The United States, 1945–1974* (New York: Oxford University Press, 1996), 531, 535; Paul K. Conkin, *Big Daddy from the Perdanales: Lyndon Baines Johnson* (Boston: Twayne Publishers, 1986), 192–93; Daniel Patrick Moynihan, *Maximum Feasible Misunderstanding: Community Action in the War on Poverty* (New York: The Free Press, 1969), 29; Jim F. Heath, *Decade of Disillusionment: The Kennedy-*

Johnson Years (Bloomington: Indiana University Press, 1975), 170–71; Johnson, *The Vantage Point,* 72.

5. Robert Dallek, *Lone Star Rising: Lyndon Johnson and His Times, 1908–1960* (New York: Oxford University Press, 1991), 8, 169, 379–81, 518–27. As a New Deal congressman, LBJ made sure black farmers from his district received the same loans as white farmers from Farm Security Administration programs. Milo Perkins, an FSA official, said that Johnson "was the first man in Congress from the South ever to go to bat for the Negro farmer." See Dallek, *Flawed Giant,* 120; Steven F. Lawson, *Civil Rights Crossroads: Nation, Community, and the Black Freedom Struggle* (Lexington: University Press of Kentucky, 2003), 59.

6. Carl Brauer, "Kennedy, Johnson, and the War on Poverty," *Journal of American History* 69, 2 (June 1982):104, 118–19.

7. Adam Fairclough, *To Redeem the Soul of America: The Southern Christian Leadership Conference and Martin Luther King, Jr.* (Athens: University of Georgia Press, 1987), 134–35, 150–53.

8. John F. Kennedy, "Special Message to the Congress on Civil Rights and Job Opportunities," 19 June 1963, *Public Papers of the Presidents of the United States: John F. Kennedy, Containing the Public Messages, Speeches, and Statements of the President* (Washington, D.C.: GPO, 1964), 483–85, 488; Heath, *Decade of Disillusionment,* 113–14; Bruce Miroff, *Pragmatic Illusions: The Presidential Politics of John F. Kennedy* (New York: David McKay Co., 1976), 225; Allen J. Matusow, *The Unraveling of America: A History of Liberalism in the 1960s* (New York: Harper and Row, 1984), 120–21; Robert Lampman, oral history interview, 17 July 1974, 7–9; James T. Patterson, *America's Struggle Against Poverty, 1900–1985* (Cambridge: Harvard University Press, 1981, 1986), 134–35.

9. Office of Economic Opportunity History, vol. 2, Documentary Supplement, *Economic Report of the President,* January 1964, 203–4, Record Group 381, Office of Economic Opportunity Papers, National Archives 2, College Park, Md. (hereafter OEO papers); House Committee on Education and Labor, *Hearings on H.R. 10440,* 88th Cong., 2d sess., 17–20 March, 7–10, 13–14 April 1964, 247 (hereafter House, *Hearings on H.R. 10440*); Patricia Sullivan, *Days of Hope: Race and Democracy in the New Deal Era* (Chapel Hill: University of North Carolina Press, 1996), 64–65; William Warren Rogers, Robert David Ward, Leah Rawls Atkins, and Wayne Flynt, *Alabama: The History of a Deep South State* (Tuscaloosa: University of Alabama Press, 1994), 524, 530; Sar A. Levitan, *The Great Society's Poor Law: A New Approach to Poverty* (Baltimore: Johns Hopkins Press, 1969), 12.

10. Harry McPherson, *A Political Education: A Washington Memoir,* 3 editions (Austin: University of Texas Press, 1972, 1988, 1995), 135; Irving Bernstein, *Promises*

Kept: John F. Kennedy's New Frontier (New York: Oxford University Press, 1991), 236; Kari Frederickson, *The Dixiecrat Revolt and the End of the Solid South, 1932–1968* (Chapel Hill: University of North Carolina Press, 2001), 215.

11. Conkin, *Big Daddy*, 135; Miroff, *Pragmatic Illusions*, 231; Moynihan, *Maximum Feasible Misunderstanding*, 6; Matusow, *Unraveling of America*, 217; Irving Bernstein, *Guns or Butter: The Presidency of Lyndon Johnson* (New York: Oxford University Press, 1996), 106.

12. R. Sargent Shriver, oral history interview 1, 20 August 1980, 18–19, 38–39; James L. Sundquist, oral history interview 1, 7 April 1969, 22–24.

13. Johnson, *The Vantage Point*, 76; Joseph A. Califano, Jr., *The Triumph and Tragedy of Lyndon Johnson: The White House Years* (Simon and Schuster: New York, 1991), 76; Bernstein, *Promises Kept*, 268; Levitan, *Great Society's Poor Law*, 74; Shriver, interview 1, 20 August 1980, 34–35, interview 2, 23 October 1980, 52–53; Kermit Gordon, oral history interview, tape 4, January–April 1969.

14. Adam Yarmolinsky, oral history interview, 13 July 1970, 18, interview, 21 October 1980; Shriver, oral history interview 1, 20 August 1980, 71; Lampman, oral history interview, 24 May 1983, 27–28, 43–44; John A. Baker, oral history interview 3, 21 April 1981, 3–4; William P. Kelly, oral history interview 1, 4 April 1969, 6. See also Levitan, *Great Society's Poor Law*, 29–30; Poverty and Urban Policy transcript, John F. Kennedy Library, Boston, 183–84; Moynihan, *Maximum Feasible Misunderstanding*, 98; *Congressional Record—Extensions of Remarks*, 12 June 1968, E5347; Administrative History of OEO, vol. 1, pt. 1:49–50.

15. Patterson, *America's Struggle*, 136; Administrative History of the OEO, vol. 1, pt. 1:37–38.

16. No date, Section by Section Analysis of the Economic Opportunity Act of 1964, Box 2, Legislative Background—Economic Opportunity Act, LBJ Library; Administrative History of the OEO, vol. 1, pt. 1, 35; memorandum, 2 March 1964, to the Director [of the Bureau of the Budget] from Charles L. Schultze, "Outline of the Poverty Bill and Issues Raised Therein," box 1, Legislative Background—Economic Opportunity Act, LBJ Library; "The War on Poverty: A Congressional Presentation," 17 March 1964, box 7, 4–5, General Counsel Records Regarding the President's Task Force in the War Against Poverty, OEO papers.

17. Poverty and Urban Policy transcript, 231–32, 247–49, 254, 258; William Cannon, oral history interview, 21 May 1982, 24–25; Bruce J. Schulman, *Lyndon B. Johnson and American Liberalism: A Brief Biography with Documents* (Boston: Bedford/St. Martin's Press, 1995), 183.

18. Sundquist, oral history interview, 7 April 1969, 7–8; John Baker, oral history interview 2, 21 April 1981, 30–31; Dan T. Carter, *The Politics of Rage: George Wallace,*

the Origins of the New Conservatism, and the Transformation of American Politics (New York: Simon and Schuster, 1995), 154; memorandum, 2 March 1964, to the Director [of Bureau of the Budget] from Charles L. Schultze.

19. Dallek, *Flawed Giant*, 142; Johnson, *The Vantage Point*, 74–75.

20. Doris Kearns Goodwin, *Lyndon Johnson and the American Dream* (New York: St. Martin's Press, 1976, 1991), 227; Johnson, *Vantage Point*, 77.

21. *Washington Post*, 17 March 1964; 1964 Scrapbook, 88th Cong., 2d sess., Phil Landrum Papers, Offices of Susan Landrum and Phil Landrum, Jr., Jasper, Georgia (hereafter Landrum Papers); Johnson, *The Vantage Point*, 77–78; Califano, *The Triumph and Tragedy of Lyndon Johnson*, 76; Shriver, oral history interview 2, 23 October 1980, 45–46; Stephen J. Pollak, oral history interview 2, 29 January 1969, 14; Unger, *The Best of Intentions*, 91; *The Daily Times*, Gainesville, Georgia, 17 March 1964, Poverty Clippings File, Landrum Papers.

22. Shriver, oral history interview 2, 23 October 1980, 46–47; Donald M. Baker, oral history interview 1, 24 February 1969, 1; Virginia Van der Veer Hamilton, *Lister Hill: Statesman from the South* (Chapel Hill: University of North Carolina Press, 1987), 267; *Congressional Quarterly Almanac, 88th Congress, 2nd Session . . . 1964* (Congressional Quarterly Service: Washington, D.C., 1964), 20:27.

23. Hamilton, *Lister Hill*, 236, 249, 253, 255, 266; see also Frederickson, *Dixiecrat Revolt*.

24. House, *Hearings on H.R. 10440*, 17–20 March, 7–10, 13–14 April 1964, pt. 1:433; Bernstein, *Guns or Butter*, 56; Administrative History of the OEO, 1:42–43; Yarmolinsky, oral history interview, 21 October 1980, 33; Levitan, *Great Society's Poor Law*, 41; Donald Baker, oral history interview 1, 24 February 1969, 203; Pollak, oral history interview 2, 29 January 1969, 17; *Congressional Record*, 12 June 1968, E5347, Box 660, Office Files of John Macy, LBJ Library.

25. House, *Hearings on H.R. 10440*, pt. 1:19, pt. 3:1521; Administrative History of OEO, 1:42–44; Drew Pearson editorial, 21 May 1964, Poverty Clippings File, Landrum Papers.

26. House, *Hearings on H.R. 10440*, pt. 1:321–23, 465.

27. Statement, 8 April 1964, Poverty Clippings File, Landrum Papers; House, *Hearings on H.R. 10440*, pt. 1:379; Marjorie Hunter, "Landrum Defies G.O.P. on Poverty," *New York Times*, 10 April 1964.

28. Senate, Committee on Labor and Public Welfare, *Hearings on S. 2642*, 88th Cong., 2d sess., 17, 18, 23, 25 June 1964, 54 (hereafter Senate, *Hearings on S. 2642*).

29. Ibid., 177, 181, 183–84, 186.

30. Major Amendments to H.R. 11377 [aka H.R. 10440] Made by the Senate Labor and Public Welfare Committee, Anti-Poverty Legislation File, Landrum Papers; Select Subcommittee on Labor and Public Welfare, Executive Meeting Minutes,

30 June 1964, box 444, Labor and Public Welfare Committee, Lister Hill Papers, W. S. Hoole Special Collections, University of Alabama, Tuscaloosa (hereafter Hill Papers).

31. Shriver, oral history interview 2, 23 October 1980, 80–81; Joseph W. Sullivan, *Wall Street Journal,* 29 July 1964; Johnson, *The Vantage Point,* 80.

32. Memorandum for the President from Sargent Shriver, Box 39, White House Aides Files—Bill Moyers, LBJ Library.

33. *Congressional Record,* 22 July 1964, 110, pt. 13:16659, 23 July 1964, 16722–16723, 16727; Michael L. Gillette, *Launching the War on Poverty: An Oral History,* (New York: Twayne Publishers, 1996), 130.

34. *Congressional Record,* 23 July 1964, 110, pt. 13:16705.

35. Ibid., 16726, 16786–16787.

36. Ibid., 16727, 16741, 16768, 16790. Senator Gore explained why he voted against the governors' veto: "I was about to say that in programs in which the contractual relationship is between the Federal Government and the municipality or a county or regional organization, I see no justification for interposing the power of the Governor to veto. This is not wise. This is not the practice that has been followed. I see no necessity for starting it now"; Gillette, *Launching the War on Poverty,* 129.

37. Yarmolinsky, interview, 21 October 1980, 11–12; Shriver, interview 2, 23 October 1980, 76–77; Cannon, interview, 21 May 1982, 55–56.

38. *Congressional Record,* 23 July 1964, 110, pt. 13:16706, 16757, 16764; John Baker, interview 2, 24 February 1969, 33; Sullivan, *Days of Hope,* 124–29. Thurmond feared the family farm corporation precisely because of its connection to the New Deal's FSA. Sullivan wrote, "FSA administrators were sensitive to the interconnections of rural poverty, social isolation, racial discrimination, ignorance, and the political impotence of the masses of southern people. . . . In addition to providing loans and grants, the FSA promoted economic and social interaction among its client families through cooperative associations, collective farming techniques, and neighborhood action groups; it cooperated with the Southern Tenant Farmers Union, the CIO, and other progressive groups toward this end. Blacks and union members served on local FSA committees" (128–29).

39. Joseph W. Sullivan, *Wall Street Journal,* 29 July 1964; *Congressional Record,* 23 July 1964, 110, pt. 13:16726, 16786–87. Those southerners who voted for the bill were Ervin, N.C.; Fulbright, Ark.; Gore, Tenn.; Johnston, S.C.; Jordan, N.C.; Long, La.; Smathers, Fla.; Talmadge, Ga.; and Walters, Tenn. Those voting against the bill included Byrd, Va.; Eastland, Miss.; Ellender, La.; Hill, Ala.; Holland, Fla.; McClellan, Ark.; Robertson, Va.; Russell, Ga.; Sparkman, Ala.; Stennis, Miss.; Thurmond, S.C.; and Tower, Tex. Tower was a Republican.

40. Johnson, *The Vantage Point,* 80; Unger, *Best of Intentions,* 97; Bernstein, *Guns*

or Butter, 109. On 28 July the House Rules Committee voted out the bill. Eight voted yes (all Democrats), seven opposed (five Republicans and two southern Democrats, Smith of Virginia and Colmer of Mississippi).

41. *Congressional Record,* 5 August 1964, 110, pt. 14:18198.

42. Ibid., 18208; Unger, *Best of Intentions,* 98. The 18 July uprising in Harlem spread to Bedford-Stuyvesant in Brooklyn and more riots occurred in Rochester and Jersey City.

43. *Congressional Record,* 5, 6 August 1964, 18221, 18263, 7 August 1964, 18575.

44. Ibid., 6 August 1964, 18264, 7 August 1964, 18575; *Elberton Star,* n.d., Poverty Clippings File, Landrum Papers.

45. *Congressional Record,* 6 August 1964, 18325; *Congressional Quarterly Almanac, 89th Congress, 1st Session. . . . 1965,* 21:406.

46. *Congressional Record,* 6 August 1964, 18634, 19023. The vote breakdown for the southern states except Mississippi was: Alabama for, Elliott, Jones, Raines, against, Andrews, Huddleston, Roberts, Selden; Arkansas for, Mills, Trimble, against, Gathings, Harris; Florida for, Fascell, Fuqua, Gibbons, Matthews, Pepper, against, Bennett, Cramer (R), Gurney (R), Haley, Herlong, Rogers; Georgia for, Davis, Landrum, Pilcher, Stephens, Vinson, Weltner, against, Flynt, Forrester, Hagan, Tuten; Louisiana for, Boggs, Herbert, Long, Morrison, Thompson, Willis, against, Waggonner; North Carolina for, Bonner, Colley, Fountain, Henderson, Taylor, Whitener, Kornegay, against, Broyhill (R), Jonas (R), Lennon, Scott; South Carolina for, Rivers, against, Ashmore, Dorn, McMillan, Watson; Tennessee for, Bass, Davis, Everett, Evins, Fulton, Murray, against, Baker (R), Brock (R), Quillen (R); Texas for, Brooks, Gonzales, Mahon, Patman, Pickle, Poage, Purcell, Roberts, Thomas, Thompson, Wright, Young, against, Alger (R); Virginia for, Gary, Hardy, Jennings, against, Abbitt, Broyhill (R), Downing, Marsh, Poff (R), Smith, Tuck. See Johnson, *The Vantage Point,* 81; Donald Baker, interview 1, 24 February 1969, 14; Norbert Schlei, interview, 21 April 1981, 36, 44; Sundquist, *On Fighting Poverty: Perspectives from Experience* (New York: Basic Books, Inc., 1969), 4.

47. Levitan, *Great Society's Poor Law,* 45–46; Kelly, interview 1, 4 April 1969, 12–14; Shriver, interview 1, 20 August 1980, 41.

48. Memorandum from Claude R. Kirk, n.d., resumé Claude R. Kirk, n.d., letter to Jack T. Conway from George C. Wallace, 4 November 1964, all in Box SG 22390, Alabama Governors Files, Alabama Department of Archives and History (ADAH); James Bennett, "Wallace to Discuss Anti-Poverty Program," *Birmingham Post Herald,* 30 September 1964, Box 37.56, Albert Boutwell Papers, Birmingham Public Library; memorandum to Poverty Bill File from Jim Solomon, 1 October 1964, Box SG 22379, letter to Governor George C. Wallace from C. Herbert Oliver, 12 December 1964, Box 22390, memorandum to George C. Wallace from Cecil C. Jackson, Jr.,

"Economic Opportunity Act Office," 20 November 1964, Box SG 22403, all part of Alabama Governors Files, ADAH; memorandum to Theodore M. Berry from Frederick O'R. Hayes, "Alabama," 20 March 1965, Box 1, CAP Office Records of the Director, State Files 1965–1968, OEO papers; letter to George Wallace from Jesse M. Hamil and James E. Hamil, 28 February 1965, Box SG 22390, Alabama Governors Files, ADAH; memorandum to Governor Wallace from Claude R. Kirk, "Economic Opportunity Grants," n.d., Box SG 22403, Alabama Governors Files, ADAH.

49. Anonymous, "Assessment of the Anti-Poverty Situation in Alabama," 6 April 1965, Box 1, CAP Office Records of the Director, State Files 1965–1968, OEO Papers; memorandum to Bill Moyers from Marvin Watson, "Memo from Buford Ellington Poverty Program in Alabama," 7 June 1965, Box 56, White House Aides Files—Moyers, LBJ Library.

50. Glenn T. Eskew, *But for Birmingham: The Local and National Movements in the Civil Rights Struggle* (Chapel Hill: University of North Carolina Press, 1997), 166, 182, 256, 277; "Statement of Erskine Smith," 5 January 1965, Box 38.14, Boutwell Papers; Gillis Morgan, "City's Anti-Poverty Action Could Reach into 42 Areas," *Birmingham News*, n.d., and Ted Bryant, "Mayor Appoints New Development Group Head War on Poverty Here," *Birmingham Post Herald*, both in Tutweiler Southern History Collection (TSHC), Clippings Files, Birmingham Public Library.

51. Minutes of Meeting of the BACDEO, 22 January 1965, Box 38.10, Boutwell Papers; letter to W. C. Hamilton from Erskine Smith, 9 February 1965, Box 38.13, ibid.; letter to George Wallace from Erskine Smith and Freida Coggin, 16 February 1965, and telegram to Sargent Shriver, Frieda Coggin, WBRC-TV, WAPI-TV, and Erskine Smith from Claude Kirk, both in Box SG 22390, Alabama Governors Files, ADAH; Ted Brant, "Smith Key to Poverty Funds," *Birmingham News*, n.d. [ca. March 1965], TSHC; Gillis Morgan, "Poverty Experts Explain Program to 400 Alabamians," *Birmingham News*, 28 February 1965, TSHC; "Agenda Alabama State Economic Opportunity Conference," 26–27 1965, Box 38.15, Boutwell Papers; letter to Sargent Shriver from Harold J. Wershow, 12 March 1965, Box 24, Records of the Office of the Director Relating to the Administration of the Civil Rights Program in the Regions, 1965–1966, OEO Papers.

52. Letter to Albert Boutwell from Jesse Lanier, March 1, 1965, Box 38.15, Boutwell Papers; "Anti-Poverty Meeting Set by County: Establishment of Committee to be Discussed," *Birmingham Post Herald*, 2 March 1965, ibid.; "Minutes of the Meeting of the Jefferson County Association of Municipal Mayors," 3 March 1965, ibid.; "Wendell Named Successor: Smith to Resign as Chief of Anti-Poverty Group," *Birmingham News*, 10 March 1965, TSHC; memorandum to Cecil C. Jackson from Economic Opportunity, "Progress Report as of March 12, 1965," 12 March 1965, Box SG 22390, Alabama Governors Files, ADAH.

53. Lou Isaacson, "War Behind Poverty War: Mayor Asks Smith to Quit," *Birmingham News*, 7 March 1965, TSHC; letter to Albert Boutwell from Erskine Smith, 9 March 1965, and memorandum to Members of the BACDEO from Erskine Smith, 9 March 1965, both in Box 8.12, Boutwell Papers; "Smith to Resign as Poverty Chief," *Birmingham Post Herald*, 10 March 1965, TSHC; letter to Erskine Smith from Albert Boutwell and M. E. Wiggins, 10 March 1965, Box 8.12, Boutwell Papers; Paul G. Smith, interview by author, Birmingham, 9 May 1998, 10, transcript on file at the Birmingham Public Library, Archives and Manuscripts Division; "Antipoverty Aid Says Wallace Sought Ouster: Head of Birmingham Program to Resign Today—Tells of Threat to Veto Projects," *New York Times*, 12 March 1965.

54. "Antipoverty Aid Says Wallace Sought Ouster," ibid.

55. Anonymous, memorandum, "Assessment of the Anti-Poverty Situation in Alabama," 6 April 1965, Box 1, CAP Office Records of the Director, State Files, 1965–1968, OEO Papers; memorandum to Theodore M. Berry from Frederick O'R. Hayes, "Alabama," 20 March 1965, memorandum to Sargent Shriver from Theodore M. Berry, "Alabama," 24 March 1965, both ibid.; memorandum to Sargent Shriver, Jack T. Conway, William Haddad, Frederick O'R. Hayes from Theodore M. Berry, "Birmingham Veto," n.d., ibid.; Ted Bryant, "Smith Key to Poverty Funds," *Birmingham News*, n.d., TSHC; resolution of the BACDEO, 12 March 1965, Box 38.6, Boutwell Papers.

56. Marjorie Hunter, "Wallace Defied on Poverty Funds: Federal Grants Are Made to Alabama Biracial Groups," *New York Times*, 14 April 1965. Huntsville–Madison County, Aniston–Calhoun County, and Tuskegee also received OEO funds at the time that Birmingham's program development grant was announced. See Roy Reed, "Wallace Vetoes a Poverty Grant: Action on Birmingham Aid is Attributed to Politics," *New York Times*, 13 May 1965; minutes of Meeting BACDEO, 23 April 1965, Box 38.10, Boutwell Papers.

57. "Editorial: Mayor Lanier, Anti-Poverty," *Birmingham News*, 3 May 1965, TSHC; Letter to Sargent Shriver from George Wallace, 7 May 1965, Box 22390, Alabama Governors Files, ADAH.

58. Press release from the Governor's Office, n.d. [ca. May 1965], Box SG 22390, Alabama Governors Files, ADAH; memorandum to Bill Haddad from Bob Martin, "Huntsville, Alabama (Preliminary Report)," 5 April 1965; memorandum to Edgar May, Robert Clampitt, Jack Gonzales from Frank Prial, "Huntsville, Madison County, Alabama," 1 November 1965; memorandum to Edgar May through C. B. Patrick and Robert L. Martin from Bill Seward and Al From, "Huntsville, Alabama, CAP," 20 July 1966; memorandum to Bill Haddad and Bob Clampitt from A. Frank Grimsley, Jr., "Calhoun County—Anniston, Alabama Program," 2 April 1965; report,

"Calhoun County, Alabama County Seat: Anniston," n.d. [ca. 1965]; all memoranda and report in Box 1, Inspection Reports Evaluating CAP, OEO Papers.

59. Anonymous, "Administrative Confidential re: Governor's Veto," n.d. [ca. 14 May 1965], Box 1, CAP Office Records of the Director, State Files 1965–1968, OEO Papers; "State Poverty Veto Periled: Amendment Takes Aim at Governors," *Birmingham Post Herald*, 14 May 1965, TSHC; Marjorie Hunter, "House Group Votes Poverty-Veto Curb," *New York Times*, 14 May 1965, TSHC; Marjorie Hunter, "Governors to Get Antipoverty Veto: House Panel Limits Power as it Votes to Pass Bill," *New York Times*, 21 May 1965, TSHC; "Editorial: The Anti-Poverty Veto," *Birmingham News*, 21 May 1965, TSHC.

60. Patricia Sullivan, ed., *Freedom Writer: Virginia Foster Durr, Letters from the Civil Rights Years* (New York: Routledge, 2003), 374, 376.

4

Is There a Balm in Gilead?

Baptists and Reform in North Carolina, 1900–1925

Richard D. Starnes

When the noted professor and theologian Walter Rauschenbusch took the podium before the Southern Sociological Congress in 1913, his audience recognized him as the nation's leading advocate of the social gospel. In the face of tremendous suffering caused by industrialization, immigration, and urbanization—widespread poverty, poor public health, illiteracy, malnutrition, inadequate housing—the social gospel challenged believers to address the earthly problems of their fellow man as a route to salvation and the eventual establishment of the kingdom of God on earth. Such an idea moved beyond the ancient notions of Christian charity, as it placed man's earthly needs at least on par with needs spiritual. "There is an immense unfilled social program contained in the personality and mind of Jesus Christ," Rauschenbush told his audience. "This is the call of the new age to the ancient church."[1]

This belief clearly resonated with his audience of the region's most active social reformers. Yet, Rauschenbusch's concepts sprang from a northern urban context, and the organization he identified as having the best-developed church-based reform program, the Federal Council of Churches, reflected the same bias. Such an approach could hardly be successful in the rural South. Another speaker, William Louis Poteat, a biologist, president of North Carolina's Wake Forest College, and influential social reformer, suggested another way for southerners to apply the spirit of the social gospel in their region. His solution was to center social uplift efforts in individual congregations. "The local Church," Poteat argued, "is responsible for the regeneration of the men and women about it and for the regeneration of the society in the midst of which it stands as a city on the hill." Churches and individual believers had as their mission "to relieve suffering and remove the cause of it, to forestall the increase in defectives and dependents, to check the havoc wrought by disease among the effective agents of the kingdom, to clean out the nests of vice," and to root out "moral evil which is everywhere the root of social unrighteousness." For Poteat and many other North Carolina Baptists, blending religion and social reform was less about adopting the social gospel theology and more about applying the teachings of Christ to daily living.[2]

Perhaps it was easier for him to evoke visions of a type of social Christianity in North Carolina. Like the biblical healing place of Gilead, by the early twentieth century the state boasted a powerful reputation as the most progressive in the South. Poteat also clearly linked religion and social reform in both his personal life and his public pronouncements. Still, southern church people remained divided on such questions, and scholars of the region have long differed on the degree of connection between southern social reform and the region's churches. C. Vann Woodward set the tone for a generation of historians when he proclaimed that "the dominant conservatism of the Southern church" prevented the social gospel from playing a substantive role in the region, even though such ideas were "not unknown to Southern clergymen." Other scholars such as Samuel S. Hill Jr. and John B. Boles agreed with Woodward's assertion that the social gospel did not take root in Dixie. Hill observed that while certainly southern church people extended Christian charity to people in need, "the southern church has never devoted its energies to the redemption of the social structures, and certainly warrants no identification with the 'social gospel' tradition."[3] Certainly, the social gospel did not take root as a theology in the South to the degree that it did in the North, but in the early twentieth century southern church leaders like Poteat who were influenced by it increasingly saw the connection between religion and reform. Later, scholars such as Wayne Flynt, John Patrick McDowell, Keith Harper, and Ralph E. Luker suggest that southern church people did bring together matters of faith and their desire, indeed their charge from God, to look after the welfare of others. Moreover, such efforts led to a gradual realization that even if social programs were secondary to the salvation mission of the church, such programs played a crucial role in fulfilling the charge of the Gospels. In a study of Alabama Baptists and social reform, Flynt urged historians to look again at southern churches and social reform, arguing that a conservative theology with its emphasis on literal interpretation of scripture did not mean that southern Protestants looked past the earthly problems confronting their society. Among Baptists specifically, the region's most conservative and most fundamentalist denomination, Flynt argued that "the presence of institutional church programs, church-employed social workers, and improved rural education" suggested that Alabama Baptists actively developed programs to improve their lives. At the same time, "there was a change of attitude and philosophy which helped prepare the way for political and social change."[4]

The case of North Carolina offers an opportunity to examine the themes and limitations of southern social Christianity and to reassess its importance. In the early twentieth century, North Carolina's most prominent voices for social reform were closely connected to the state's largest religious denomination. Individual reform advocates, such as William L. Poteat, Josiah W. Bailey, Livingston Johnson, Watson Smith Rankin, Clarence Poe, and Fannie Heck, were prominent Baptist laypersons and, together with like-minded clergy, comprised a small but highly influential elite that sought to improve the state's social conditions. Likewise, in individual churches, the State Baptist Convention, and through the denominational press, Tar Heel Baptists pushed a reform agenda informed by, and sometimes inspired by, the social gospel. This reform impulse was effective. On issues in which North Carolina Baptists took interest, such as education, child labor, public health, temperance, or the care of the mentally ill, public or private initiatives emerged to improve social conditions. In North Carolina, Baptists did not limit their advocacy for social reform to denominational forums. Just as social issues emerged as important topics in the denominational discourse, Baptists rose to leadership roles in secular private or public reform agencies throughout the state. But in the eyes of Tar Heel Baptists not every issue warranted attention. Notions of racial superiority, paternalism, social class, and a support of the economic status quo defined the contours of their social Christianity. Still, the combined influence of the church as an institution and the efforts of individual members linked religion and reform. In the early decades of the century, North Carolina Baptists emerged as the arbiters of the state's reform ethos, and their efforts and influence dictated the direction of social reform.[5]

North Carolina Baptists and their reform ethos evolved with the state's unique social, economic, and political structure. The state's "progressive plutocracy" that political scientist V. O. Key discussed in his seminal book *Southern Politics in State and Nation* had deep roots. In some ways, the new century saw a continuation of a pattern of power that dominated North Carolina society and politics from the mid-nineteenth century. Since before the Civil War, the state's social and political elite worked to maintain their own position by stifling democracy, dividing voters on the grounds of class

or race, and preventing lower-class whites from establishing their own meaningful voice. But these leaders did express interest in the state's social welfare.
Since the 1840s, state leaders had advocated reforms in the form of a common schools system, state-funded internal improvements, a strong public
university, and state institutions for the mentally ill.[6] The political environment remained relatively stable from the end of Reconstruction until the
1890s, when the tensions of the New South led to the merger of white Populists and Republicans of both races that won control of state government.
One attraction of this so-called Fusion movement was the promise of reform.
North Carolinians at the bottom of society hoped that the changes these new
leaders offered would not simply ease their burdens but would reshape the
fundamental nature of the state's society. It was not to be. In 1898, Democratic leaders led by Furnifold Simmons, Josephus Daniels, and Charles
Brantley Aycock pitted white Populists and black Republicans against each
other in one of the most brutal and divisive white supremacy campaigns ever
waged in the annals of southern politics. Despite the defeat of the Fusion
movement, it reintroduced social and economic reform as an issue in the
public discourse.[7] The lesson was clear: Reform was possible, and would even
be celebrated, so long as it did not threaten the established power structure.
Still, as in other southern states, racial tension, illiteracy, poverty, industrial
conditions, public health, and other problems plagued North Carolina well
into the twentieth century. The result of the election of 1900 was the reestab-
lishment of a white elite that had held the reins of power in North Carolina
since the 1850s, and they brought with them their particular notions of progressive reform. But the state's response to such problems earned it, justly or
unjustly, the reputation as the region's most progressive state. Church people,
specifically Tar Heel Baptists, were at the center of this reform impulse.[8]

Two denominational factors allowed ideas concerning social Christianity
to gain wide influence in North Carolina. The first was the presence of an
active denominational press. As in other southern states, North Carolina
boasted a widely read state Baptist paper, and its pages reflected the changing
relationship between Baptists and the society in which they lived. Founded
in 1834 by the Reverend Thomas Meredith, the *Biblical Recorder* offered readers information and opinions on a variety of topics ranging from suggestions
for Sunday School lessons to political commentary. The three men who edited the paper between 1900 and 1925—Josiah W. Bailey, Hight C. Moore,
and Livingston Johnson—all believed that the religious press should play a
role in shaping public opinion on the issues that confronted society. "We
hold that no good thing to do or say can be secular," Bailey opined in 1900.

"To think so is almost to deny God, certainly it is to circumscribe him." Bailey certainly was aware of the power of the denominational press. In the late 1890s, he had supported efforts by Furnifold Simmons, the leader of the state Democratic Party, to win back control of both the legislature and the governor's mansion through a bitter and divisive campaign that centered on race. But he also saw the paper as a forum to set the Baptist agenda in North Carolina, a function Moore and Johnson later endorsed. Each of these editors became active in reform causes, though their specific interests differed widely. Bailey led the state temperance movement and was a vocal supporter of public education, while Moore and Livingston were more interested in eradicating child labor and improving public health. However, all supported the basic idea of social Christianity and used the paper to reinforce it in the minds of Tar Heel Baptists.[9]

The second internal factor shaping Baptists' social Christianity in North Carolina grew from the dynamic economic and intellectual atmosphere that gripped the denomination during the early twentieth century. As historian Paul Harvey observed, the early twentieth century was a time in which the physical realities were changing for southern Baptists. The forces of the New South moved them to the city, into industry, and, for some, into the middle class, all while they clung to a faith rooted in tradition. Baptists comprised the state's largest religious denomination in 1900, a community of believers numbering 355,987 in 3,000 churches. Yet changing social and economic circumstances challenged the innate conservatism that underlay Baptist thought. On theological matters such as salvation through grace, infant baptism, and the divine inspiration of the scriptures, Baptists remained resistant to change. North Carolina Baptists had little patience for those who challenged traditional Baptists' ideas, especially through new theological positions emerging from higher criticism. "The only hope of the Bible against the ill effects of Higher Criticism is that we Christians read the Bible," Josiah Bailey reminded readers. "Denounce the critics less and read the Bible more."[10] No doubt the rapidly changing, increasingly complex world altered by industrialization, urbanization, and the trappings of modernity reinforced this traditional religious outlook. It also generated human suffering on a scale larger and more apparent than at any time since the Civil War. Baptists took an interest in addressing the suffering caused by the social and economic changes of the new century, but clearly such efforts remained secondary to matters more eternal. Hight C. Moore reminded his readers, "our doctrine of salvation must ever take precedence above our doctrine of philanthropy. Let us not magnify the second above the first nor keep the first aloof from the second." Later, he opined, "the salvation of the individual comes first; then his enlistment in social services follows, or should follow as a matter of course. Orthodoxy should be coupled with orthopraxy, for neither is complete without the other."[11]

Tar Heel Baptists undertook social reforms across a wide spectrum during the early twentieth century, but such interests developed amid an evolving awareness of the relationship between the spiritual and secular roles of the church. Though reform ideas circulated earlier, Baptists created institutions to implement their agenda by the century's second decade. In 1912, the State Baptist Convention recognized the growing importance of the church's role in social reform by appointing a Committee on Social Conditions chaired by President William Louis Poteat of Wake Forest College. The committee, which included John Alexander Oates, Hight C. Moore, and W. R. Collum, reported that even the ancient church was called to minister to the earthly needs of early Christians. That heritage was important for modern Christians to understand, as the modern church faced a crisis if it "insists on being aloof from the world." The problems of modern life had spawned all manner of "humanitarian movements and schemes of social uplift and reform," yet the committee realized that many Christians did not feel moved to address such concerns. The committee reminded their fellow Baptists that unless churches took an active role in social reform, they were not only abandoning the cause of reform to secular groups, but they were also shirking a component of their charge from God. "The mission of the church is twofold," the committee reported, "to make people good and to make society just." The next year, the Southern Baptist Convention followed North Carolina's lead, establishing a permanent Social Services Commission replacing several ad hoc committees that had studied the church's role in social reform in previous years. The state committee played an important role articulating the Baptist agenda and urging members to put it into practice.[12]

The Committee on Social Conditions evolved by 1914 into the Committee on Social Services, the new name suggesting a shift from studying the state's social problems to developing programs to address them. The committee, chaired by Baptist state orphanage director M. L. Kesler, observed, "we believe that our convention, as an organized body of Christian people, should take a deep and abiding interest in the complete welfare of our entire commonwealth." Such work—which the committee suggested some Baptists might prefer to call "Christianity applied to life and conditions around us"—required Baptists' attention as "we have more people within the range of our life than any other denomination" and as social reform "is demanded

by our State Mission ideals." The committee set forth a plan for Baptist reform efforts that reflected the links between denomination initiatives and
secular reform movements in North Carolina. It recommended continued
support of the Baptist orphanage and suggested assistance for widows as a
logical extension of such work. Though unwilling to endorse state pensions
for widows, the committee reminded the convention that the Apostles pioneered church support for widows, labeling it perhaps the earliest "form of
applied Christianity." They advised churches and pastors to "cooperate in
every proper way with the Anti-Saloon League," so long as such support did
not lead to partisan politics. The committee also urged support for public
health initiatives and for churches "to take more active interest in the North
Carolina Conference for Social Service, an organization representing Christians in all denominations" and a group that consistently insisted "that social
service not be divorced from church activity."[13]

    To illustrate this point, the committee praised the work of Raleigh's Tab-
ernacle Baptist Church. Founded in 1874 as the Second Baptist Church of
Raleigh, the congregation grew rapidly and embraced social welfare programs as an essential part of its ministry. As early as 1889, the church organized a free medical clinic for the city's indigent population. Renamed Tabernacle Baptist Church in 1910, the congregation continued its social outreach
programs. The Committee on Social Service commended Tabernacle for its
"Social Center" program that furnished "wholesome conditions of life for
working girls and students who come as undefended strangers within the
gates of our cities." The message to the convention was clear. Social reform
was an aspect of ministry that the modern church had to embrace.[14] In subsequent years, the Committee on Social Service continued to exhort Baptists
to take a larger role in programs designed to ease the suffering of those at the
bottom of society. Though the main efforts of the committee centered on the
orphanage, widows' relief, and providing for retired pastors, other initiatives
emerged and the committee attempted to keep the issue of social reform on
the minds of Baptists across the state.

    This institutional advocacy for social Christianity led to official support
for secular efforts. In 1916, M. L. Kesler, frequent member of the Committee
on Social Service, introduced a successful resolution to support the creation
of a State Board of Public Welfare. Such an institution "would be a constructive agency for social progress and development of the State" which would
lead to "the advancement of Christian morality and citizenship." Also in
1916, the committee report included a call for Baptists to support both the
Southern Sociological Congress and the North Carolina Conference for So-

cial Services. Even though neither was "an ecclesiastical or denominational organization," committee members reminded Baptists, "both are intensely Christian in their sympathies" and "our people ought to be encouraged to have a lively interest and active participation in such organizations." Though clergy support for these kinds of groups and the reform agenda they advanced remained important, reformers urged pastors to keep their congregations informed of such initiatives and to elicit help from them when possible. In 1920, the committee advised Baptist ministers to "familiarize themselves with the several lines of public work in these fields now being undertaken by public and social agencies generally and interpret them to the members in frequent sermons and discourses and otherwise."[15]

This denominational interest coincided with increased participation by Baptists in other reform movements. Those prominent in denominational reform efforts often emerged as leaders in secular organizations, broadening their influence and that of Baptist notions of reform. No Baptist reformer elicited more respect than William Louis Poteat. A biologist, active Baptist layman, and skilled college leader, Poteat rose to prominence in social reform movements both within his denomination and in secular circles. According to biographer Randal L. Hall, Poteat's reform ideology centered on fostering moral conduct, building a stronger society, and helping people deal with the problems created by modern life. The presidency of Wake Forest, which he assumed in 1905, gave Poteat an influential position from which to trumpet reform initiatives. Already a leading advocate of temperance and improved public education, by 1910 he turned his attention to other causes such as child labor, the care of the mentally ill, improved race relations, and public health. But his vocal pronouncements concerning the relationship between religion and social uplift outweighed his efforts on individual issues. Though not ordained, Poteat emerged as the voice of Baptist social Christianity in North Carolina and beyond.[16]

Poteat's denominational activities on behalf of social reform were extensive. In 1911, he addressed the World Baptist Alliance on the need for Baptist conventions to form social welfare committees, something his own state convention had done in 1912 and something that the Southern Baptist Convention (SBC) would do the next year. In fact, Poteat chaired the inaugural SBC Social Service Commission. From that post, he reminded the convention of "an all embracing social ideal to be realized in the reign of righteousness in the earthly life of man," achieved through the efforts of church people applying Christ's teachings to their interactions with their fellow man. Such sentiments, repeated often in various forums, established Poteat as a Baptist progressive visionary. Though replaced as chair, possibly because his views were too liberal for many SBC leaders, he served on the Social Service Commission for over two decades, helping to guide Baptist reform efforts at a regional level. Poteat also frequently chaired the state convention's Committee on Social Services, but his reform activities extended far beyond Baptist circles. Active in the Southern Sociological Congress, he served on that body's Committee on Church and Service in 1915. He also belonged to other social welfare organizations, like the North Carolina Conference for Social Service (NCCSS). If Poteat's notions about faith-based social reform struck some as too liberal, they had clearly defined limits. He embraced interracialism as a way to deal with the region's racial problems, fought for better facilities for the mentally ill, and railed against child labor. Yet, like many other progressives, he supported sterilization for mental patients deemed to be beyond treatment and did not challenge the state's socioeconomic elites or the economic system that kept so many North Carolinians impoverished in mill villages or sharecropper shacks. His continued popularity as a Baptist leader suggests that his active support of social reform did not undermine—and probably enhanced—his standing in denominational circles.[17]

Clarence Poe, an active Baptist layman and editor of the popular *Progressive Farmer* newspaper, also emerged as a prominent proponent of social Christianity. Though he trumpeted this message in different venues, his most important was the NCCSS formed in 1912 to "unite all the now scattered forces of social service upon this threefold program: investigating conditions, awakening the people, and securing remedies." Poe chaired the NCCSS for three years and remained active in its causes. Poe's leadership and reputation attracted official support of the NCCSS from Baptists in the annual state convention. Hight C. Moore and Livingston Johnson regularly endorsed Poe's group editorially in the *Biblical Recorder* and reported favorably on its activities. Yet, Poe's support of social reform also had its limits. Though quite willing to lead movements advocating improved education, temperance, and changes in child labor, Poe drew the line at race equality. To ease the tension in southern society, he favored a program of rural segregation. He envisioned cooperative, interdependent, but segregated, agricultural communities replacing the scattered settlements of the rural South. Though it never came to fruition, Poe's ideas concerning rural segregation demonstrate the limits of his progressive vision. Men like Poe and Poteat bridged secular and sectarian reform movements, and their influence in both camps demonstrates the ways in which Baptists guided the course of progressive reform in North Carolina.[18]

While such leaders influenced reform in various ways, for most North Carolina Baptists social reform remained a component of missionary work aimed at the salvation of the unchurched. For some it also represented an opportunity to become more active in Baptist life. Fannie E. S. Heck brought together social reform, missionary work, and a broader role for women in denominational circles. Born in Virginia in 1862, her family moved to Raleigh following the Civil War. Her father was a prominent businessman, and both parents were members of Raleigh's First Baptist Church. Heck, who remained unmarried, devoted her energies to church work, specifically the cause of missions and work among the poor in Raleigh. She founded the Woman's Missionary Societies of North Carolina in 1886, a body that she led until her death in 1915, and led the SBC Women's Missionary Union from 1892 to 1894. Like Poe and Poteat, she participated in numerous reform groups such as the North Carolina Society of Social Work and even served a term as vice-president of the Southern Sociological Congress. But it was her role as a leader of Baptist women that placed her in the forefront of social reform.[19]

Heck urged Baptist women to challenge the social conditions in the world around them. In a speech to young women at the Baptist Woman's Missionary Union Training School in Louisville—an institution she helped found—Heck asked them "are you satisfied?"

Are you satisfied with the state of things in your own country? Is life here as pure and Christian as it should be? Is the government run on the plan on the Sermon on the Mount? No, not even the Ten Commandments. Are you satisfied with the conditions that you find in your city or town? However sheltered your own life has been you have some knowledge of the dark spots in your city; the wrong and pain of the home life; the crime in young lives; the evil of drink; the ruin of manhood and womanhood. You are not satisfied. Though custom may ordinarily make you take these things for granted, there come times when they sorely trouble you. You see, perhaps by accident, into the dark ways of life. A drunken man reels by you in the street; you see a miserably clad child snatch a half eaten apple from the street or a woman lurking in the shadows. A great questioning overwhelms you. Why should these things be?[20]

She encouraged women to seek solutions to social problems caused by poverty—in their churches, in civic clubs, and even in their daily interactions. For Heck, reform efforts offered a way for Baptist women to exercise leadership in a church dominated by a strict patriarchy, improve the lot of the less fortunate, and fulfill the Great Commission. When she died in 1915, she was memorialized as a visionary in terms of both social work and the rôle of women in the church, a fitting tribute for a leader who challenged the prevailing winds on both scores.[21]

The issues Baptists embraced demonstrate how they applied their brand of social Christianity to the problems around them. Prohibition elicited support from North Carolina Baptists like no other social reform cause. Following the election of 1900, Josiah Bailey hailed "the revival of prohibition sentiment" in the Old North State. In calling for a renewal of the prohibition movement, Bailey reminded his readers that such efforts were a religious responsibility. "Christianity," he wrote, "is not a refuge for wrecks, but a savior for society." Fighting the cause of prohibition meant assailing state political leaders, who tended to shift the burden of prohibition to county and city officials through local option legislation. Such measures meant little to prohibition proponents who blamed alcohol for a litany of social problems ranging from violent crime to poverty. Between 1900 and 1907, Bailey often dedicated his editorials to prohibition, labeling alcohol as "the greatest curse of our civilization."[22]

Baptist efforts in support of prohibition extended beyond the pages of the *Biblical Recorder*. Individual Baptists were prominent in the North Carolina Anti-Saloon League (NCASL), a statewide committee that Bailey chaired from 1903 to 1907. For Baptists who joined the movement for prohibition, the link between their cause and the social mission of the church was clear. John Alexander Oates, a layman from Fayetteville and an active member of the NCASL, reminded his fellow Baptists that the "social service side of [the church's] mission has been largely forgotten in the campaign for creed and conquest." "The restless regiments of unwashed humanity are being heard in the plaintive appeal for a strong hand to rescue and save," he observed. The church's efforts were "being felt on the steering wheel of law and society as never before," a fact that would allow the church to better fulfill its God-given mission on earth.[23] Not surprisingly, Baptists provided the core of North Carolina's temperance movement. The legislature passed the Watts Act of 1903, which established rural prohibition largely because of the widespread support among North Carolina Baptists as well as other Protestants. Leaders such as Bailey, future governor Clyde Hoey, and laypeople in churches throughout the state continued to lobby for an end to local option laws, and the *Biblical Recorder* frequently reminded readers of the moral implications of the prohibition constitutional amendment. The success of Baptist prohibitionists in mobilizing supporters in the cause of reform represents their greatest but not their only success.[24]

Aside from temperance, the cause of public education elicited the greatest response from both clergy and laity. North Carolina had claimed a system of publicly funded common schools since 1840, and by the Civil War the state's education system was the best in the South. In many ways, this achievement was far from superlative. Students seldom attended school for longer than four months, and the state lacked both public high schools and schools for free blacks. The war destroyed the common school system, and financial problems and a lack of leadership on the issue meant that public education in the late nineteenth century was much worse than it had been before the Civil War. Still, public education remained on the minds of North Carolinians across the economic spectrum. Leaders such as novelist Walter Hines Page, Populist leaders Marion Butler and Leonidas L. Polk, and University of North Carolina president Kemp P. Battle raised education as a social, economic, and political issue by the 1890s.[25]

Of course, Tar Heel Baptists maintained a strong interest in education. They saw it not only as a way to prepare children for their earthly duties but also as a method to instruct them in subjects such as moral conduct and matters of the soul. "There is no task more serious than that of the education of one's son or daughter," Bailey reminded his readers. "God is concerned in it; His purposes are involved."[26] The denomination's own institutions reflected growing support for education. After struggling for a number of years during and immediately after Reconstruction, enrollment at Wake Forest College began to grow and the endowment increased substantially. In 1889, Baptist layman and agrarian activist Leonidas L. Polk pushed the Baptist State Convention to create a college for women in North Carolina. Chartered two years later, Baptist Female University opened in Raleigh in 1899, dedicated to providing opportunities for higher learning to the state's young Baptist women. The state convention also supported a number of colleges and academies throughout the state, such as Mars Hill College, Chowan College, and the Burnsville Academy.[27]

The issue of public support for education was more divisive in Baptist ranks. Since the 1890s, state Baptist leaders had been vocal in their opposition to publicly funded educational institutions, but that animosity was directed more at the University of North Carolina and other public institutions of higher learning than at the common schools. Many leading Baptists believed that public higher education undermined denominational colleges by attracting students with cheaper tuition and a more liberal social environment. Such opposition defined the public position of North Carolina Baptists throughout the 1890s, but the new century brought a change in the way they viewed public education.[28]

Education emerged as the state's defining political issue after Charles Brantley Aycock, a Baptist and Democrat from Wayne County, was elected governor in 1900. Aycock believed that that the greatest issue facing North Carolina was its inadequate public education system.[29] In his inaugural address, he noted that "the Good Book tells us that the strong should bear the infirmities of the weak and the lessons of that great authority are of utility in our political life. . . . It will be a glorious day for us if our people in the hour of their prosperity and wonderful growth and development can realize that men can never grow higher and better by rising on the weaknesses and ignorance of their fellows, but only by aiding their fellowman and lifting them to the same high plane which they themselves occupy."[30]

Aycock's vision appealed to his fellow Baptists at the same time they were beginning to express interest in the link between social reform and religion. As Aycock set the public agenda for improving public education, Baptists grew more vocal in their support. The *Biblical Recorder* supported educational improvements even before Aycock took office. Bailey correctly reminded readers, "we have set forth time and again the distressing conditions of the free schools." Not only did Bailey support Aycock's proposed improvements to the public school system, but he also supported the more controversial idea of compulsory education.[31] After the election, the paper came out strongly in favor of Aycock's educational reforms even though it continued to disagree with the governor on state support to higher education. In 1901, Bailey even called for volunteer teachers to staff North Carolina's public schools. Both Governor Aycock and Superintendent of Public Instruction Thomas F. Toon heartily embraced Bailey's suggestion, though the matter never came to fruition. By 1903, the Baptist State Convention concluded, "it is the duty of the state to provide a common school education for all her children as a safeguard to a democratic form of government."[32]

But support for public education had its limits. Criticism of funding the state university continued, but other issues reflect the limits of Baptist progressivism in educational matters. Denominational leaders disapproved of Baptist academies accepting public funds to educate students in areas that lacked adequate facilities. This practice had become relatively common in the most rural areas of the state, particularly the western mountains. Bailey viewed such cooperation as a blurring of the line between church and state, declaring, "it is just as wrong for Baptists to make an alliance with the state as it is for Roman Catholics." Just as he questioned state-supported universities, Bailey also questioned the motives and practices of the Southern Education Board, a group he believed wielded too much power in the state public schools.[33]

Other reform efforts tested Baptist connections to the state's political and economic elite. Like their fellow believers across the South, North Carolina Baptists eagerly supported the growing tide of industrialization sweeping the region in the late nineteenth and early twentieth centuries. The growth of the textile, lumber, and manufacturing industries transformed the state in dramatic ways. The state Baptist newspaper often announced the opening of new mills and changes in management and generally heralded industrial development and the hope it held for the state and its people. In January 1900, the *Biblical Recorder* lauded Charlotte resident D. A. Tompkins's book *Cotton Mill Processes and Calculations,* claiming that "we have not had an abler or more encouraging book in many a day." The book outlined, and the editor endorsed, the widespread development of the textile industry as a way both to curb agricultural decline and to build the regional economy. "The question [of North Carolina's economic future] is to be answered in the development of the manufacture of the staple [cotton] at home," the *Biblical Recorder* declared. "By this means the farmer will not only get a better price for his cotton, but markets will be created for his other products." Such industrial development would not only employ thousands of North Carolinians directly but also would benefit "the merchant, the school-teacher, the physician, and the preacher."[34]

Such endorsements reflected the strong ties between North Carolina Baptists and the state's economic elite. Still, while North Carolina Baptists welcomed the new industrial order, they also recognized the problems industrialization generated, such as long hours, poor conditions, child labor, inadequate pay, and the new moral temptations of the mill villages. Baptists attempted through moral suasion to convince mill owners that they could improve conditions for their workers and still turn a profit. In 1901, the *Biblical Recorder* profiled J. D. Moore, manager of the Modena mill in Gastonia and an active Baptist layman. Moore was the personification a middle-class Baptist dealing with the social and economic issues of the New South. He reported that his workers put in shifts of 60 to 66 hours, with Saturday evening and Sunday off. Moore even suggested that mill owners who employed a child who was subject to the compulsory school attendance law be cited with a misdemeanor. The Modena mill provided a teacher for mill children ten months of the year, and Moore reported that 90 percent of the mill's

employees attended church. Still, the undercurrents of conservatism, paternalism, and class tensions prevented Modena from becoming an experiment
in social reform. Moore made clear the strict discipline with which he managed the mill, firing men and women who did not meet production or his
moral standards. Moore's approach, according to the editor, "shows us the
Christian way of dealing with a question that is coming home in our state."[35]

Not all mill owners emulated Moore's example, and mill villages remained
bastions of poverty, illiteracy, and disease. In 1905, former mill worker and
Baptist minister I. N. Loftin reported the poor social conditions in the state's
mill villages to the Contemporary Club in Henderson. Although others
who examined the villages labeled residents as "the poor white trash of the
South," Loftin argued that mill workers were drawn from families who had
owned land, and even slaves, before the Civil War. He observed general
moral decline among textile workers once they arrived in the villages. Men
left their families, young women turned to prostitution, and young men became petty criminals. Most troubling to Loftin, and no doubt his audience,
was the resulting decline in religiosity. In his experience, only about 30 percent of mill workers attended church, some avoiding formal religion out of
disinterest and others because, as one woman told Loftin, "the children ain't
got nothing to wear and dem folks out there are ready to poke fun at rags."
Loftin called on his fellow Baptists to help ease these people's worldly burden so as to improve their hope for salvation. "In this way," he concluded,
"the religious atmosphere cannot be much, when in many cases there is nothing conducive to such a life, and when night has often been converted from
hours of sleep and rest for children to a time of work among humming
spindles and clanking shuttle-boxes, where morals do not grow and the
beauty of youth fades long before the age of manhood is reached." Men such
as Loftin embraced the link between social reform and the church's salvation
mission and tried to put it into practice among the state's downtrodden.[36]

For the next two decades, reports presented at the State Baptist Convention reflected continuing interest in social conditions in the state's industrial
communities. While their newspaper and the State Baptist Convention expressed great concern with the social problems present in the state's mill villages, Tar Heel Baptists had few positive things to say about labor unions. In
1901, the *Biblical Recorder* expressed concern that labor leaders would use
their positions not simply to benefit workers but as stepping-stones to political power, a position the paper would maintain toward organized labor.[37]

Baptist progressives did not pursue radical change, nor did the lot of average workers improve dramatically as a result of denominational programs,

but Baptist efforts did bring relative relief in some areas of the new industrial society. Baptists identified child labor as early as 1901 as a problem worthy of their attention. Josiah Bailey admitted the problem of child labor but questioned the motives and utility of national reform organizations such as the National Child Labor Committee, even when that body's efforts in the state were led by Alexander J. McKelway, a Presbyterian minister. Still, Baptists were well represented by Clarence Poe on the NCLC's state committee even though he shared some of Bailey's concerns. When industrial interests defeated a child labor bill in 1905, the *Biblical Recorder* published a series of letters from mill village missionaries outlining in great detail the harsh conditions for children in the mills. Despite such vocal protests and much attention for Baptists leaders, North Carolina remained without substantial child labor legislation until the 1930s. If Baptist efforts for prohibition and education stood as examples of successful social reform campaigns, the efforts to regulate child labor remained disappointing, perhaps because it represented too direct a challenge to the state's economic elite.[38]

By World War I, North Carolina Baptists expressed a growing interest in public health. In some ways, secular attention to this issue preceded and outdistanced Baptist reform efforts in the state. North Carolina created a State Board of Public Health in 1877, but until the early twentieth century inadequate funding prevented state officials from addressing disease, sanitation, and other concerns in a systematic way. Still Baptists recognized the practical social implications of the biblical injunctions concerning caring for the sick. In 1902, in an effort to alleviate the shortage of physicians in rural communities and improve the health care available to Tar Heels statewide, the trustees at Wake Forest College created a two-year medical school that received accreditation from the American Medical Association two years later.[39]

One of the professors at Wake Forest's new medical school hoped to make a larger contribution to public health reform in North Carolina. A native of Mooresville, Dr. Watson Smith Rankin was an active Baptist layman with a medical degree from the University of Maryland. He came to Wake Forest as a professor of medicine in 1903 and became the medical school's second dean two years later. As dean, he brought a zeal motivated by a desire to increase the number of doctors in the state, improve their professional training, and improve the health of North Carolinians generally. His combined interest in physician training and public health led to trips to Panama to learn about malaria control. Once back home, he disseminated his findings, contributing to a decrease in the disease in North Carolina. He also researched methods to stem the spread of hookworm. Such efforts gained the attention of state leaders, and in 1909 Rankin was appointed North Carolina's first full-time secretary of the State Board of Public Health, a post he held until 1925. As secretary, Rankin pushed for stronger public health legislation, sought to empower local officials to deal with public health issues at the county level, and urged the development of both better medical education and community hospitals across the state. It is unclear how Baptist ideas of social Christianity shaped Rankin's professional activities, but Baptists across the state praised his efforts. During the influenza epidemic of 1919, the *Biblical Recorder* quoted extensively Rankin's advice to the public and praised a monthly public health bulletin published by the State Board of Public Health, advising readers that it "should be read by our people every month."[40] In another issue, editor Livingston Johnson noted, "We do not know any department of our State Government service that is rendering better service than the State Board of Health. Dr. Rankin, Secretary of the Board, and his assistants are 'on the job.' "[41]

More important, North Carolina Baptists responded to Rankin's call for better hospitals, especially one where the poor might seek care for free or at reduced cost. Local and state officials began opening hospitals in rural communities, most often financed by both public funds and local philanthropists, but the number of hospitals grew slowly. The *Biblical Recorder* admonished readers that "we, as a denomination, have neglected entirely too long the important work of ministering to the sick. We should begin as soon as possible to make amends for our past neglect."[42] Such efforts included a call for hospitals for black North Carolinians as well. As the *Biblical Recorder* noted, "Emergency hospitals have been opened for white people in several cities, but we have not noticed that any municipality has opened such a hospitals for negroes [*sic*]." As such municipal hospitals opened free of charge or charged only minimal fees, they "have been real blessings wherever opened." Black citizens not only needed such facilities but also, as taxpayers, deserved them. "Negroes pay taxes to support city government," the editor proclaimed, "and are entitled to the benefits that come from governments supported by taxation." To critics who might argue that blacks paid fewer taxes than whites, he countered that blacks were generally poorer than whites and that was "the reason that they should have the service of charitable institutions. The poor people in any community need more charity than those who are better off."[43]

Tar Heel Baptists applied such ideas of improving public health by establishing a modern Baptist hospital to treat indigent whites and generally improve the level of medical care in the state. The Baptist State Convention began to plan for establishing such a facility during its 1919 meeting, forming a Hospital Commission and beginning to raise funds for such a facility. The convention set aside $100,000 to begin construction of a facility when a location was selected and proposed that the city selected as the home of the Baptist hospital raise a matching amount. In 1921, Baptist leaders announced Winston as the site of the new facility, a site selected as much for the zeal of its boosters as its central location. Dedicated in 1923, the new hospital boasted 80 beds and a construction cost of $192,628. During the 1920s, its focus on providing care to the poor put the institution in dire financial straits that only worsened during the Great Depression. Still, through the efforts of Baptists across the state, the institution survived, a testament to dedication of Baptists to improved health care in North Carolina.[44]

Biblical Recorder editor Livingston Johnson reminded his readers in 1920 that initiatives such as Baptist Hospital went beyond simple notions of Christian charity. In fact he argued that a hospital was an important extension of social Christianity in the state, as it would be both an institution designed to treat the sick and another way to offer the unsaved the route to salvation. "The need for hospitals under Christian influence cannot be a question with those who have given careful thought to the matter," he argued. After all, Catholics "get their strongest hold on people by their hospital and other charitable work." "Christ has set us an example in caring for the sick," Livingston concluded. "He used the power to heal as a valuable aid in reaching the souls of men." Likewise, at the 1920 Baptist State Convention, R. F. Beasley, chairman of the Committee on Social Services, noted that his body had issued a report that year that concluded that "public health, public morals, public child welfare, better living conditions, preventable deaths, preventable neglect and poverty exploitation of women and children" and other social ills "are a primary concern to the Church and to church members."[45]

As in other southern states, race remained an issue on which North Carolina Baptists struggled for direction. Certainly blacks felt the same hardships as their white brethren in terms of inadequate educational facilities, poor public health, and other social ills. Such problems were magnified by the system of segregation. Earlier support for white supremacy in the form of the disfranchisement amendment of 1900 placed white Baptists on the side of the state's Democratic Party. At the turn of the century, the pages of *Biblical Recorder* were filled with articles pointing out the inequality of black southerners and calling for the restriction of voting rights. In fact, once the disfranchisement amendment passed the legislature, editor Josiah Bailey declared that "the race issue in North Carolina died August 2d, 1900" and predicted a new era of social and economic progress. Yet, as white Baptists began to expand their view of the church's role in social welfare, they also recognized the role that race played in shaping social realities in the state and began modest, but nonetheless significant, steps to tame the excesses of Jim Crow without challenging the system itself. At the end of its 1918 annual report, the Committee on Social Services identified "two evils to which we feel it our duty to call attention." The first was lynching, a practice that the committee felt "should be discountenanced and denounced by all good citizens" and perpetrators punished with "the full penalty of the law." The second issue involved equal justice for black and white citizens in the state. The committee criticized "the tendency of juries in certain sections of the State to fail to convict violators of the law, no matter what crime, no matter what evidence," a practice especially common "if the prisoner at the bar is a white man charged with an offense against a negro." They asked that despite "social distinctions that exist between the races," "no guilty man should escape punishment because the man against whom he commits an offense belongs to another race." In 1922, the committee asked individual churches to "encourage the work of the Inter-racial Commission now at work in North Carolina." Moreover, it asked "that the agencies co-operating with this Convention continue and extend all possible assistance in training and guiding negro ministers and other leaders and where possible co-operate with them in alleviating existing destitution." Despite this rhetoric, North Carolina Baptist reformers stopped well short of calling for equal treatment for their black neighbors, another serious limitation of their progressive ideology.[46]

At the dawn of the twentieth century, North Carolina Baptists faced the same social, economic, and theological challenges as their fellow Protestants throughout the South. Their experiences with social Christianity suggest a number of things about the link between religion and reform in the Progressive-era South. North Carolina Baptists confirm the findings of earlier scholars who argue that southern churches did articulate and practice a broad-ranging reform ethos informed by the social gospel and designed to apply Christian teachings to the changing world around them. But the case of North Carolina suggests that Baptists did more than call for social change. They used their influence in denominational circles, in secular organizations, and in politics to improve public education, to address pressing public health needs, to begin to reform child labor, and to institute strict temperance legislation. In a state where conservatism, a traditional elite, and business interests ruled the day, it is easy to see why social reform in the Old North State had its limits. Baptists did not change industrial conditions in factories or the mill villages that surrounded them. They did not push for equality for black North Carolinians, and much of their reform vision remained unrealized. But North Carolina Baptists were also the heirs of a progressive tradition that tolerated, even celebrated, social reform initiatives as long as those reform efforts did not threaten the social and economic status quo. Within this narrow field of opportunity, North Carolina Baptists emerged as the state's progressive conscience.

Notes

1. Walter Rauschenbush, "The Social Program of the Church," in *The South Mobilizing for Social Service: Addresses Delivered at the Southern Sociological Congress, Atlanta, Georgia, April 25–29, 1913*, edited by James E. McCulloch (Nashville: Southern Sociological Congress, 1913), 504–11, quote on 511.

2. William Louis Poteat, "The Social Task of the Modern Church," in McCulloch, ibid., 534–40, quote on 540. For a compelling analysis of Poteat and his reform ethos, see Randal L. Hall, *William Louis Poteat: A Leader of the Progressive Era South* (Lexington: University Press of Kentucky, 2000). Hall actually suggests such a comparison between Rauschenbusch and Poteat.

3. C. Vann Woodward, *Origins of the New South, 1877–1913* (Baton Rouge: Louisiana State University Press, 1951), 452; Samuel S. Hill Jr., *Southern Churches in Crisis* (New York: Henry Holt, & Company, 1966), 171; John B. Boles, "The Discovery of Southern Religious History," in *Interpreting Southern History: Historiographical Essays in Honor of Sanford W. Higginbotham* ed. John B. Boles and Evelyn Thomas Nolen (Baton Rouge: Louisiana State University Press, 1987), 540–41. Another book that supports this perspective is James J. Thompson, *Tried as by Fire: Southern Baptists and the Religious Controversies of the 1920s* (Macon, Ga.: Mercer University Press, 1982).

4. Wayne Flynt, "Dissent in Zion: Alabama Baptists and Social Issues, 1900–1914," *Journal of Southern History* 35 (November 1969):542. Flynt pioneered this reexamination of the importance of the social gospel in the South. See his "Southern Protestantism and Reform, 1890–1920," in *Varieties of the Southern Religious Experience* ed. Samuel S. Hill (Baton Rouge: Louisiana State University Press, 1988), 135–57; "Feeding the Hungry and Ministering to the Brokenhearted: The Presbyterian Church in the United States and the Social Gospel, 1900–1920," in *Religion in the South* ed. Charles Reagan Wilson (Jackson: University Press of Mississippi, 1985), 83–138; and *Alabama Baptists: A History of Baptists in the Heart of Dixie* (Tuscaloosa: University of Alabama Press, 1999), chap. 7. For a useful examination of this debate, see Keith Harper, *The Quality of Mercy: Southern Baptists and Social Christianity, 1890–1920* (Tuscaloosa: University of Alabama Press, 1996), 1–14, and Paul Harvey,

Redeeming the South: Religious Cultures and Racial Identities Among Southern Baptists, 1865–1925 (Chapel Hill: University of North Carolina Press, 1997), 197–99.

5. For scholars who view social Christianity as having an important role in southern reform movements, see John Patrick McDowell, *The Social Gospel in the South: The Women's Home Missionary Movement in the Methodist Episcopal Church, South, 1886–1939* (Baton Rouge: Louisiana State University, 1982); Ralph E. Luker, *The Social Gospel in Black and White: American Race Reform, 1885–1912* (Chapel Hill: University of North Carolina Press, 1991); John C. Eighmy, *Churches in Cultural Captivity: A History of the Social Attitudes of Southern Baptists* (Knoxville: University of Tennessee Press, 1972), chaps. 4 and 5; and Harper, *The Quality of Mercy*. For more on the larger context of social reform in the early-twentieth-century South, see William A. Link, *The Paradox of Southern Progressivism, 1880–1930* (Chapel Hill: University of North Carolina Press, 1992). This study examines only white Baptists affiliated with the North Carolina Baptist State Convention.

6. Paul D. Escott, *Many Excellent People: Power and Privilege in North Carolina, 1850–1900* (Chapel Hill: University of North Carolina Press, 1985), 15–31, 184–85, 196–219, 241–62. For more on the social order of post–Civil War North Carolina, see Dwight B. Billings, *Planters and the Making of a "New South": Class, Politics, and Development in North Carolina, 1865–1900* (Chapel Hill: University of North Carolina Press, 1979). For more on North Carolina's reputation as a progressive state, see V. O. Key, *Southern Politics in the State and Nation* (New York: Alfred A. Knopf, 1949), 205–28; Paul Leubke, *Tar Heel Politics: Myths and Realities* (Chapel Hill: University of North Carolina Press, 1990), 1–17; and George B. Tindall, *Emergence of the New South, 1913–1945* (Baton Rouge: Louisiana State University Press, 1967), 7, 31–32.

7. Escott, *Many Excellent People*, chap. 10. See also the essays in *Democracy Betrayed: The Wilmington Race Riot of 1898 and Its Legacy* ed. David S. Cecelski and Timothy B. Tyson (Chapel Hill: University of North Carolina Press, 1998), and Helen G. Edmonds, *The Negro and Fusion Politics in North Carolina, 1894–1901* (Chapel Hill: University of North Carolina Press, 1951).

8. For more on Baptist social thought before 1900, see Rufus B. Spain, *At Ease in Zion: Social History of Southern Baptists, 1865–1900* (Nashville: Vanderbilt University Press, 1967), and Eighmy, *Churches in Cultural Captivity*, 3–21. Flynt also noted the legacy of southern populism as an influence on religious reform efforts. See Flynt, "Southern Protestantism and Reform," 138.

9. *Biblical Recorder,* 4 April 1900; Frederick A. Bode, *Protestantism and the New South: North Carolina Baptists and Methodists in Political Crisis, 1894–1903* (Charlottesville: University Press of Virginia, 1975), 127–31, 141–44. See also the *Biblical Recorder,* 2 May, 29 August 1900 for more on the paper and its perceived role. Josiah W. Bailey

edited the paper from 1893 to 1907, Hight C. Moore from 1908 to 1917, and Livingston Johnson from 1917 to 1931.

10. *Biblical Recorder,* 21 February 1900.

11. Bureau of the Census, *Special Reports: Religious Bodies: 1906: Part I: Summary and General Tables* (Washington, D.C.: Government Printing Office, 1906), 242; *Biblical Recorder,* 6 November 1912, 23 September 1914.

12. *Annual of the North Carolina Baptist State Convention, 1912* (Raleigh: Edwards & Broughton, 1912), 73–75; Harvey, *Redeeming the South,* 209–10.

13. *Annual of the North Carolina Baptist State Convention, 1914* (Raleigh: Edwards & Broughton, 1914), 90–91.

14. Ibid., 91; Jerry B. Cooper and Mary S. Kelley, *The First One Hundred Years of Tabernacle Baptist Church* (Raleigh: Bynum Printing Company, 1974).

15. *Annual of the North Carolina Baptist State Convention, 1916* (Raleigh: Edwards & Broughton, 1916), 35, 85–86; *Annual of the North Carolina Baptist State Convention, 1920* (Raleigh: Edwards & Broughton, 1920), 97. The Southern Sociological Congress was a loose coalition of academics, clergy, and social reformers who sought solutions to the region's pressing social problems. See Tindall, *Emergence of the New South,* 7–8, 175–76.

16. Hall, *William Louis Poteat,* 76–78.

17. *Annual of the Southern Baptist Convention, 1914* (Nashville: Southern Baptist Convention, 1914), 36–37. Poteat later served on the North Carolina Commission for Interracial Cooperation and became somewhat involved in the regional movement. He was a member of the North Carolina Society for Mental Hygiene, a group that promoted eugenics. See Hall, *William Louis Poteat,* 99–102, 190–91.

18. Clarence Poe, *My First 80 Years* (Chapel Hill: University of North Carolina Press, 1963), 149–50; *Biblical Recorder,* 31 January 1917, 19 February 1919; Joseph A. Cote, "Clarence Hamilton Poe: The Farmer's Voice, 1899–1964," *Agricultural History* 53, 1 (1979):30–41; Jack Temple Kirby, *Darkness at the Dawning: Race and Reform in the Progressive South* (Philadelphia: J. B. Lippincott, 1972), 119–30. Josiah W. Bailey also served on the North Carolina Committee on Rural Race Problems, the organization Poe used to publicize his rural segregation ideas. See also Cote, "Clarence Hamilton Poe: Crusading Editor, 1881–1964" (Ph.D. diss., University of Georgia, 1976).

19. Deborah Beckel, "Roots of Reform: The Origins of Populism and Progressivism as Manifest in Relationships among Reformers in Raleigh, North Carolina, 1850–1905" (Ph.D. diss., Emory University, 1998), 222–88; Mrs. W. C. James, *Fannie E. S. Heck: A Study of the Hidden Springs in a Rarely Useful and Victorious Life* (Nashville: Broadman Press, 1939), 10–15, 28–40, 64; Fannie E. S. Heck, *In Royal Service: The Mission Work of Southern Baptist Women* (Richmond: Southern Baptist Convention, 1913), 101–18, 121–29.

20. "Series of Talks on Harmony, Joy, Beauty, and Power Given at the Baptist WMU Training School, Louisville, Kentucky, May 24–27, 1913," Fannie Exile Scudder Heck Papers, North Carolina Baptist Historical Collection, Wake Forest University.

21. Raleigh *News and Observer*, 26 August 1915; Raleigh *Times*, 1 September 1915; *Biblical Recorder*, 26 August 1915.

22. *Biblical Recorder*, 28 November 1900. See also issues of 19 February 1902, 21 January, 18 March 1903, 13 April, 18 June 1904.

23. "Temperance and Law Enforcement," undated speech (ca. 1907), John Alexander Oates Papers, North Carolina Baptist Historical Collection, Wake Forest University.

24. Link, *Paradox of Southern Progressivism*, 99–106; *Biblical Recorder*, 9 May, July, 23 August, 6 September, 15 November 1916, 11 April 1917, 20 March 1918, 16 June 1920. For more on prohibition in North Carolina, see David J. Whitener, *Prohibition in North Carolina, 1715–1946* (Chapel Hill: University of North Carolina Press, 1946).

25. William S. Powell, *North Carolina Through Four Centuries* (Chapel Hill: University of North Carolina Press, 1989), 290–92, 418–20; Hugh Talmadge Lefler and Albert Ray Newsome, *North Carolina: The History of a Southern State*, 3d ed. (Chapel Hill: University of North Carolina Press, 1973), 589–95. For an excellent study of education in North Carolina, see James L. Leloudis, *Schooling the New South: Pedagogy, Self, and Society in North Carolina, 1880–1920* (Chapel Hill: University of North Carolina Press, 1996).

26. *Biblical Recorder*, 13 June 1900.

27. Hall, *William Louis Poteat*, 22–32; M. A. Huggins, *A History of North Carolina Baptists, 1727–1932* (Raleigh: The General Board of the Baptist State Convention of North Carolina, 1967), 292–97, 307–8.

28. Leloudis, *Schooling the New South*, 109–17; *Biblical Recorder*, 5 September 1900, 14 August 1901, 26 February 1902. See also H. Leon Prather, *Resurgent Politics and Educational Progressivism in the New South: North Carolina, 1890–1913* (Rutherford, N.J.: Associated University Presses, 1979), 128–30.

29. Oliver H. Orr, Jr., *Charles Brantley Aycock* (Chapel Hill: University of North Carolina Press, 1961), 197–203. The degree to which Aycock's reform impulse was motivated by religion is debatable. Orr noted that Aycock was a Baptist who took comfort in reading the Bible, but at least one associate labeled him "not very churchy" (ibid., 17, 36).

30. "The Ideals of A New Era," 15 January 1901, in *The Life and Speeches of Charles B. Aycock* ed. R. D. W. Conner and Clarence Poe (Garden City, N.Y.: Doubleday, Page & Company, 1912), 236–37.

31. *Biblical Recorder*, 30 June 1900, 27 March, 17 April, 1 May 1901, 12 March 1902.

32. Ibid., 1 May 1901; *Annual of the North Carolina Baptist State Convention, 1903* (Raleigh: Edwards & Broughton, 1903), 69. For more on the limits of educational reform in North Carolina, see J. Morgan Kousser, "Progressivism—For Middle Class Whites Only: North Carolina Education, 1880–1910," *Journal of Southern History* 46 (May 1980):169–94.

33. *Biblical Recorder,* 8 October, 24 December 1902, 21 January 1908. Later, editor Livingston Johnson continued vocal support for public schools and the work they did. He also helped to organize Baptist academies to better equip them to survive the competition posed by public educational institutions. See ibid., 15 March, 14 June, 11 October, 13 December 1916, 14 February 1917. The Baptist State Convention's Board of Education undertook new initiatives designed to accomplish this goal. Still, many Baptist institutions struggled in the face of improved public education.

34. Ibid., 16 January 1900. For references to mill openings and related news, see ibid., 14 February 1900, 23 January 1901. For more on Tompkins, see George Taylor Winston, *A Builder of the New South, Being the Story and Life Work of Daniel Augustus Tompkins* (New York: Doubleday, Page, & Company, 1920), and Howard Bunyan Clay, "Daniel Augustus Tompkins, an American Bourbon" (Ph.D. diss., University of North Carolina, 1950).

35. *Biblical Recorder,* 23 January 1901. For more on conditions in the state's mill villages, see Jacquelyn Dowd Hall, James Leloudis, Robert Korstad, Lu Ann Jones, and Chris Daly, *Like A Family: The Making of a Southern Cotton Mill World* (Chapel Hill: University of North Carolina Press, 1987), chap. 1.

36. *Biblical Recorder,* 19 April 1905.

37. Ibid., 5 June 1901, 26 April 1905, 6 September 1916, 3 April 1918, 14 May, 12 November 1919. For more on Baptist views of labor unions, see Wayne Flynt, "Alabama White Protestantism and Labor, 1890–1920," *Alabama Review* 25 (July 1972):192–217.

38. *Biblical Recorder,* 2 January 1901, 11 February 1903, 19 May 1905, 27 April 1913; Link, *The Paradox of Southern Progressivism,* 177–80.

39. Jesse P. Chapman Jr. and Richard Janeway, *Miracle on Hawthorne Hill: The Medical Center, Bowman Gray School of Medicine of Wake Forest University and North Carolina Baptist Hospital* (New York: Newcomen Society of the United States, 1988).

40. Mattie U. Russell, "Watson Smith Rankin," *Dictionary of North Carolina Biography* ed. William S. Powell, 5 vols. (Chapel Hill: University of North Carolina Press, 1979–94), 5:174–75; Thomas C. Ricketts, with Jim Vickers and Sara McEwan, *Family and Friends: Rural Health Policy in North Carolina* (Chapel Hill: Cecil G. Sheps Center for Health Services Research, University of North Carolina at Chapel Hill, 1998), 5; *Biblical Recorder,* 27 August 1919.

41. *Biblical Recorder,* 11 February 1920.

42. Ibid., 9 June 1920.

43. Ibid., 25 February 1920.

44. Chapman and Janeway, *Miracle on Hawthorne Hill,* 8–10; Huggins, *A History of North Carolina Baptists, 1727–1932,* 345, 350, 352; *Biblical Recorder,* 5 January 1921.

45. *Biblical Recorder,* 9 June 1920; *Annual of the North Carolina Baptist State Convention, 1920,* 96.

46. *Biblical Recorder,* 11, 25 April, 6 June, 11 July, 8, 15 August 1900; *Annual of the North Carolina Baptist State Convention, 1918* (Raleigh: Edwards & Broughton, 1918), 98; *Annual of the North Carolina Baptist State Convention, 1922* (Raleigh: Edwards & Broughton, 1922), 119. His support of the disfranchisement amendment earned Bailey accusations of partisanship that he attempted to deny. See *Biblical Recorder,* 10 October 1900.

5

The Beginnings of Interracialism

Macon, Georgia, in the 1930s

Andrew M. Manis

With good reason has historian Dan T. Carter characterized the 1930s and '40s as a turning point, if not a watershed, in the Age of Segregation. The Great Depression, of course, shaped the psyche of a generation of Americans and hit the South particularly hard. In 1937 the region's per capita income of $314 was roughly half that of the rest of the country, and a year later President Franklin D. Roosevelt called the South "the nation's number one economic problem." Of course, Roosevelt's efforts to address the ravages of the depression transformed the nation's political and economic history.[1]

In Macon, Georgia, the 1930s also marked the beginnings of interracial efforts to soften the blows of Jim Crow. Whites and blacks in this decade cautiously began to challenge warnings about "race mixing" to meet and work together to alleviate the harsher aspects of segregation. In instigating the process that eventually became the civil rights movement, these became the first successful efforts to close the unutterable separation between white and black citizens of Macon. These efforts at interracialism launched both indigenous and transplanted efforts among whites and blacks to take timid half-steps toward racial justice. Certain of these cooperative efforts, conducted mostly by Christian denominations, had "made in Macon" stamped on them, while others were imported into Macon from earlier regional organizations of racial uplift. Chief among these organizations were the Commission on Interracial Cooperation (CIC), founded in the wake of Red Summer by an Atlanta Methodist minister, Will W. Alexander, and the spin-off Association of Southern Women for the Prevention of Lynching (ASWPL), founded by Jessie Daniel Ames in 1930.

One of the important themes in the work of Wayne Flynt has been to go against the grain of southern religious historiography to argue in many articles, books, and public addresses that the religion of white southerners has not been as captive to racism as it has been cracked up to be. Some historians look at groups of persons and lump them together to form a generalized "rule," while others look for the exceptions to the rules. John B. Boles has called these kinds of historians "lumpers" and "splitters." The question of the southern white church's racial captivity has been debated for a generation with Samuel S. Hill "lumping" most southern white religionists into the "captive" category. With good-natured but respectful arguments to the contrary, Flynt has argued with Hill as his meticulous historical spadework has found the exceptions.

Two points may be raised about Flynt's eagerness to highlight the exceptions. First, he has always acknowledged the truth of the generalization. Most of the celebrated scholars of southern religious history have expounded on this theme, and no contrarian can ignore the findings of so luminous a lineup. Hill's many books and articles can almost single-handedly make the case. The works of other established scholars—for example, Kenneth K. Bailey, John B. Boles, Donald Mathews, Brooks Holifield, and John Lee Eighmy—have sounded these notes, as have midcareer interpreters like Charles Reagan Wilson, Ted Ownby, Paul Harvey, Mitchell Snay, and myself. Flynt's work on southern religion maintains his friendly dialogue with the dominant view, but a second point must be emphasized: Flynt also mines the field for opportunities to explode the myth that the South has been so religiously solid and racially conservative because he loves his native region and *wants* to find *his kind of religion* in it. He is philosophically inclined toward a complexity capable of nodding in agreement with the claim that the white South has been dominated by racial conservatism while adding a mischievous "Yes, but . . . " to the discussion.[2]

One of Flynt's seminal essays arguing against the grain of other historians of southern religion was his 1977 article "Religion in the Urban South: The Divided Religious Mind of Birmingham, 1900–1930."[3] In this and many other articles, Flynt has touched on the developing Social Gospel in the South and the limited ways in which it challenged Jim Crow. Most recently, in his definitive *Alabama Baptists: Southern Baptists in the Heart of Dixie,* Flynt continued to look for the surprising exceptions to the acknowledged rule of conservative domination. As one of Wayne Flynt's students, I have gone into almost every research project of my own with a question that reflects a student's respect for a teacher: in tackling this topic, I continually ask, "What would Wayne do?" Following my honored mentor's example, this piece focuses on the urban South in the 1930s to ask what religious interracialism looked like in a smaller city like Macon, Georgia.[4] While my work has generally tended to agree more with the majority report, here I find Flynt's model compelling, as I draw the outlines of those racial moderates in the 1930s who, though still segregationists, hoped to palliate the sharper pains of the Jim Crow system against the backdrop of the radical racism of the vocal majority.

During the 1930s, political reaction in Georgia against FDR and the New Deal provided the context for interracial work between white and black Christians in Macon. Racially progressive whites working with African Americans were encouraged by Roosevelt's policies, and especially by the sympathetic ear of First Lady Eleanor Roosevelt. At the same time, they worked within a state over which champion race-baiter Governor Eugene Talmadge presided. Linked with the Klan and issuing frequent warnings of a "Nigra takeover," Talmadge and his followers, who elected him twice in the thirties and again in the 1940s, made Georgia a dangerous place for interracial activity that could easily be mischaracterized as "race mixing."[5] This chapter looks at the rise of interracial activities in Macon during the depression era and the local and state political milieu that made interracial activities difficult and sometimes dangerous.

The Depression and Racial Discrimination

The depression exacerbated an already tenuous economic picture for the South. In the mid-1920s the boll weevil devastated the entire region's cotton production. One Georgia county saw production plummet from 20,000 bales in 1919 to 333 in 1922. Macon, with its eleven textile mills, was suffering even before the market crashed in 1929. Annual income of southern farmers fell from $206 during the 1920s to a low of $83 during the depression. As the farm economy weakened, food became scarcer in Macon. Farmers made little profit selling their harvests and planted only enough to feed their families. As national unemployment hit a high of 24.9 percent in 1933, soup kitchens sprung up around town and lines of clients lengthened.[6]

By 1930, Macon's African Americans numbered 32,906, almost 43 percent of the total Bibb County population of 77,042. Unemployment in the county increased during the decade for both whites and blacks, though growth in black joblessness outpaced that for whites by almost two and a half times. In 1940, 7.29 percent of whites in Bibb County were unemployed, compared with 12.85 percent of blacks. With the number of black-owned or -operated farms falling by 37.1 percent between 1930 and 1940, compared to only 7.2 percent among whites, black farmers in Bibb County lost their farms during the 1930s at a rate of more than five times that of white farmers.[7]

In the face of such difficulties, blacks received little help from New Deal legislation. The reduction in acreage mandated by the Agricultural Adjustment Act further reduced the meager income of many Georgia tenant farmers, driving them to day labor or unemployment. The codes of the National Recovery Act required higher wage scales and led many businesses to eliminate marginal workers. Not surprisingly, blacks were the first to be displaced. Thus, as historian Paul Bolster argued, New Deal programs "produced frustration and a will to dissent" among African Americans.[8]

Throughout the South this increasing competition for jobs made scarcer by the economic upheaval escalated racial tensions. Clark H. Foreman, a field agent for the Julius Rosenwald Fund and from 1938 to 1967 president of the Southern Conference for Human Welfare, described a situation in which jobs formerly given to blacks were during the depression being taken by whites. White resentment over having to do "nigger jobs" or seeing blacks with jobs that could have been held by other whites sparked new racial animosities. Foreman wrote, "When you have unemployment in the South, you have race trouble, for it is among the unemployed element, comprising large numbers of under-privileged white unskilled labor in economic competition with Negroes, that race prejudices are most prevalent and most easily stirred."[9]

One group that was stirred up was called the American Order of Fascisti or the "Black Shirts," an American spin-off of Mussolini's organization that drew some 40,000 members in Georgia, with branches in Atlanta, Macon, Savannah, and Columbus.[10] In September 1930, however, in a hint of the interracial efforts that would develop during the decade, an organization of Macon's African Americans named The Forum called a mass meeting at Stewart's Chapel AME Church to discuss employment and other matters affecting them. The audience passed a resolution thanking prominent whites in Macon who had registered their opposition to the Black Shirts: "Whereas, certain organized forces in Georgia have begun a movement to stir up race hatred and prejudice and oust the men of our race from all gainful employment in the municipalities of this state and elsewhere, making the next a hard winter for the Negroes of Georgia and have him out of every job a white man would care to hold. . . . Whereas, many of our white friends in Macon promptly accepted the challenge and have been unremitting in their efforts to make constructive sentiment favorable to us in this present crisis." The resolution then thanked W. T. Anderson, various civic clubs, and the churches for their "courageous and humanitarian stand . . . in behalf of our race in this crisis."[11]

Beyond the economic difficulties of both black and white citizens of Macon, a pair of outsiders observed the troubling racial realities of the city. Studying white-black inequities in education and city services in 1934, Jesse O. Thomas, the southern field secretary of the National Urban League, concluded that Macon was "one of the most backward cities in the whole South."[12] When Mayor G. Glen Toole told a gathering of the Junior Chamber of Commerce that "the Negro is the greatest curse in the community today," blacks rescinded their invitation to the mayor to speak to them regarding black Sunday Schools at a "Harvest Drive." Angered by the insult, white Methodist pastor Walter Anthony called the mayor's comment a "weird and grotesque example of crooked thinking."[13]

Black citizens of Macon also suffered more specific areas of discrimination. Voting remained one of those areas. In November 1933 the black General Missionary Baptist Convention met in Macon, where delegates adopted a report complaining that "the church has been too much divorced from politics, so that we have today too many demagogues in our legislatures and not enough statesmen." Thus, the Baptists continued, "our people should be taught how to vote, when to vote, and for whom to vote." Still, too few blacks in Macon managed to get on the voter registration lists. On one occasion in the 1930s, a black minister, the Reverend M. E. Moon, sought out a liberal white attorney to take a case involving police brutality. Anticipating a future run for public office, the attorney declined to take the case because blacks did not vote in sufficient numbers.[14]

Reasons for this dearth of black voters were not difficult to ascertain. White registrars exercised inordinate authority in choosing who could register. In 1939, a Bibb County tax collector admitted to an interviewer that he asked potential black voters to explain the Supreme Court jurisdiction clause of the Constitution, bragging, "I can keep the president of the United States from registering in Macon if I want to." That same year H. R. Harris, manager of the Georgia Baptist College, spoke to members of a club in the student activity building at Mercer about the problem of voting among blacks. Un-American groups, he complained, had the right to vote, but "the Negro remains disfranchised." He blamed African Americans' disinterest in voting on poor educational facilities, noting that Bibb County spent more money educating white students than educating blacks. Such conditions gave blacks "little incentive to vote in the South." Still, he argued, blacks were preparing themselves for the opportunity to vote when it came.[15]

A white speaker hit on a similar theme as Buford Boone, managing editor of the *Macon Telegraph,* addressed a Mercer Forum on "The Southern Negro in Politics." Boone pointed out the federal government's doctrine that "all men are created free and equal and that no one's right to vote shall be abridged by, among other things, color." With this he contrasted the white primary among Democrats, designed to exclude blacks from the only elections of any consequence in the one-party South. Boone told his audience that the solution of the Negro problem lay "in raising the level of the Negro through recognition of his rights of suffrage," as well as, Boone added significantly, "the admission that he deserves better opportunities."[16]

Discrimination in medical care gave the African Americans of Macon additional reason for concern, especially when a black Bibb County farmer named Albert Glover was severely injured when a car crashed into his wagon on Forsyth Road. Taken home by a friend, he was later examined by county physician Dr. Herring Winship, who found Glover able to move his right arm and leg only with great difficulty and his left arm and leg not at all. Winship's request that Glover be admitted to the Macon Hospital was rejected by hospital superintendent Howard V. Williams, who concluded Glover was not sufficiently hurt to be considered "a hospital case." Angered by this decision, Winship took the case before a meeting of the Bibb County commissioners. Calling for Glover to be admitted, he told them, "I believe he will die if he is left where he is." The occasion induced another visit by Williams, who commented that Glover was "getting along alright," adding, "if we took in everybody with a sprained shoulder, the hospital would have to be three times as big as it is."[17]

Within a few years this and similar incidents led the Macon Hospital to establish a separate wing for black patients. While this move increased the black community's access to health care, the medical situation for blacks remained tenuous and in some ways the Jim Crow wall was buttressed. Later, Dr. C. W. Dyer, administrator of Macon's black St. Luke's Hospital, wrote a letter to the *Telegraph* suggesting that black doctors and nurses were not getting sufficient training at the Macon Hospital's Negro wing. Suggesting a solution, he called on the city to enlarge and take over the funding of St. Luke's Hospital, while leaving control of it in the hands of Macon's black citizens. Dyer's letter, labeled "The Negro in Macon," ranged beyond discrimination in medical care to address other concerns. Believing that "the

South is a great place for blacks," Dyer informed white readers that blacks would find it ideal if the South would address inadequate public education and "justice in the courts."[18]

Such injustice has of course continued over the decades, and Macon blacks in the 1930s also experienced discriminatory treatment by local law enforcement agencies. For example, on 14 January 1933, police raided several black dance halls under "dive and gaming" ordinances passed the previous summer. In what one detective called the largest raid in his recollection, a squad of plainclothes officers led by Chief Detective T. E. Garrett raided a dance hall on Broadway and Hawthorne streets, arresting owner Son Wright for operating a dive and 103 patrons for loitering in a dive. Police Chief Ben T. Watkins had received several complaints about the noise produced by Wright's dances and used four patrol wagons and all available police cars to transport the "chattering Negroes" to headquarters. On the same afternoon and evening police also raided several other halls, including one owned by C. H. Douglass, where 18 persons were arrested for assembling for purposes of gaming. In all, some 140 blacks were incarcerated in the incidents.[19]

In light of these intimidations, black parents often warned their teen-age offspring to exercise caution and deliberate self-restraint whenever in the downtown area. Frank Hutchings Jr. recalled his father insisting that he and his brothers come straight home after school and not linger anywhere in downtown Macon. Parents often recounted the fate of "Cocky" Glover, a victim of a notorious 1922 lynching. Often embellishing the already sordid story to include Glover's body being tied to an automobile and dragged through black neighborhoods, black parents implored their children to avoid brushes with the law at all costs, with stern warnings that arrests could lead to dire consequences.[20]

In the following days, *Macon Telegraph* publisher W. T. Anderson wrote to Mayor Glen Toole to protest the wholesale arrests. Anderson and other spokespersons from the black community complained that patrons who were not drunk or disorderly or committing any other crime were indiscriminately picked up in the mass arrests. Such persons, they argued, should be allowed to participate in social events without police interference or intimidation. Toole replied to Anderson that whiskey was reportedly served, in violation of federal prohibition policy, and that Wright had been repeatedly warned to keep order. He added, "I have much sympathy for the Negro, and you may rest assured that I will always see . . . that they will have the best of the breaks." Toole, Recorder Court Judge M. Felton Hatcher, and Police Chief Watkins conferred with Anderson early in the week and negotiated the blacks' release after four days in jail. Eventually Hatcher dismissed the charges on all but two of the defendants but warned the others: "It must be pretty bad if Negroes will call on officers to report complaints on their own race in a matter like this. If you are brought before me again on charges like these, it won't be this way next time."[21]

Wholesale arrests subsided for a while, but later in the decade police began another campaign in which various black homes or "dives" were raided in May 1938. This flare-up saw some 50 black citizens arrested for drunkenness, being a public nuisance, or operating illicit dives.[22] The crusade continued into 1939, when police arrested sixteen-year-old Sara Scott for disorderly conduct and resisting arrest. On 8 February, Officer A. J. Millirons ordered a number of black teens to stop roller-skating on the Main Street sidewalks. When she refused to take off her skates in accordance with his order, Millirons warned Scott that if she did not comply he would be forced to take her before a judge. "Damn the judge and damn you," came the girl's impertinent reply, followed by her efforts to slap and kick the officer. Claiming to be defending himself, Millirons later admitted striking her but only after her attacks had begun. Brought to trial on 14 March, Scott claimed the officer had grabbed her and twisted her arm when she could not get her skates off quickly enough. According to her testimony, her resistance to his manhandling led the officer to hit her in the nose. Recorder's Court Judge George M. Nottingham found Scott guilty but suspended her sentence.[23]

Blacks in Macon became convinced that both the arrest and conviction were unjust. Frank J. Hutchings wrote the *Telegraph* calling on the "superior race" to show its supposed superiority by treating the "inferior race" with fairness and justice. Doubting that the 108-pound girl would attack a large, armed police officer without provocation, Hutchings questioned the veracity of the frequent claim that white southerners were the blacks' only friends: "We might tell ourselves it is true, but the burden of proof rests with the white man, as actions speak louder than words."[24]

Vouching for Scott's character, Ballard High School assistant principal Lewis H. Mounts told readers of the *Telegraph*, "No member of the family gave any trouble beyond slight matters of normal mischief, nor ever constituted a deportment problem." He further expressed doubts about the negative picture of his former student presented by the prosecution, adding, "I am fully convinced that she would have given no trouble whatsoever if dealt with in any proper fashion. I have had her daily as a pupil in my classroom for over two and a half years and have never found any need of unusual measures for her control. I must state in conclusion that I know personally that serious damage has been done to the Macon Negro's confidence in the white man's justice, and that there is grave needs that something be done to retrieve the loss." Singling out of blacks in this manner, Mounts asserted, had hurt black-white relations in Macon. Despite progress accomplished by burgeoning interracial cooperation, the Scott incident and others like it had "done much to undo the work of past years so far as faith in the Southern white man's sense of fair play is concerned."[25]

Discriminatory practices on the local scene, however, were not the only items on a list of factors inhibiting interracial progress in Macon. The political atmosphere across Georgia in the 1930s was poisoned, especially for whites and blacks committed to interracial cooperation, by the state's flamboyant governor, Eugene Talmadge. His demagoguery and race-baiting accusations against Roosevelt's New Deal made interracialists feel unwelcome in Talmadge country.

Eugene Talmadge and the Racist Resistance

Born fifteen miles north of Macon on the family plantation near Forsyth, Eugene Talmadge attended the University of Georgia, practiced law in Atlanta for a year, and eventually married and settled on a farm in Telfair County. First elected to public office as a state representative in 1920, he rode his strong rural appeal to three terms as commissioner of agriculture beginning in 1926 and to the governorship in 1932. His enthusiastic ruralism and his flamboyant rhetoric made him one of the most popular politicians in Georgia history. As the state's chief executive, Talmadge accepted federal largesse but came to bitterly oppose Roosevelt's New Deal for enlarging the federal bureaucracy and its willingness to incur government debt.[26]

By 1935 the governor's distaste for Roosevelt had sunk so low that it expressed itself in a grossly insensitive remark that "the next president we should have should be able to walk a two-by-four."[27] He also told a gathering of Kiwanis and Rotary Clubs in Rome, Georgia, that the evils of communism were mild compared to the shortcomings of the New Deal. "I've never seen anything in Communism as bad as the New Deal," he said, "and there are things in Communism that are revolting." Hinting that he might challenge FDR for the Democratic nomination, he predicted that 1936 presidential contest would be a matter of "Americanism vs. Communism."[28] By the mid-1930s such associations between Roosevelt, or the New Deal, and communism especially resonated with white southerners. The 1931 Scottsboro Case, handled by the Communist Party's International Defense League, had

caused most whites to discern communist intrigue in even the most timid
efforts toward racial equality. Opponents of interracial cooperation now had
an additional epithet to fling at racial do-gooders; they were communists as
well as "nigger-lovers."

Just as significantly, elements of the Roosevelt administration also challenged the views of Talmadge's rural constituency, which had less contact
with education or educated blacks than city folk and were thereby more sus-
ceptible to racial appeals. Near the end of 1935, Talmadge traveled to New
York to make a radio speech called "Georgia Answers Roosevelt," part of
a national effort to deny Roosevelt a second term. In collaboration with
wealthy Texas oil man John Henry Kirby and author Thomas Dixon, among
others, Talmadge formed an organization called the Southern Committee to
Uphold the Constitution and made plans to launch the national effort with
a "Grass Roots Convention" in Macon.[29]

In the days before the meeting, the *Telegraph* replied to requests to get off
the fence regarding Talmadge's machinations. Committing themselves, the
editors "preferred not to say anything that would appear to be unduly critical
of friends within our gates." They nonetheless pointed out the paper's disagreements with FDR. They also scored Senator Richard B. Russell's overly
enthusiastic defense of the New Deal. On Talmadge's criticisms, the *Telegraph* held that "practically all of [the governor's] charges against Roosevelt
for deserting the Democratic platform and going over to the Socialists and
Communists are true."

The Grass Roots reply to White was unmistakable. Planners greeted the
"delegates" with a giant Confederate flag draped behind the platform and an
issue of *The Georgia Women's World* in every seat. Published by the Atlanta-
based National Women's Association of the White Race, the magazine pic-
tured Eleanor Roosevelt speaking with at black professor at Howard University. Inside the covers, one article fumed, "Surely no other roamed the
country at will as she does. . . . surely the white women of the nation, at least
those of the South, have not shared the cordial comradeship which is so
freely bestowed to and among the Negroes of the nation." Another complained about black appointments in the Roosevelt administration. Reading
the magazine were some 3,000 partisans, mostly Georgia farmers "united to
oppose Negroes, the New Deal and . . . Karl Marx."[30]

The convention delegates gained permission to enter Talmadge's name on
primary ballots, after the governor's speech called on Democrats nationwide
to "run that boondoggling crowd out of Washington." Representing Macon,
city attorney E. W. Maynard chaired local arrangements for the rally and

welcomed visitors to Macon. Denouncing the president, Maynard asked, "How can you depend on him to protect this county against Socialism when he is in favor of Socialism? How can you depend on him to protect the rights of the states when he is against states' rights?"

Macon's general response to Talmadge may be judged by its election results. In 1932, Talmadge received just under 24 percent of the votes in Bibb County, compared to 37 percent two years later.[31] After the Grass Roots Convention, however, while the *Telegraph*'s editors remained respectful of the governor's efforts, at least two readers took different perspectives. "A Roosevelt Booster" regarded the convention as a laughingstock, deriding Talmadge with the comment that "every time this clown opens his mouth Mr. Roosevelt gets a vote. . . . as Governor you are an insult to the voters of Georgia." During the following days letters to the editor brought another anonymous comment—indicative of a racially progressive white author who feared racist intimidation enough to avoid signing a name.

We people of the South have been fortunate in our relations with our Negroes. They did not come here in the first place on their own choice. For years they . . . made the South the richest spot in the country. During the war they tended the crops and took care of the women and children while their masters were fighting a war to keep them in slavery. Since the war they have made the best of help on the farms and the best of house servants. They have gotten less and less justice in courts than menials in most countries. They do not try to vote yet pay their taxes and are patriotic. . . . I think we owe the Negro too great a debt to condemn him because a few of his race have committed the unpardonable crime. I think it is unpardonable in a Governor who will condone the instigation of race prejudice for political purposes or any other cause.[32]

In 1940, Talmadge sought another term as governor after a four-year absence. In an effort to campaign as what Stephen Tuck has called the "protector of white Georgia," Talmadge made race and the specter of black voting the central issues of his winning campaign. While Talmadge drew weaker poll numbers in Macon than in more rural parts of Georgia, his populist appeal as the champion of white supremacy made him a formidable enemy for racial liberals in the state. Beyond this, his down-home antics and rural sensibilities endeared him to common folk who often supported him to spite their more sophisticated neighbors.

Once back in office, his third term was dominated by his efforts to fire

Walter Cocking, dean of education at the University of Georgia, for advocating the racial integration of Georgia's schools. Running for reelection in 1942
against Ellis Arnall, Talmadge again made race and education the central
issues of his campaign.[33] Leading up to the primary election, the Georgia
State Democratic Committee passed a resolution praising the governor "for
his manhood and courage in thus upholding the sacred traditions of this
state and the constitution he swore to defend." In the committee's discussions, one member said, "I like Negroes. I like 'em in their place. And their
place in the cotton field, hoeing and chopping cotton." Regarding support
for Talmadge, he added, "In my section you're either for Talmadge or against
him. And if you say you're gonna vote against him, we'll ask you whether
you're for racial equality, and I can tell you'll have a fight on your hands."[34]
    The controversy over racial integration at the University of Georgia spread
to the state's other colleges and universities. Talmadge's efforts to dominate
the state university system's Board of Regents eventually led to the loss of
accreditation for all the state-sponsored colleges in Georgia and cost him the
election. In Bibb County, Talmadge received 46 percent of the vote in 1942.[35]
The political atmosphere dominated by his racist politics, however, guaranteed that people in Macon involved in interracial work would, indeed, have
a fight on their hands.

Local Roots of Interracial Cooperation

Despite the larger milieu of resistance to racial change in Georgia and the
city, blacks and white citizens of Macon worked together to a much greater
extent in the 1930s than ever before. Two factors contributed to this birth of
interracialism. First, new regional organizations for dealing with racial problems were founded in the post–World War I era. These organizations, most
notably the CIC and the ASWPL, established beachheads in a number of
southern cities, including Macon. Making the soil fertile for these interracial
organizations in Macon and other cities, however, were cooperative efforts
during the Great War, the depression, and the New Deal era. Such efforts
were the second element giving rise to Macon's interracial experiments of the
1930s.
    For example, in conjunction with their white counterparts, African Ameri-
cans conducted Liberty Bond drives, a War Savings Stamp parade, and Red
Cross drives. During the depression, in the first year of the Roosevelt presidency, the Macon Chamber of Commerce spearheaded the city's campaign
to urge businesses to comply with the Blue Eagle Drive of the National Re-

covery Administration. John L. Morris, head of the local effort, met with black leader Minnie Singleton to coordinate canvassing of the black sections of the city. Singleton also enlisted the local branch of the National Urban League to participate in the effort. Some 300 citizens fanned out across the city to convince all employers to sign voluntarily a blanket code as a pledge to pay a minimum wage of 40 cents an hour for a 35-hour work week. A second campaign put 800 citizens to work calling on consumers to patronize only businesses that displayed the Blue Eagle sign and its slogan, "We Do Our Part." Later more than 25,000 participated in a massive NRA parade in Macon.[36]

On at least one occasion during the campaign, Macon blacks held mass meetings at First African Baptist Church, where they urged their members to trade only with firms or individuals who observed the codes and were also "giving the Negro a chance to work along with all other people." Along with encouraging such cooperative efforts, however, the leaders also criticized discriminatory administration of the codes and other New Deal projects. For example, H. A. Hunt, principal of the Fort Valley Normal and Industrial School, had called on the "New Deal" to become a "Square Deal" aiding black relief work projects and lessening the gap between white workers earning 90 cents a day compared to 40 cents for black workers. In response a mass meeting led by L. J. May, Dr. C. W. Dyer, A. W. Barrow, Charles H. Douglass, and W. C. Lee adopted a resolution against employers who refused to comply with the codes. Under the law, the resolution asserted, minimum wage benefits "belong to all wage earners, regardless of race, color or creed. . . . To deny the Negro equal wages for identical work flouts the program of the administration [and] defeats the great purpose of the NRA."[37]

Macon blacks also volunteered as Red Cross workers in large numbers. In October 1938, for example, black women in Macon formed an auxiliary of the American Red Cross. Mattie Hubbard Jones was elected to chair the auxiliary and to work closely with Dorothy White, executive secretary of the Macon Red Cross chapter. Meeting at the black section of the Washington Library, White oriented 30 black volunteers to work in "war, disaster, peace, for safety, and other services." They also volunteered to work in a national campaign to fight polio and registered their rejection of communism by participating in a 1938 rally of the American Loyalty League, where a white Catholic priest and two black Protestant ministers warned the audience against communist efforts to recruit black members.[38]

While the activities continued to separate white organizations from their black counterparts, they ran along parallel tracks and showed both whites and blacks in the city that both races were working in similar ways for similar goals. Since blacks worked alongside whites for "white" goals, they also called upon the white community to contribute to their own goals. Chief among these were fund-raising campaigns to strengthen certain black institutions. In the fall of 1933 the Reverend J. H. Gadson, president of the black Baptist Central City College, led a drive to raise funds for capital improvements and an endowment fund to strengthen the school and put it on par with Atlanta University. After a trip to New York when he induced contributions from the National Baptist Convention, Gadson donated an entire year's salary of $1,800 to the project. That same week he garnered five contributions, including at least one anonymous white citizen who gave $100 in honor of his two black servants and in memory of his former African-American nurse. While contributions from black church rallies and the annual meeting of the black Georgia Missionary Baptist Convention continued to come in, the turning point in the campaign was the decision of Macon industrialist James H. Porter, head of the college's white advisory board, to pay $5,000 for all the assets of the college. He later turned the college back over to the black Georgia Baptist Convention.[39] When the campaign ended, Frank J. Hutchings Sr., a veteran of the Great War and owner of the Hutchings Funeral Home, wrote a shrewd thank-you note to white citizens through the *Telegraph* "for showing a Christian spirit in improving the educational facilities of Central City College," which he believed illustrated "a very close bond of friendship" in Macon's black-white relations. Hoping, however, to gain white help on a similar matter, he added: "I am wondering if there isn't some way the same whites cannot be induced, encouraged or implored to say just a few words about the dilapidated, overcrowded 'janitorless' fire traps which we citizens of Macon commonly call the Bibb County Negro Public schools."[40]

In the 1920s Macon boasted but ten public schools for blacks. Only one of these, Hudson Industrial, was a secondary school. Salaries for school administrators were grossly unequal, with white male high school principals earning $125 a month, compared to $75 a month for a white female principal. At the elementary level white male principals earned $60 a month, in contrast to the highest black principal who was paid $40 month. By the end of the decade, African-American students in Macon constituted 39 percent of the total, while only 9 percent of expenditures went to black education. One study reported that statewide, blacks received only about one-twenty-fifth of the total amount spent for public education, while figures compiled by the New Deal era Works Progress Administration showed that the state of

Georgia spent $35.42 on the education of its white students compared to $6.32 for black students.[41]

Black private education centered on several schools in Macon. Ballard Normal School was operated by the American Missionary Association and Macon's First Congregationalist Church since just after the Civil War. Central City College, which began elementary and secondary instruction in 1889, began its college department in 1920. The next year, a public school teacher named Minnie L. Smith founded Beda-Etta Business College, which gave instruction in typing, shorthand, bookkeeping, and banking. The St. Peter Claver Catholic School also educated black citizens of Macon.[42] In 1923, black Macon made fund-raising efforts to help rebuild Central City College after its buildings were destroyed by fire in 1921.[43]

Black educator R. S. Ingram wrote to the *Macon Telegraph* appealing for help in developing the new Negro High and Industrial School. Adopting a Bookerist perspective, he sought to assure whites that instruction at the school would be safely vocational. Styling the new school as a Tuskegee in the making, Ingram emphasized the "service" character of vocational training—"not merely the giving of information, theoretically, but actually doing the work with the hands, well and intelligently." Highlighting courses in shop work and carpentry for boys and sewing and domestic science for girls, he rejected a DuBoisian liberal education as "inflated and superficial." Disparaging mere "book learning," Ingram argued that when "taught to be more industrious, prosperous, more dependable and self-reliant through better methods of industrial education," blacks would improve their conditions and become more content with life in the South. He concluded his letter by underscoring that instruction at the new school would not challenge southern traditions of race relations: "This city is fortunate because its Board of Education and its Superintendent of Schools are wholly sympathetic toward a progressive industrial education program. The teachers of the several vocations here received their training at the best industrial institutions— Hampton, Tuskegee and Cheyney. . . . They are all Southern-born and reared and fully understand and respect the fixed sentiments and customs established for our goings that are conducive to peace and prosperity for us all." Commenting on the letter, editor W. T. Anderson complimented Ingram's philosophy as sound and sane. "Many well-intentioned people who have no fundamental understanding of the colored race and its needs," he wrote, "have been championing the higher education for the Negro in the South." Such an error, he argued, betrayed an "unpardonable stupidity."[44]

At the same time, however, Anderson found problems in the more activist perspective reflected in the recently organized National Association for the Advancement of Colored People (NAACP), which had begun membership drives in most Georgia cities, including Macon. In a 1921 column, he lamented that "radical and shallow" leaders like W. E. B. DuBois were replacing "the deeper, saner and more practical men of their race like Moton of Tuskegee." Noting the NAACP's meetings throughout Georgia, he warned that criticisms of the South and other efforts to estrange blacks from whites would retard rather than advance the status of blacks. If, on the contrary, blacks would "take the advice of his Best Friend and aspire to become a good servant in the large and best sense as well as the menial sense, there is nothing the better element of the white race in the South will not do for him."[45]

In addition to periodic requests that white Macon address inequities in the black public schools, most of which went largely ignored, blacks in Macon also sought white help when the depression hurt the financial base of the privately funded Ballard Normal School. In February 1933, for the first time in the school's 65-year history, Ballard principal Raymond G. von Tobel launched a fund drive to make up for cuts in contributions from its northern benefactor, the Congregationalist Church's American Missionary Association. Hard economic times had reduced Ballard's enrollment from 400 to 215, leading Tobel to write the *Telegraph* to appeal for help. The principal allayed white fears that the instruction received at Ballard would not upset southern social conventions. Emphasizing a curriculum focused on "manual training" for boys and "domestic arts and science" for girls, Tobel said that the school produced good citizens, asserting, "There is little lawlessness among Ballard students." Noting that Ballard graduates made up 80 percent of the teachers in the black public schools, he assured whites that "Whatever question there may have been . . . has been answered by the excellent work that the faculty has done in helping to adjust the Negro students to the white viewpoint. The school has served, indeed, a most useful purpose not only in the educational field, but also in the field of race relations." Tobel also recruited George N. White, a vice-president of the First National Bank, to be secretary of the campaign and Police Chief Ben P. Watkins to help raise funds. Fund-raising rallies also included written appeals from Mayor G. Glen Toole and W. T. Anderson. Whites in Macon, however, apparently were not moved to great beneficence, as reports of collection totals at the campaign's end amounted to only $451.80, collected from Ballard students and the African-American churches.[46]

The 1930s also saw efforts of interracial cooperation aimed at improving medical care for African Americans. Most of the activity centered on

St. Luke's Hospital, which began as a clinic treating black patients in 1928, because black physicians were denied access to the wards of the Macon Hospital. On the eighth anniversary of the hospital, administrator C. W. Dyer and other black physicians conducted an open house for both black and white citizens to become acquainted with the facilities. They also invited white surgeons to come and share their knowledge of newer procedures with their black counterparts. Dyer's 250 invitation letters to white citizens included requests for financial donations, but by the time of the event, only 23 contributions had been procured.[47]

The following spring, St. Luke's established a plan for affordable hospital insurance at a cost of 35 cents a week. As Dyer's brainchild, the plan covered only hospital expenses of $22 a week. In one of the first plans of its kind in Georgia, the plan enrolled 400 clients from some 90 black families in its first year. The arrangement trained Macon blacks to look to the hospital in times of illness, contributing to higher cure rates. With his penchant for gently tweaking white sensibilities, Dyer noted, "White people talk about the danger of disease spreading from servants but talking about it is about all they do. We are trying to do what we can to lift the health standards of the Negro race, and a Negro hospital, well supported, together with hospital insurance for those who ordinarily have hospital attention will do something to help us reach that goal."[48]

Dyer's pithy remark may have hit its intended target, because a year later there was some movement in the effort to elevate St. Luke's to full hospital status. His efforts were a vivid example of the clever interracial dance blacks engaged in to gain concessions from whites for the purpose of ameliorating the harsher realities of Jim Crow. Strategists like Dyer shrewdly maintained their polite pressure on white Macon, exploiting all inconsistencies in white arguments and gently goading whites into humanizing the system of segregation. Along the way, blacks managed to win over sympathetic whites by tapping their eagerness to see themselves as magnanimous caretakers of "their colored people." This self-conscious dance among blacks and the traditions of noblesse oblige of whites makes it impossible to differentiate efforts at interracial cooperation from the paternalism southern whites inherited from the previous century.

Thus in August 1938 Dyer led a group of black leaders to ask the Bibb County Commission to join with the city to sponsor either the building of a new hospital for blacks or for the city or county to take over the privately run St. Luke's. Aiding their argument with a crucial statistic, Dyer and the others reminded the white leaders that the black death rate in Bibb County was three times that of whites. In addition, he reported that the Macon Hospital's black wings had only 27 beds, a figure later corrected to 62, for a black population of some 32,000. Initially the commissioners referred the matter to the Macon Hospital Commission and the county Board of Health.[49]

By October the black medical leaders and the Bibb County Medical Society launched a campaign to build a new 60-bed hospital for blacks, to be staffed by a black staff. Four white doctors lent their vigorous support to the effort. Administrator C. L. Ridley told political leaders that the facilities at Macon Hospital had reached "the end of the row," pointing out that the current situation had been established 40 years earlier when Macon had a population of 23,000. Hospital capacity, he argued, was simply inadequate to the current task of caring for a county of some 75,000 potential patients. Joining the argument, Dr. C. C. Harrold called on city leaders to help provide a district hospital operated with public funds, from the local to the federal level. Harrold sent out letters to the commissioners to meet with all interested parties at the grand jury room of the county courthouse. "We have found that all these groups have been working for the same thing," Harrold explained, "and these letters are to request the entire groups to meet" on 3 November for further discussions. These cooperative efforts successfully led to the incorporation of St. Luke's Hospital in November 1939.[50]

All these fledgling interracial efforts, usually initiated by black organizations for pragmatic purposes, involved soliciting white financial help to strengthen separate, unequal, and weaker black institutions in Macon. Or, as in the case of parallel programs during the Great War and depression, these efforts helped fight the Germans abroad and economic dislocation at home. In the development of interracialism in Macon, however, they laid the groundwork for cooperative efforts aimed specifically at softening the blows of Jim Crow. In that great struggle, the churches and self-consciously interracial organizations like the Commission on Interracial Cooperation and the Association of Southern Women for the Prevention of Lynching would lead the efforts.

Interracial Efforts on Racial Issues

One of the earliest interracial religious efforts in twentieth-century Macon grew out of the long-standing tradition of Methodism. After emancipation, black Methodists in the South were beset with choices. Staying within the Methodist Episcopal Church South with their white coreligionists remained only a short-term possibility, as most blacks wanted church communion where Christian equality and their own African-based religious practices could be honored. Before long, it became clear that they would leave for a black denominational structure. Early on, the only other choice was the African Methodist Episcopal Church, which was rapidly moving into the South and recruiting former slaves who were Methodists. As a northern-based denomination, however, the AME was considered a dangerous Yankee influence on southern blacks. Thus, by 1870 white Methodists helped certain "loyal" (read "uninfluenced by AME radicalism") black members to form a new conference that evolved into the Colored Methodist Episcopal Church. This new denomination, sometimes derided by AMEs as "the slave church," maintained less independence from and thus closer ties with white Methodists in the South. Reflecting this tradition, the educational and missionary convention of the CME met for its annual assembly in Macon on 12 September 1916. Several white ministers from Atlanta's Emory University and from Macon's Wesleyan College and Mulberry Street Methodist Church were invited to instruct their black ministerial brothers. Such Christian mixing, the gathering held, "shows that a friendly feeling is in the heart of the best people of both races" and nurtured "the hope of racial adjustment in the South."[51]

By the 1930s, some Macon congregations began to participate in Race Relations Day, scheduled for the Sunday nearest to Valentine's Day. But again blacks initiated them. In 1932 the black First Baptist Church observed the occasion by inviting three white laypersons to speak. In the fairly paternalistic affair, Lincoln McConnell, vice president of the City Bank and Trust Company, remarked on the southern white man's friendship toward blacks. John L. Morris, manager of the Chamber of Commerce, urged his black audience to educate themselves, advising that "the world pays more for good manners and a pleasing personality than it pays for anything else." Reiterating that theme, Walter P. Jones, superintendent of schools, told the congregation that "education would do more to abolish hatred and prejudice than mere force." Welcoming the white leaders and adding to their comments were black ministers E. G. Thomas of the First Baptist Church and M. A. Fountain, pastor of the Steward Chapel AME Church, as leaders of the ceremonies. Both a black choir and a white quartet provided music for the service. Black-initiated efforts cropped up periodically, beginning late in the decade, such as a 1938 series of services sponsored by a number of black churches held at Macon City Auditorium to express their appreciation to whites who had contributed to the black community in various ways.[52] Still, the white churches stayed away from this sort of activity.

The exceptions to this were Wesleyan College, the Methodist school for women, and the Baptist-run Mercer University. Among white Christians in Macon, these two schools would provide important leadership in more progressive race relations in Macon. Often professors at the schools, and usually at great peril to their permanent employment, surreptitiously subverted their students' racial orthodoxy. In the early twentieth century, a Mercer philosophy professor, J. Rufus Moseley, became known for both his Christian spirituality and his cross-racial ministry. Although resigning his position in 1900 after a short tenure at Mercer, Moseley remained a respected but quirky public figure in Macon. After having a radical spiritual experience that he often likened to Christ's resurrection appearances to his disciples, he left Mercer because of his "radical new developments in religious thought" and because he wished to avoid involving the school in what, he later wrote, "might prove to be some controversial matters." He then began an unpaid ministry to the poor and imprisoned. From the mid-1920s to his death in 1954, he wrote a regular column for the *Macon Telegraph,* mostly focusing on various spiritual topics. During the heyday of lynching in Macon during the 1920s, an unarmed Moseley once broke up a small lynch mob, who "were filled with fear and fled." Some thirty-five years after his death, an elderly black janitor told a visitor to the *Telegraph* offices everything he could remember about Moseley. "If you had no coat, he would give you his," he reported.[53] Much later, in 1963, when Mercer University drew criticism for the decision to admit black students, its president, Rufus C. Harris, received a letter from a supportive alumnus, Class of 1911: "Your side is sure to win in the final," adding, "This letter is likely due to the seed sown in English class at Mercer where I sat under Professor Carl Steed. He was a great advocate of the rights of the Negro even then, and did not wait until Sunday to say so."[54]

Another way the denominations, working in conjunction with their schools, managed to "integrate" at least the mental universes of their students was by inviting black ministers to speak at meetings of their student organizations. For example, in 1933 the South Georgia Methodist Conference invited W. A. Bell, a black leader of interracial religious work in Atlanta, to speak at its Young People's Assembly at Wesleyan College. Celebrating the work of the black Methodist Paine College in Augusta, Bell told the young audience, "I am confident that your church and mine—and your people and my people—have not caught a glimpse of our possibilities for service— possibilities of wiping out the unnecessary differences between races and building a great Christian brotherhood." Two years later the Mercer Ministerial (Student) Association invited Central City College president J. H.

Gadson to address their regular meeting held in Roberts Chapel. In surprisingly frank comments, Gadson told the young ministers that southern whites were not giving proper attention to the plight of blacks: "Whatever Negroes are in America, whether good or bad, is due to the white man."[55]

Beyond these small-scale efforts, the more significant interracial work in Macon, as in other southern cities, came from local committees operating under the guidance of the CIC and the ASWPL. The CIC was organized as Will W. Alexander's answer to the post–World War I violence. Based in Atlanta, the commission organized local interracial committees in various towns and cities throughout the South in an effort to bring together the "better element" of both races. In perhaps its most important work, the CIC's interest in social issues and social science evolved into the publication of numerous articles, pamphlets, and books in opposition to lynching. Chief among these was Arthur F. Raper's *The Tragedy of Lynching*, which significantly contributed to reducing such mob violence after its publication in 1933.[56]

The racial ideology and methods of the CIC, however, were a conservative half-step away from the dominant racial views of most white southerners of the 1920s and '30s. Cautiously progressive, the CIC never challenged segregation itself, taking great pains to avoid appearing to advocate social equality or "race mixing." Generally accepting of "separate but equal," the CIC emphasized its work to ensure the equality of the South's racial arrangements but did not address their separateness. Its chosen pace for racial change was slow and gradual, and that gradualism often antagonized blacks who participated in CIC activities. Many, such as Morehouse College president Benjamin E. Mays, complained that its white leaders did not encourage frank discussion from black members. At one such meeting, black sociologist E. Franklin Frazier once interrupted a sedate discussion, asking pointedly, "If I am arrested . . . what can Dr. Alexander and the rest of you do to see that I get justice and that I am not subjected to the usual brutality of which Negroes are so often the victims?" His question was never answered and, he later reported, "it was found convenient to adjourn."[57] By 1944 the CIC disbanded to make way for its successor organization, the Southern Regional Council.

Founded by Jessie Daniel Ames in 1930, the ASWPL grew out of the Women's Division of the CIC. Ames had been an activist for woman's suffrage until the adoption of the Nineteenth Amendment in 1920, after which she became involved in the Texas affiliate of the CIC. In 1929 she moved to Atlanta to become director of the Women's Division but became somewhat rankled by the male-dominated CIC leadership. Advocating a higher profile role for women in the CIC, She organized the ASWPL as a kind of sister organization to focus attention on the antilynching crusade. Numbering some 40,000 members throughout the South, made up mostly of the wives of upper middle-class professionals, the ASWPL pressured local police and politicos to see that no lynchings took place in their communities. In those counties where the ASWPL was most active, lynchings declined from 20 to 5 a year. Many came to believe that the organization's success had rendered federal antilynching legislation unnecessary, leading to the ASWPL's demise in 1940.[58]

By 1936, some 40 Macon women, all white, had signed the ASWPL "Declaration and Personal Pledge" to work in the community to create a "new public opinion, which will not condone for any reason whatever acts of mobs or lynchers." Mrs. Marshall J. Ellis led the Macon contingent of ASWPL women and represented Macon on the Executive Committee of the Georgia Council of the ASWPL. In this capacity she met quarterly with Ames and other committee members to carry out locally the overall program of the ASWPL. Between May 1936 and early 1937, Ellis began making periodic trips to various southern venues conducting institutes on the "American Negro." As part of this campaign, the Macon ASWPL, along with other branches, led their communities in the study of a book titled "A Preface to Racial Understanding." In April 1937, she conferred with Ames and other Georgia leaders on how to build on momentum generated by such study sessions.[59] Apparently serving as the secretary for the Macon branch, Mrs. C. C. (Louise) Harrold corresponded regularly to enlist Jessie Daniel Ames to address various women's church groups in Macon. A member of St. James Episcopal Church, Harrold invited Ames to speak to her Women's Auxiliary on 6 May 1936. Before speaking to some 30 women at St. James, she also gave an address at Wesleyan College.[60]

Over the next several years Ames continued to make contacts in Macon, working either under ASWPL or CIC auspices. One of those contacts was W. Lowry Anderson, a young Methodist minister in Roberta, a town some 30 miles west of Macon. Interested in race matters, Anderson became a part-time field agent for Macon's Committee on Interracial Cooperation, an affiliate of the CIC. In 1941 he sent Ames a copy of an editorial from the *Macon News* criticizing the ASWPL for supporting the Costigan-Wagner antilynching bill in Congress. The column defended the paper's record against lynching as "unequaled by any Southern newspaper" but rejected the bill, believing "that the South was amply able to look after its own affairs." Then in a swipe at the ASWPL and perhaps at Ames's marital status, the commentary concluded, "We cannot, therefore, countenance such calculated propaganda as that released by the Association. . . . More men were beaten to death at a recent Detroit auto strike than have been lynched in the South in the last twenty years. . . . for the South's sake, Miss or Mrs. Ames, let's not make this another Scottsboro case." Along with the clipping, Anderson sent Ames his own commentary: "The editorial, to me, is obviously unfair and based from beginning to end on false assumptions and false interpretations. Knowing something of the prejudicial opinions and petty selfishness of Jack Tarver, it is my guess that he wrote it. And it is like his procedure to try to imply that your letter is an unpatriotic act." Ames in reply suggested that Anderson drop into the *Macon News* offices to "relieve the confusion of the writer . . . as to my legal title. It seems that he was more disturbed over knowing whether to call me 'Miss' or 'Mrs.' than was necessary."[61]

The most significant interracial work in Macon began in November 1937 when the Reverend George E. Clary, pastor of the Mulberry Street Methodist Church, called together a group of white and black citizens to help build "positive good will in a bi-racial society." This group soon affiliated with the CIC and became known as the Macon District of the Georgia Committee on Interracial Cooperation, more commonly called the Macon Interracial Committee. Before long George Clary began to spearhead CIC activities in Macon, planning the group's first district meeting for 3 November 1938. The state chair of the Georgia committee invited a number of prominent citizens to join the group. Blacks who eventually became involved were Dr. C. W. Dyer, Dr. R. S. Smith, Minnie Singleton, Frank Hutchings, and Willis B. Sheftall, and white members were Dice R. Anderson and J. W. Daniel, both of Wesleyan College, attorney Harry S. Strozier, the Reverend Michael M. Warren, pastor of Christ (Episcopal) Church, Mrs. C. C. Harrold, J. Rufus Moseley, and H. N. Massey of Georgia State College for Women.[62]

At a conference focused on "Education in the Macon Area," Aaron Brown, a professor at nearby Fort Valley State College, gave an address titled "Loopholes in the Education Law." Addressing educational inequities in Georgia according to race, Brown criticized the willingness of the state to tolerate one-teacher schools for black students, citing statistics indicating that such schools made up 71 percent of all black elementary schools, compared with 2 percent of white elementary schools. Brown cited many other inequities. Georgia had state approval for 473 white high schools, compared to 54 black schools. More than 90 percent of white teachers had state certificates, compared to less than 55 percent of black teachers. The average distance from a school was 18 miles for black students, 6 miles for whites, with transportation provided for the white students but not for the blacks. Some 144,000 white students were transported to their schools, compared with fewer than 2,000 black students. Out of 2,630 buses only 35 served black students, with comparative expenditures for transportation $188,934 for white children, $16,000 for blacks.[63] The committee held three conferences in 1939, at the Mulberry Street Church or at the parish house of Christ (Episcopal) Church, continuing variations on the education theme. Registration for all three meetings totaled 38 whites from 8 counties and 66 blacks from 10 counties.[64]

Between its conference and regular meetings, the Macon Interracial Committee helped develop "racial understanding" through acquaintances and frank discussion. In 1939 it hired W. Lowry Anderson as a field agent. The disparity between the number of whites and blacks attending the committee's educational conferences suggested a larger Macon community that discouraged interracial work and intimidated many whites who might have attempted it. Lowry Anderson's observations confirm this. "The friendly interest on the part of white people," he noted, "is almost always held in check if not indeed dissipated by fear of group or political disapproval. This is true of your County Commissioners, school teachers, preachers, school superintendents, mayors, businessmen." He criticized as paternalistic the practice of many white organizations that helped pay educational expenses of selected African-American students, who typically felt paralyzed to attempt to change oppressive conditions of their people. Anderson also condemned the air of superiority he had detected in some black members of the Macon committee for less prosperous members of their race. Anderson believed blacks with such attitudes "not only make them aliens from their own people but also make impossible their ever commanding the respect of white friends who would and could do most for their race. The white people who want Negroes who ask them for cooperation to assume an attitude of superiority toward the race of which they are members are not the white people who really went to work for equal opportunity."[65]

In 1940 Anderson reported to the Macon Interracial Committee an incident in Roberta. When police beat a young black man, Anderson challenged the offending officer, suggesting that the violence had been unnecessary. When both police officials and the mayor defended the officer, the young minister addressed the issue of police brutality against blacks and unfair administration of justice in the courts in a sermon. He denounced the police officer's assumption that the right to arrest a black man gave him the right to beat him. He told the congregation that "the race prejudice which makes it hard for a colored person to get justice in courts would no longer be tolerated." The sermon received from many in the congregation "a cold and noncommittal quietness," and by the end of the year Anderson's bishop had moved him to a new congregation, the Cross Keys Methodist Church in Macon.[66]

By far the most important success of the Macon Interracial Committee in the 1930s was its role in establishing the Booker T. Washington Community Center. The committee combined its work with that of the local Community Chest and the federal Works Progress Administration. In September 1938 the WPA's Recreation Division developed a program to establish black community centers under the sponsorship of local committees in 12 cities. These centers purposed to coordinate welfare programs for blacks, to aid local agencies, and to test new WPA programs. After a WPA survey determined the needs of the cities, Macon was selected as one of the venues. Bureaucratic tangles slowed the plan's development until spring 1939 when the Macon Interracial Committee discovered other local surveys. These reports coincided with certain statements of needs in the city by the Department of Health, the Board of Education, the Juvenile Court, the City Recreation Department, and industrial leaders. Chief among these was a report indicating that almost 73 percent of the city's juvenile delinquency came from black children. In addition, young males were responsible for almost 60 percent of black delinquency. The Interracial Committee quickly saw the WPA community center plan as the short-term answer to this cluster of problems and decided to marshal its efforts to make the center a reality.

The committee communicated with WPA officials, along with leaders of the Macon Community Chest, appealing for funding. Eventually, the WPA committed to paying the salary of a director, while the Community Chest put the center in its annual budget. Before the year ended a 24-room house on Broadway was rented, furnished, and prepared for a three-pronged program of health, education, and recreation. The center's health agenda focused on fighting venereal disease and providing general health information to combat fear and superstition regarding local hospital facilities. Its education program emphasized literacy and vocational training, while its recreational program was designed to counter tendencies toward delinquency by directing youth toward worthwhile activities.

Willis B. Sheftall, a Macon black with social work training and five years' experience, was chosen as the center's first director. In its first three months of operation the Booker T. Washington Community Center, as it was eventually named, conducted a camp for 30 underprivileged boys, examined 871 patients through its health clinic, and formed 3 recreational clubs involving another 36 boys. The Macon Interracial Committee provided leadership, making up the center's first board of directors. White members included George Clary, George Burt, executive editor of the *Macon Telegraph*, Methodist laywoman Callie D. Cutter, Louise Harrold, the Rev. C. Logan Landrum, pastor of the Tattnall Square Presbyterian Church, and Jimmie Wright, a member of the Junior Chamber of Commerce. Blacks on the board were Matthew L. Flemming, a local tailor, Frank J. Hutchings, Ruth Hartley Moseley, a nurse with the Bibb County Board of Heath, Relliford S. Smith, M.D., the Rev. Douglas L. T. Robinson, pastor of Stewart Chapel AME Church, and Alma Edwina Williams, president of the Progressive Federated Club. Three board officers, Clary, Landrum, and Harrold, were white, while Hutchings was the only African American among the officers.[67]

The Macon Interracial Committee experience acquitted many of the board members well. Carrying methods and attitudes of the committee over to the Washington Center board, the members continued to foster a non-paternalistic ethos of equality and avoided the perception of white charity for blacks. In its public relations efforts with Macon's white community, the board emphasized that aiding the black segment would produce healthy effects for the whole city. A fund-raising letter warned that, if ignored, the problems of the black population could endanger "the social solemnity of the whole community."[68]

Such strategies suggested the difficulties of interracial work in this period, as Washington Center leaders feared that most white citizens would object to a program aimed almost exclusively at black needs. WPA guidelines required local funding for the community centers, making it necessary for board members to tap white support cautiously. Concerns about attracting white donors to the project, for example, led the board to scrap its original name, the Interracial Commission Center, in favor of the safer name of Booker T. Washington.[69]

These concerns accompanied the decision to seek funding from the Macon Community Chest, which to that date had never contributed to any black organizations. The board thus submitted a proposal filled with statistics regarding the plight of African Americans. For example, a black in Macon was four times more likely than a white to die of tuberculosis or of murder. Ninety-four percent of Macon's syphilis cases occurred among blacks. Black school attendance was 53 percent of its total enrollment. Blacks were responsible for 66 percent of the city's crime. Nonetheless, the board placed partial blame on white-controlled "environmental conditions" which could be aided by the work of the center. This cautious appeal carried the day with the Community Chest board, which, fortunately for the center, included Louise Harrold as one of its members.[70]

Historian Robert Burnham has argued that the Washington Center built a strong financial foundation and eventually succeeded in becoming part of the city's establishment. As this process began in the center's first year, the 1940s dawned with two major problems on the horizon. At the state level, Governor Talmadge focused his 1940 gubernatorial campaign on race and devoted virtually his entire term to ferreting race-mixers out of the faculties of Georgia colleges and universities. By September 1941, the Macon Interracial Committee scheduled white minister Robert W. Hicks to address one of its meetings on the subject of "Georgia's Problems of Biracial Education and Race Prejudice." Lowry Anderson anticipated that Hicks would "have something to say about our pig-headed Governor." This and a subsequent meeting, however, were poorly attended. Many of those in attendance believed that Talmadge's "recent anti-Negro political moves" had intimidated some members away from the gathering.[71]

The other problem lay across the Atlantic, as the United States inched closer to involvement in World War II. Even before Pearl Harbor, Lowry Anderson had begun gathering information regarding the issue that had exacerbated race relations during the previous "war to end war"—the treatment of black soldiers at Camp Wheeler. Another war would renew the problem. He discovered poor treatment of blacks by military police and found that five northern black soldiers were punished for disciplinary violations by being retained in southern stations, such as Camp Wheeler or Fort Benning. Anderson sought to bring to the Macon Interracial Committee discussions of the black soldier's status in the new war effort. Even here, however, the intimidating racial milieu scared him away from rhetorical strategies soon to be used by the black press. In a letter to Jessie Daniel Ames, the young minister suggested a more prudent approach: "What we can do is instead of saying anything about the similarity of our treatment of Negroes and Hitler's treatment of the Jew, we have got to discuss the things going on in our community which nullifies democracy and Christianity."[72]

In the face of these present and approaching problems, and to give Macon's churches and interracial efforts a shot in the arm, several members of the Macon Interracial Committee helped schedule an evangelistic crusade by the renowned Methodist missionary and evangelist E. Stanley Jones. Because Jones was well known in part for refusing to speak at racially segregated events, Lowry Anderson viewed this event as "one of the most encouraging facts about the interracial prospects in Macon." An interracial group of four white and four black ministers hatched the plan to invite Jones to Macon, then recommended to the white Macon Ministerial Association and the black Ministers' Evangelical Union that they issue the evangelist a joint invitation. The white group initially balked, insisting that Jones be informed that separate seating must prevail at the services even though attendance would be open to both races. The black group agreed to this, so long as the Ministerial Association agreed that seating be equally divided between blacks and whites. Albert Grady Harris, pastor of First Presbyterian Church and president of the Ministerial Association, led a small contingent of white ministers in objecting to Jones's appearance at any black churches or schools. The Reverend D. L. T. Robinson, pastor of the Steward Chapel AME Church, dismissed the problem as hypothetical, reminding the white ministers that no black church had even extended an invitation.[73]

After all the ministerial compromises had been effected, Jones spoke in Macon on 19–22 October 1941. In the evenings he spoke at the city auditorium, while addressing chapel services at Mercer, Wesleyan, Central City College, and Ballard Normal School in the mornings. He also spoke at ministers' conferences at the white First Baptist and First Presbyterian churches. Black ministers, however, were welcomed to both churches. In his message at Mercer, Jones seemed to anticipate America's involvement in another European war, heralding America as the "mediator of a new world order based on the central idea of democracy." His definition of democracy, however, no doubt raised some eyebrows when he told the students, "We should give equality of opportunity to everyone within our own borders. Democracy means social and economic democracy as well as political democracy."[74]

While encouraged by Jones's visit to Macon, if only because young ministers love to bask in the glow of more famous preachers, Lowry Anderson showed small signs of disillusionment. The problems of race relations during the coming war bothered him, as did white ministerial wrangling over racial policies during the Jones crusade. A few days before Jones arrived in Macon, Ames wrote Anderson a letter indicating her surprise that Jones sacrificed his previously "inflexible principles" to accept the Macon invitation under racially segregated conditions. She wistfully commented that "this work of race relations is quite the same as clearing a dense forest with heavy undergrowth." In reply, the young idealist lamented the fact that too few prominent laypersons had joined the effort. He wrote, "The thing that has limited it [interracial work] so much in Macon—most of them have been preachers who have been interested. . . . It seems to me that the preachers have fallen down lamentably on the job in failing to interest their boards of stewards and deacons. Of course, we have to confess to that failure."[75] The failures of "unutterable separation," especially within Macon's ministerial class, would continue for a good while longer.

Notes

1. Dan T. Carter, "From Segregation to Integration," in *Interpreting Southern History: Historiographical Essays in Honor of Sanford W. Higginbotham,* ed. John B. Boles and Evelyn Thomas Nolen (Baton Rouge: Louisiana State University Press, 1987), 414–15; John Shelton Reed and Dale Volberg Reed, *1001 Things Everyone Should Know About the South* (New York: Doubleday, 1996), 53.

2. Samuel S. Hill Jr., *Southern Churches in Crisis* (New York: Holt, Rinehart, and Winston, 1966); Kenneth K. Bailey, *Southern White Protestantism in the Twentieth Century* (New York: Harper and Row, 1964); John B. Boles, *The Great Revival, 1787–1805: The Origin of the Southern Evangelical Mind* (Lexington: University Press of Kentucky, 1972); Donald G. Mathews, *Religion in the Old South* (Chicago: University of Chicago Press, 1977); John Lee Eighmy, *Churches in Cultural Captivity: A History of the Social Attitudes of Southern Baptists,* rev. ed. (Knoxville: University of Tennessee Press, 1988); E. Brooks Holifield, *The Gentlemen Theologians* (Durham: Duke University Press, 1978); Charles Reagan Wilson, *Baptized in Blood: The Religion of the Lost Cause, 1865–1920* (Athens: University of Georgia Press, 1980); Mitchell Snay, *Gospel of Disunion: Religion and Separatism in the Antebellum South* (Chapel Hill: University of North Carolina Press, 1977); Paul Harvey, *Redeeming the South: Religious Cultures and Racial Identities among Southern Baptists, 1865–1925* (Chapel Hill: University of North Carolina Press, 1997); Ted Ownby, *Subduing Satan: Religion, Recreation, and Manhood in the Rural South, 1865–1920* (Chapel Hill: University of North Carolina Press, 1993); Andrew M. Manis, *Southern Civil Religions in Conflict: Civil Rights and the Culture Wars* (Macon: Mercer University Press, 2002), and *A Fire You Can't Put Out: The Civil Rights Life of Birmingham's Reverend Fred Shuttlesworth* (Tuscaloosa: University of Alabama Press, 1999).

3. Wayne Flynt, "Religion in the Urban South: The Divided Religious Mind of Birmingham, 1900–1930," *Alabama Review* 30 (April 1977):108–34.

4. This article constitutes one of the early chapters in my book, *Unutterable Separation: Blacks and Whites in Twentieth Century Macon, Georgia* (Macon: Mercer University Press, 2004).

5. Stephen N. G. Tuck, *The Civil Rights Movement in Georgia* (Athens: University of Georgia Press, 2001), 18.

6. *Macon Telegraph,* 24 October 1979, 1A, 9A (hereafter *MT*).

7. U.S. Census figures for 1930 and 1940 indicate these ratios for total and partial unemployment in Bibb County: 1930 unemployment, whites 5.28 percent, blacks 8.35 percent; 1940 unemployment: whites 7.29 percent, blacks 12.85 percent. Over the decade white unemployment grew by 2.01 percent, compared to 4.5 percent for blacks. Over the same decade, white-owned or -operated farms in Bibb County fell from 642 to 596, a 7.2 percent decrease. By contrast, black-owned or -operated farms fell from 370 to 233, a 37.1 percent decrease. For U.S. Census figures for 1930 and 1940, see http://fisher.lib.virginia.edu/census.

8. Paul Douglas Bolster, "Civil Rights Movements in Twentieth Century Georgia" (Ph.D. diss., University of Georgia, 1972), 44–45, 47.

9. "Depression and the Race Problem: A Confidential Statement," n.d., Commission on Interracial Cooperation Papers, Woodruff Library, Atlanta University Center, Atlanta, Reel 4, Item 72.

10. Bolster, "Civil Rights Movements," 39; John Hammond Moore, "Communism and Fascists in a Southern City: Atlanta, 1930," *South Atlantic Quarterly* 67 (Summer 1968):445–46; Ann Wells Ellis, "'Uncle Sam Is My Shepherd': The Commission on Interracial Cooperation and the New Deal in Georgia," *Atlanta History* 30 (Spring 1986):48.

11. *MT,* 2 September 1930, 2A.

12. Jesse O. Thomas, "The Negro Looks at the Alphabet," *Opportunity* 12 (January 1934):12.

13. *MT,* 20 September 1931, 1, 11, 21 September 1931, 1.

14. *MT,* 17 November 1933, 7; Donald L. Grant, *The Way It Was in the South: The Black Experience in Georgia* (New York: Carol Publishing Group, 1993), 352.

15. Tuck, *Civil Rights Movement,* 16; Ralph Bunche, *The Political Status of the Negro in the Age of F.D.R.,* ed. Dewey E. Grantham (Chicago: University of Chicago Press, 1973), 404; *MT,* 11 January 1939, 9A.

16. *Mercer Cluster,* 1 December 1939, 3.

17. *MT,* 4 May 1932, 8A.

18. *MT,* 14 July 1938, 4.

19. *MT,* 15 January 1933, 1, 9.

20. Interview with Frank Hutchings Jr., 13 February 2004, in possession of the author, Macon, Ga.

21. *MT,* 19 January 1933, 1, 5, 21 January 1933, 12, 9 May 1938, 7.

22. *MT,* 9 May 1938, 7.

23. *MT,* 15 March 1939, 1.

24. *MT,* 19 March 1939, 4.

25. *MT,* 23 March 1939, 4.

26. James F. Cook, *The Governors of Georgia: 1754–2004* (Macon, Ga.: Mercer University Press, 2004), 228–31.

27. William Anderson, *The Wild Man from Sugar Creek: The Political Career of Eugene Talmadge* (Baton Rouge: Louisiana State University Press, 1975), 111.

28. *MT,* 28 August 1935, 1.

29. Anderson, *Wild Man,* 136–37.

30. Sullivan, *Days of Hope,* 159–60; "Blunt Criticism," reprint of *Georgia Women's World* article in *Columbia Observer,* n.d. [1936], FDR Papers, Office Files 93, box 2; Anderson, *Wild Man,* 136–40.

31. *MT,* 13 September 1940, 19.

32. *MT,* 2 February 1936, 4, 3 February 1936, 4.

33. Tuck, *Civil Rights Movement,* 19; Cook, *Governors of Georgia,* 232.

34. *MT,* 7 June 1942, 1, 2, 9 June 1942, 1.

35. *MT,* 10 September 1942, 3.

36. Annual Report, Macon Chamber of Commerce, 1933, Spright Dowell Files, Mercer University, Macon, Box 7, Folder 357; *MT,* 2 September 1933, 5A; David M. Kennedy, *Freedom from Fear: The American People in Depression and War, 1929–1945* (New York: Oxford University Press, 1999), 183.

37. *MT,* 23 April 1933, 4, 13 September 1933, 2.

38. *MT,* 22 October 1938, 9A, 18 January 1939, 7A, 3 June 1938, 2, 7 June 1938, 9.

39. *MT,* 28 August 1935, 7, 1 October 1933, 11, 23 October 1933, 11, 2 November 1937, 3, 18 November 1933, 9.

40. *MT,* 11 December 1933, 4; *Macon Courier,* 6 December 1978, 1, 7, 12.

41. Sesquicentennial Edition of the *Macon Telegraph,* 28 September 1973, Section IV, 4; Catherine Meeks, *Macon's Black Heritage: The Untold Story* (Macon: The Tubman African American Museum, 1997), 58, 64; T. J. Woofter Jr., *Progress in Race—Relations in Georgia* (Atlanta: Report of the Secretary of the Georgia Committee on Race Relations, 1922), 14; Works Progress Administration, *Georgia: The WPA Guide to Its Towns and Countryside* (Columbia: University of South Carolina Press, 1990; originally published 1940), 85.

42. Macon City Directory, 1927, 14; Grant, *The Way It Was in the South,* 229–30.

43. Letter to editor, H. Taylor, *MT,* 8 September 1923, 4.

44. Both Ingram's letter and Anderson's editorial comments are found in the *MT,* 26 March 1923, 4.

45. *MT,* 20 May 1921, 6.

46. *MT,* 31 January 1933, 5; *MT,* 7 February 1933, cited in Titus Brown, *Faithful, Firm, and True: African American Education in the South* (Macon: Mercer University Press, 2000), 113; *MT,* 28 February 1933, 5, 2 March 1933, 11.

47. *MT,* 20 November 1936, 7.

48. *MT,* 11 May 1937, 9, 1 September 1937, 11.

49. *MT,* 30 August 1938, 7.

50. *MT,* 5 October 1938, 1, 2, 28 October 1938, 1, 10; Meeks, *Macon's Black Heritage,* 48.

51. *MT,* 17 September 1916, 5.

52. *MT,* 15 February 1932, 5.

53. *MT,* 23 March 1941, 5; Wayne McClain, *A Resurrection Encounter: The Rufus Moseley Story* (Minneapolis: Macalester Park Publishing Company, 1997), 112–13, 122, 164, citing R. Moseley, *Manifest Victory* (St. Paul, Minn.: Macalester Park Publishing Co., 1986), 185–87.

54. Quoted in Will Campbell, *The Stem of Jesse: The Costs of Community at a 1960s Southern School* (Macon: Mercer University Press, 1994), 65.

55. *MT,* 16 June 1933, 8; *Mercer Cluster,* 1 March 1935.

56. Morton Sosna, "Commission on Interracial Cooperation," in the *Encyclopedia of Religion in the South* (Macon: Mercer University Press, 1984), 179–80; Ann Ellis, "The Commission on Interracial Cooperation, 1919–1944: Its Activities and Results (Ph.D. diss., Georgia State University, 1975).

57. Benjamin E. Mays, "Realities in Race Relations," *Christian Century* 48 (1931): 404; E. Franklin Frazier, "Memorandum submitted by Dr. Guy B. Johnson," Myrdal-Carnegie Papers, CIC Papers, Reel 4, 13–13C; Bolster, *Civil Rights Movements,* 55–56; Ellis, "Commission," preface.

58. Morton Sosna, "Association of Southern Women for the Prevention of Lynching," in the *Encyclopedia of Religion in the South,* 77–78; Jacquelyn Dowd Hall, "The Legacy of Jessie Daniel Ames," *South Today,* n.d., 7, in Southern Regional Council Papers, Reel 218, Robert W. Woodruff Library, Archives Department, Atlanta University Center, Atlanta; Jacquelyn Dowd Hall, *Revolt Against Chivalry: Jessie Daniel Ames and the Women's Campaign Against Lynching* (New York: Columbia University Press, 1979).

59. Reports, 1936, CIC Papers; Letters, Jessie Daniel Ames to Mrs. E. B. Harrold, 15 May 1936, Mrs. Marshall J. Ellis to Mrs. Robert H. McDougald, 30 September 1936, Ames to Ellis, 1 April 1937, all in Association of Southern Women for the Prevention of Lynching (ASWPL) Papers, Reel 5, Archives Department, Woodruff Library, Atlanta University Center.

60. Letters, Mrs. Louise C. Harrold to Jessie Daniel Ames, 6, 18 April 1936, Ames to Harrold, 21 April, 15 May 1936, all in ASWPL Papers, Reel 5.

61. Editorial from *Macon News,* 2 June 1941; W. Lowry Anderson to Jessie Daniel Ames, 4 June 1941, Jessie Daniel Ames to W. Lowry Anderson, 30 June 1941, both in CIC Papers, Reel 50, Item 123, Archives Department, Woodruff Library.

62. W. Lowry Anderson to Dr. R. L. Russell, 1 October 1938, CIC Papers, Reel 51, Section 144; W. Lowry Anderson, 21 August 1942 Report, CIC Papers, Reel 50, Item 123.

63. Aaron Brown, "Loopholes in the Educational Law," Macon Conference, Georgia Committee of the CIC, 3 November 1938, CIC Papers, Reel 51, Section 144.

64. Report, Georgia Committee on Interracial Cooperation, October 1938–July 1939, and Interracial Conference, Macon, Georgia, 3 November 1938, both in CIC Papers, Reel 45, Item 46.

65. Anderson to Clary, Report on Work Done for Interracial Cooperation [July–September 1939], September 29, 1939, CIC Papers, Reel 51, Section 144.

66. Report on work done by W. Lowry Anderson, June 1940, and George E. Clary to Ames, 11 November 1940, both in CIC Papers, Reel 51, Section 144.

67. Biennial Report, Department of Education, 1940, CIC Papers, Reel 29, Item 13; History of the Booker T. Washington Community Center, [1939]; Anderson to Clary, Report on Work Done for Interracial Cooperation, CIC Papers; Robert A. Burnham, "Interracial Cooperation in the Age of Jim Crow: The Booker T. Washington Community Center of Macon, Georgia," *Atlanta History* 42 (1999):19, 22.

68. Burnham, "Interracial Cooperation," 22–23; Macon Negro Demonstration Project, 4; BTWCC, Board of Directors, Minutes, 29 May 1939, and form letter to Mr. John Doe, 1 September 1939, both in BTWCC Office Files.

69. Burnham, "Interracial Cooperation," 20–23; Macon Negro Demonstration Project, 4; BTWCC, Board of Directors, Minutes, ibid.

70. Burnham, 25; "Information Submitted to Community Chest," CIC Papers, Reel 51.

71. W. Lowry Anderson, 5 September 1941 Report, 10 October 1941 Report, both in CIC Papers, Reel 50, Item 123.

72. W. Lowry Anderson, 5 September 1941 Report, and Report to Ames and Tilly, 14 December 1941, CIC Papers, ibid.

73. W. Lowry Anderson, 10 October 1941 Report, CIC Papers, ibid.

74. *MT,* 21 October 1941, 2.

75. Jessie Daniel Ames to Lowry Anderson, 14 October 1941, Anderson, Report to Ames and Dorothy Tilly, 14 December 1941, both in CIC Papers, Reel 50, Item 123.

6

Race, Class, the Southern Conference, and the Beginning of the End of the New Deal Coalition

Glenn Feldman

Although no one could know it at the time, the New Deal held within it the seeds of its own destruction. While the program would eventually develop into a political partnership of unparalleled strength and effectiveness, it would also harbor tensions and contradictions that made it, from the beginning, temporary and ephemeral—doomed to do anything but last. Nowhere would this be truer or more apparent than in the Deep South, in places like Alabama.

The New Deal in its complete sense was not one singular program or even a set of closely related goals. It was, far more accurately, a patchwork of policies, initiatives, people, and agencies—schemes to do something, *anything*, to alleviate the unprecedented crisis that confronted the country. Its goals and personalities—sometimes pacific, sometimes contradictory and competing, often confusing because of the sheer immensity and newness of the task that lay before them—reached out to and subsumed under their broad canopy a bewildering array of different Americans. By March 1933, the New Deal offered sanctuary for the weary and beleaguered from all walks of life, people of conservative nature and those with a more liberal bent, people beset by the revolutionary economic tempests of the age who had found little or no relief elsewhere. By the time Franklin Roosevelt took the oath of office as the country's thirty-second president, most of them had nowhere else to go. So the New Deal became one and the same entity that responded to the plight of the rural inhabitant and the urban dweller; to actors, artists, authors, and playwrights; bricklayers, iron molders, steel rollers, and textile workers; unskilled teens who had never spent a night away from home; country people accustomed to generations of poverty, debt, and the deprivation of electricity and even indoor plumbing; widows caring for fatherless children; the starving, educated and uneducated; the farmer and the city worker; those who worked with their hands and those who worked with their minds; the small town, the big city, and the sparsely dotted countryside.

The unprecedented exigency that became known as the Great Depression eventually made all of these, and more, partners in the great experiment called the New Deal. For a while it also made them partners in the political expression and engine that drove the experiment: the Democratic Party of Franklin Roosevelt. Yet the New Deal could not reconcile—nor did it even attempt to, in most instances—the wildly divergent worldviews, philosophies, and beliefs that the kaleidoscope who called themselves "New Dealers" or New Deal supporters brought with them to the project. The participants themselves looked on one another with curiosity at best, in some cases with suspicion and outright dislike. The New Deal contained the seeds of its own destruction because it brought together so many people with so little in common for a goal that many of its constituents understood as inherently temporary. It brought together people who viewed the culture, religion, folkways, and even the languages of other constituent members as different, foreign, even dangerous. It could not last. In fact, it is a testament to the political will and ability of its designers that the coalition managed to hold itself mostly together for the better part of four decades.

Yet it is not enough simply to observe that the New Deal coalition was made up of disparate groups and thus bound to come apart at some point. The tensions, contradictions, disagreements, and factions within the New Deal presaged, to a large degree, that which would follow once the bonds of the coalition dissolved. America's Republican ascendancy of the late twentieth and early twenty-first centuries did not materialize out of thin air and the cosmos. To a large extent the contradictions within the New Deal foreshadowed what would replace the coalition as the country's dominant political paradigm once the emergency and its residual loyalties passed. And nowhere in America were these struggles more apparent than in the South, where cultural inequivalencies, first and foremost about race, tore at the coalition's bonds of fraternity and eventually ate them away.

Actually the break was apparent even before there was a New Deal. It was there at least as early as 1924 at the national Democratic convention in New York City, where fistfights erupted, releasing simmering hostilities and tensions among the 1,100 party faithful that had finally been given full vent by consideration of a plank denouncing the Ku Klux Klan. Although the plank failed to become part of the official platform by a single vote, and although

Alabama broke regional ranks to vote for it, the issue laid bare the deep and insoluble differences between the two major wings that had merged to form the Democratic Party.[1] One was urban, industrial, unionist, largely ethnic, wet, Catholic and Jewish, identified with the political machines of the great cities of the Northeast and Midwest; many of the allegiants could trace their roots to Southern and Eastern Europe, some to liberalism, others even to radicalism. The other was southern, Protestant, dry, rural, conservative, sometimes even fundamentalist, indifferent or downright unfriendly to big-city machines and unions, and staunchly, even overwhelmingly, Anglo-Saxon in its ethnic and cultural derivation. These were people, Democrats all, animated by the most profoundly divergent ideologies and worldviews, people who found the other side's culture alien, bewildering, sometimes downright repugnant. Yet the New Deal, which glued this Democratic coalition together more firmly than ever—and added thousands, even millions, of other Americans who came to the project out of sense of desperation more than anything else—meant, at its very core, *inclusiveness:* including all who needed help in the cataclysmic days of the Great Depression. Most important, for the South, this inclusiveness extended to the races, meaning in essence that either the South or the Democratic Party would eventually have to change if the affair were to have any chance of flowering into a lifelong partnership.

Oh, the New Deal was not perfect, in this or any other way. It was beset by fits and starts and false starts and backtracking, by contradictions and half-measures, by ego, and shortsightedness, hypocrisy, and even, occasionally, greed. The Agricultural Adjustment Act (AAA) hit black tenants and croppers first and hardest. The National Recovery Act (NRA) was so bound to local customs that it became known among blacks as the "Negro Removal Act" and the "Negro Run Around." Yet, taken as a whole, the New Deal far outstripped in usefulness the alternative of the head-in-the-sand, let-them-eat-cake paralysis associated with Herbert Hoover and the two preceding Republican administrations of the 1920s that had contributed so much in the first place to the construction of depression-era economics. And while the new measures for blacks were even more imperfect than those for whites, the New Deal did something no program in American history had done since Reconstruction: it included them. At an imperfect and substandard level, to be sure, but it included them. And they knew it. It was there in hundreds of gestures large and small. It was there every time Eleanor Roosevelt spoke at a black convocation or had African Americans to the White House for tea or arranged access to her husband for a beleaguered black activist or politician. It was there when Aubrey Williams made sure his

New Deal agencies had an office to address Negro affairs. It was there whenever Harold Ickes would actually say it, out loud, that under FDR blacks had "a special New Deal of their own." Or when Roosevelt himself, so often taken to task for being cautious, hesitant, even indifferent to black concerns, would communicate to African Americans that his administration was one in which they were a part, in an America in which "there should be no forgotten men and no forgotten races." In private the president could even be more forthright, confiding to Walter White of the National Association for the Advancement of Colored People (NAACP) that he had to tread carefully where senior southern congressmen were concerned—"I did not choose the tools with which I must work"—but assuring Mary McLeod Bethune that "People like you and me are fighting ... for the day when a man will be regarded as a man regardless of his race. That day will come, but we must pass through perilous times before we realize it." And because of Roosevelt's longevity and unmatched election (before or since) to four terms, black identification transcended mere identification with the man to become mass identification with the *party* itself. "My friends, go home and turn Lincoln's picture to the wall," the editor of the *Pittsburgh Courier* offered as prescient advice to other black Americans in 1938. "That debt has been paid in full."[2]

∼

During Roosevelt's first term, the vast majority of criticism against the New Deal was contained as merely extreme and even fringe discontent. Yet after his second election in 1936, the dissent burst forth in a series of high-profile conflicts that pitted Franklin Roosevelt in direct contravention to the most serious of his southern detractors. The result was to lend significant impetus to the right-wing movement against New Deal liberalism on both race and the economy. And while it appeared only mildly distracting during the thirties, the seedling of discontent implanted itself deep within the southern and western evangelical wing of the party—a seed that one spring would bloom fully as a Republican flower. By 1940, when FDR would stand for reelection to an unprecedented third term as president, the forces of southern conservatism would be massed in considerably more impressive array against him—and the pull away from the Democratic Party toward something else would be even that much stronger.

In a significant way, Roosevelt, as other Democratic presidents would do in succeeding generations, helped load and cock the gun that his antagonists pointed at his head. In February 1937, shortly after his second inaugural, FDR announced what soon became known and widely derided as his "court-packing scheme" to name fifty new federal judges to the bench, including possibly six additional Supreme Court justices. The move sprang, of course, from the president's growing unhappiness with a Supreme Court that had struck down his National Industrial Recovery Act and the Agricultural Adjustment Act, among other pet pieces of legislation.[3] Southerners, in particular, rallied against the plan on the basis of states' rights, constitutionalism, and white supremacy. Hatton W. Sumners, a New Deal congressman from Texas, betrayed the temporal nature of the southern New Deal when he informed his fellow Democrats simply, "Boys, here's where I cash in."[4] Carter Glass of Virginia held up Harold Ickes as the type of "visionary incendiary" who might play a large role in selecting new "judicial sycophants" and reminded his southern colleagues that the New Dealer had recently criticized Dixie for practicing a segregation policy that provided separate schools for the races. According to the Virginia senator, Ickes had practically committed the Roosevelt administration to "a new Force Bill" that threatened the intrinsic "civilization of the South" with another "tragic era of reconstruction." Speaker of the House William B. Bankhead of Alabama publicly supported the plan but without his usual enthusiasm; in private, he expressed serious doubts. North Carolina's Josiah W. Bailey spearheaded a move among southern Democrats and a couple of Republicans that became known as the "Southern Manifesto." The document went far toward providing a blueprint for a southern brand of conservatism that would meld white supremacy with laissez-faire to the service of a stratified status quo. It formally rebuked the New Deal as contradictory to the bedrock principles of states' rights and the "American system of private enterprise and initiative."[5]

Strike two occurred on the issue of the economy. President Roosevelt commissioned a National Emergency Council packed with southern representatives of industry and labor (including Clark Foreman and Frank P. Graham) to craft a study released in August 1938 as the "Report on Economic Conditions in the South." While the study had been designed as an administration indictment against continued southern economic colonialism, it was received by a hyperdefensive region in an altogether different way: as a slap in the face. Roosevelt himself described the South as "the Nation's No. 1 economic problem," intending empathy but actually evoking deep resentment at what many southerners interpreted as yet another example of "damnyankee meddlesomeness."[6]

Of course the economic report hit a number of nerves, most of them accurately, which was part of the reason it was received with such hostility by the intended southern beneficiaries. It pointed out that much of the region's profits were siphoned off by outside financiers, that in general the region's tax burden fell most heavily on those least able to pay, and that efforts toward more progressive taxation were fought most ferociously by outside investors, in-state industries accustomed to paying low wages, and large landholding corporations, utilities, and mega-farm and -timber interests.[7] Nowhere was this regional state of affairs more pronounced than in the Heart of Dixie. Alabama's infamous 1901 Constitution had ensured that its tax structure would be the most malformed of any state in the Union for at least the following century.[8] Nor did it help matters much when the director of the U.S. Public Health Service dubbed the South "the No. 1 health problem of the nation," or when the report pointed out that homes in the rural South were the "oldest, have the lowest value, and have the greatest need of repairs" of any farmhouses in the country; half of them were unpainted, a third had no screens to keep out flies and mosquitoes, and six in seven had no inside water. Alabama took the dubious distinction of having the highest percentage (97) of its farmhouses lacking running water, with Mississippi, Georgia, and Tennessee trailing closely behind. The South also had markedly lower industrial wages and farm income than other regions. Per capita income in the Southeast was only $309 compared with a $573 national average; southern farmers grossed only $186 per year compared with $528 a year by farmers in other regions. Yet the profits of the South's textile mills exceeded those of the North.[9]

Perhaps one basis of the growing southern enmity sprang from the tendency of New Dealers to describe regional conditions as "medieval." No matter how accurate the comparison, nobody, especially southerners, wanted to hear what the "report" had to say on that score, that "many thousands of them are living in poverty comparable to that of the poorest peasants in Europe." Nor did they want to hear Clark Foreman praise the efforts of FDR to help the people of the South escape "feudal economic conditions" or Florida senator Claude Pepper envisage a South where "the feudal system" would remain a romantic legend but in which democracy would be the practical functioning institution. Nothing was so bad as when the president himself added his voice to this chorus of stating the obvious but uncomfortable truth. In March 1938 at Gainesville, Georgia, FDR lectured the South in uncharacteristically strong terms, telling its people that they "may just as well face the facts" that the consumption power of "millions . . . in this whole area is too low" owing to the region's notoriously low wages. Furthermore, true improvement would not come to the region if its people believed in their "hearts that the feudal system is still the best system." To this end the southern people, and Roosevelt himself, needed representatives "cast in the 1938 mold not in the 1898 mold."[10]

General discontent continued to mount over a number of economic griev-ances. The powerful Southern Farm Bureaus were angry at the New Deal tenant law. Crop controls aggravated the cotton trade. NRA codes enraged commerce even though businessmen had taken a large hand in their crafting. And federal relief threatened the regional wage differential. Economic dis-satisfaction and the "report" became factors in Franklin Roosevelt's third ma-jor controversy at this time, the "purge" elections of 1938. In a calculated gam-bit the president insinuated himself against several handpicked conservative southern Democratic opponents of his New Deal in their home state reelec-tion campaigns. The result was a disaster. If FDR thought the South had circled wagons and evoked the Reconstruction memory to thwart his judicial restructuring plan in 1937, he had not seen anything yet. In Alabama, New Deal ally John Temple Graves II broke publicly with Roosevelt and joined the reactionary industrial organ *Alabama Magazine.* Senator Walter George won big in his reelection bid, snickering at the president's involvement against him as "a second march through Georgia." In South Carolina, "Cot-ton Ed" Smith and Olin D. Johnston's primary race deteriorated into a contest in race-baiting that the incumbent won. After his victory Smith thumbed his nose in fine sectional style at FDR's attempt to see him de-feated: "No man dares to come to South Carolina and try to dictate to the sons of those men who held the hands of Lee and Hampton."[11]

In the November 1938 midterm elections, Roosevelt and the New Deal got a comeuppance as the president's Democratic margin fell precipitously in the House by 61 percent (from 223 to 136 seats) and 25 percent in the Senate (from 56 to 42 seats). Surveying the disaster later, historian George Brown Tindall accurately pointed out that the southern congressional leadership that FDR leaned on so heavily had become by 1938 "undependable and some of it hostile." Furthermore, the senators who did stick with him—Maury Maverick of Texas, Claude Pepper of Florida, and Lister Hill of Alabama— were the southern "exceptions that proved the rule."[12]

November 1938 also marked a critical turning point in Deep South esti-mations of what the New Deal was all about when the Southern Conference for Human Welfare selected Birmingham, Alabama—the heart of the Bour-bon monster—in which to hold its inaugural meeting. The brainchild of Jewish communist Joseph Gelders, and assisted by Lucy Randolph Mason's entreaties to Eleanor and Franklin Roosevelt, the SCHW constituted an impressive gathering of liberal-minded southerners by any estimation. Yet its first meeting in such an inhospitable clime probably did more to stimulate conservative backlash against New Deal liberalism in the Deep South than it did to actually further the group's progressive agenda of black voting rights and economic reform. Still, the roster of 1,200 delegates who attended on that Thanksgiving weekend read like a "Who's Who" of progressive thought in the South. Herman Clarence Nixon served as field secretary, the University of North Carolina Press director W. T. Couch was program chairman, UNC president Frank Porter Graham became the group's first chairman, Congress of Industrial Organization organizers William Mitch and Yelverton Cowherd and native Alabama communist Rob Hall made the local arrangements, and Supreme Court justice Hugo Black addressed the gathering. Blacks as well as whites attended: Mary McLeod Bethune, Eleanor Roosevelt, regional editors Ralph McGill, Mark Ethridge, Virginius Dabney, George Fort Milton, and Clarence Poe, Florida senator Claude Pepper, Arkansas Democrat Brooks Hays, historian C. Vann Woodward, and Swedish sociologist Gunnar Myrdal. In addition to Gelders, Hall, Nixon, and Black, Alabamians Aubrey Williams and Clifford and Virginia Durr and elected officials such as U.S. senators John Bankhead and Lister Hill, Congressman Luther Patrick, and Governor Bibb Graves attended. Yet at least two omens of things to come appeared during the convention proceedings. First, local conservative New Dealers such as Horace Wilkinson were conspicuously absent. The patronage master was in Montgomery arguing at the state supreme court against liquor sales at state stores, yet it is as likely that he was deeply offended by the interracial nature of the gathering. And, in perhaps the most dramatic moment of the proceedings, Birmingham police commissioner Theophilus Eugene "Bull" Connor appeared with a phalanx of officers to enforce the city's segregated seating ordinance. Eleanor Roosevelt defied Connor by moving her chair into the center aisle in silent protest, registering an indignity even the commissioner endured in order to avoid arresting the First Lady. Yet if Eleanor Roosevelt's message was clear, so was Connor's, despite the mangled syntax of his infamous declaration that "Negroes and whites would not segregate together" in Alabama.[13]

There is not much doubt that the involvement of communists in the SCHW was double-edged. Communists brought energy, commitment, and vitality to the cause of racial and economic reform. Yet their very existence also harmed the organization's chances for survival, much less effectiveness, in the South. The involvement of even one communist in the group painted a big red X on the backs of all the liberals involved and made mass denun-

ciation easier for the opponents of liberalism because of the CP's popular
identification with two things that made it absolutely unacceptable in the
South: godlessness and advocacy of the radical overthrow of the American
form of government. Even if the overwhelming majority of liberals involved
in the SCHW were not actual subversives or irreligious—quite the contrary:
guilt by association in the South could easily resolve the difference and
stretch to include anyone who consorted with such folk. The resulting perception was the same regardless of the reality. The Southern Conference was
a seedbed of godless radicals bent on the defilement of patriotism and overthrow of the republic. The indictment, however unfair or inaccurate, con-
signed the group and many of its participants to the fringes of the culture in
which they lived.

Joseph Gelders had dreamed up the idea, and he was a homegrown Alabama communist. By 1947 the House Committee on Un-American Activities would brand the SCHW a communist front organization in a report one
historian called "a masterpiece of logical fallacies, quotations out of context,
and guilt-by-association techniques." Other liberal Alabama members such
as Aubrey Willliams and the Durrs would be hounded unmercifully by the
HUAC and see their liberalism inaccurately but effectively marginalized as
radicalism and communism. Within ten years the group would be defunct,
its death knell sounded by the withdrawal of CIO money to pay for its "Operation Dixie" offensive.[14]

Yet the antiradical rejection of the SCHW was only part of a broad cultural reaction that found the group and its goals obnoxious in virtually every
way that buttressed the prevailing southern status quo: racially, morally, ethnically, religiously, civically, and in relation to prescribed gender roles and
class relations. The SCHW's advocacy of voting rights for blacks was enough
to send it beyond the pale for most white southerners, but combined with
the involvement of a communist or two among the 1,200 attendees, the product was cultural dynamite. In Alabama, plain folk did not need to know
much about the actual issues discussed at the municipal auditorium to know
that they were fervently against the SCHW. All they had to do was have a
cultural reflex that functioned in order to respond to the massive stimuli
rained down on them by the planter-industrialist machine. Hubert Baughn's
journal of hidebound conservatism dutifully led the way. The *Alabama Magazine* deplored the gathering (with a good deal of truth) as a foreign enterprise
that was not representative of the Deep South. "[W]hointhehell invited" the
SCHW to Alabama, Baughn asked. It certainly was "neither spontaneous
nor Southern."[15] Yet after accurately establishing the unrepresentativeness of

the group, Baughn went the whole neo-Kluxist distance to race-bait and Red-bait the group and its goals, quickly falling back on the tried and true reasoning of Social Darwinism.

Race as usual came first, and the ritual summoning of the Social Darwinist intellectual creed necessarily brought religious, sexual, and economic orthodoxies into the picture. It was 1901 all over again, and nothing fundamental was kept separate. The basic purpose of the "long-haired men and short-haired women" who made up the SCHW was "'off with the poll tax and votes for the darkies,'" which could only lead to the abomination of "free love" between blacks and whites.[16] The goal was to equalize the "economic, social and political condition" of blacks and whites, "a task in which nature and God Almighty [had] failed for a million years." Yet nothing positive could be gained by tampering with the natural hierarchy. Segregation is the "immutable condition to interracial tolerance and sympathy in the South." It is "changeless" and "instinctive" for both races, a relationship that has long been "settled and . . . shall stand" regardless of the machinations of Godless agitators and their "crackpot schemes to reform the South out of white government." The heretics mistakenly believed that economic reform could undo racial certainties. Taking their cue from the insulting National Emergency Council's New Deal economic report, the New Dealers actually believed that legislating high wages and short hours could "work mysterious magic in the South" and "change the I.Q. of the darkey." It was the same kind of arrogant misjudgment that thought a federal antilynching law could stop just retribution against "the intolerable crime of rape" and that if the "average darkey is given a vote he will [actually] take an interest in . . . improv[ing] the government along with himself."[17]

The gradual absorption of racial parity into the New Deal program struck at the very core of southern culture. This was so because white supremacy was not something that floated above and apart from the rest of the South. On the contrary, it was *the central underpinning* of a whole southern culture that was predicated at its most fundamental level on a strict and hierarchical order of things: a society in which blacks were subordinate to whites in much the same way that women were supposed to be submissive to men, workers to employers, children to their elders, immigrants to natives, and congregations to their ministers. This was civilization itself as most southerners understood it, blessed by nature and ordained by God. It was the "Southern way of life," something to preserve and protect.[18] And, as with other societies founded upon the intellectual mound of Social Darwinism, to tamper with any part of its foundation was to tamper with the handiwork of the Creator

Himself. To question the authority of any one of its pillars was to threaten the whole natural order of things that they supported. Race was but one—the most important one, but still one—of these foundational pillars of a whole southern culture. Yet to question the innate superiority of white over black was to threaten to bring down the broader civilization on which such premises rested. To have a political position in such a society, one did not need an extensive, or even a basic, understanding of the ins and outs of policy, an appreciation of nuance or shades of grey, or a fundamental grasp of what had previously constituted history. One needed only to have a cultural IQ—an instinctive understanding of what was held most precious, godly, good, and inviolable by dominant society. In this way, southern politics is not now—nor has it ever been—predominantly about politics. It's about culture. This is the Great Irony of southern politics, and, as the century wore on, it would increasingly become the Great Irony of American politics as well.

Essentially, this is what the father of progressive journalist Charlie Dobbins was complaining about when he said that "We don't have politics in Alabama based on issues. All our politics is race."[19] As the New Deal became increasingly about reform rather than recovery, and as blacks were included more as participants in a reformation rather than the mere recipients of relief, things looked dimmer and dimmer for an extended relationship with the South. Opponents of the New Deal, where they cropped up, began talking more and more in terms of those things that southerners held dear—not politics per se but *objects de cultur:* Americanism, the Constitution, patriotism, a way of life. Alabama's anemic Republican Party showed some brief signs of life when a young attorney named Claude O. Vardaman expressed resistance to FDR by urging the GOP to "rally to the party of constitutional government." In 1938, Alabama Republicans imported Missouri congressman Dewey Short to give the keynote address at their Constitutional Day rally. A leading opponent of Roosevelt, Short had won national attention by charging that FDR had deliberately prolonged the depression and fastened upon the American people a "type of government foreign to the fundamental principles of Americanism."[20] When conservative Democratic governor B. M. Miller proposed increasing taxes to pay for Alabama's wretchedly supported state government, a Troy physician told him that "We are taxed to death" and accused the governor of betraying the whole Democratic Party. "The 13, 14, 15, and 18 Amendments to the U.S. Constitution violate God's immutable laws and are the causes of all this trouble we are having," the Bible-verse quoting doctor explained. "The Negro and Yellow Races shall be Driven from *our Country!*"[21] After a while it would not even be necessary to say anything explicitly about race. You could just say something general about the South or about southern culture, and southerners would know by the code words what you meant. Political opponents could just say "that kind of thinking doesn't represent the true South," Gould Beech recalled. "Meaning, he's not right on the race issue." So people began to talk that way about New Dealers like Aubrey Williams. *Alabama Magazine* simply announced that Aubrey "doesn't talk like an Alabamian any more," and its conservative readership knew exactly what was meant.[22]

In such a culture, true patriotism and bona fide religion were closely bound up with what constituted socially acceptable thought and behavior on race, class, and gender questions: behavior that fell within the parameters of conduct that did not threaten the status quo. Such expectations extended to blacks as well who sometimes played along and adopted the submissive role in order to get along and, in notable instances, receive praise as "good Negroes" who "knew their place." "No one has more respect than I for our colored friends of the right sort," state Democratic Party chairman Gessner T. McCorvey announced in one statewide radio address.[23]

Still, cultural prohibitions went broader and deeper than just race, and rendered black/white cooperation a sin that made obvious the fact that the sinner must be a nut bent on overthrowing the Republic and the American way of life. Aubrey Williams was no communist, a close friend remembered.[24] Neither were the Durrs. Yet in such a rigid culture anybody who dissented on the central issues could easily be branded a communist and removed to the farthest fringes of society—marginalizing them *and* their political and economic arguments, no matter how solid. Even demonstrating sympathy for poor and starving blacks, lobbying for welfare and relief, could "automatically" make whites "red" in the repressive climate of the Deep South. Whenever Alabama whites and blacks cooperated, one bona fide black radical remembered bitterly, "that was 'them Reds.'" Hosea Hudson grew disgusted with the reluctance of poor whites to join the CIO and later the CP itself and laid the whole reason to race prejudice among the impoverished. They just did not want to "come sit down with a bunch of niggers, that's what they were saying," he bitterly concluded.[25] Yet this observation is only a partial understanding. To be sure, race orthodoxy was the core component of the predominant culture. But the outer layers were made up of other types of cultural orthodoxy, violation of which meant apostasy. Two of the most important were religion and patriotism—both directly challenged by communism. Communist identification with irreligion and revolution made it easy for white southerners to dismiss its economic critique as godless non-

sense subversive of the most sacred freedoms and American way of life—
and, by association, even the most innocuous of liberal efforts to win welfare
and relief for hungry people. This, most assuredly along with the obvious
threat to racial supremacy, damaged prospects for white recruitment to radical or even liberal causes.

The interests behind the Southern Conference for Human Welfare, according to the Bourbon opposition, were not just uncharacteristic of most
people in the South; they were actually dangerously foreign to the concept of
Americanism itself and betrayed the inherent depravity of the New Deal.
The Roosevelts themselves had sponsored the "piebald, unwashed, long-
haired movement" that was "Communist-infested," aided by "left-wing al-
lies" in the New Deal administration, "radical groups," and "pink Alabamians" bent on forcing a "left-wing program . . . spawned [by] . . . radical
eggs" on the South. The SCHW was "jam-packed with radicals, black and
white" and had an "extreme left-wing complexion," as evidenced by the
involvement of Joseph Gelders and Aubrey Williams. The whole thing
smacked of Reconstruction, Moscow-style, with an approbating nod from
the man in the White House. At root, the SCHW represented northern
hatred of the South and was the gravest design "launched against the South
for decades." Its intent was to "put the South on the defensive . . . flout
Southern ideals and traditions . . . fan [the] flames or racial unrest . . . and
jam through federal domination of Southern affairs," including universal
manhood suffrage and its ugly "by-products." This program was "anything
but Southern," yet the president was sympathetic to it because he "hates the
South" and has "never understood" anything about it except for the "darkey
vote." Naturally, the offense should arouse the "ire of the great rank and file
of Southerners as nothing else . . . since Reconstruction days."[26] In short, the
SCHW was made up of southerners who had "deserted the Democratic
party."[27]

Thus suitably instructed by the foremost barometer of conservative Alabama opinion—one that was skilled in tying together the most sacred regional shibboleths on an allied array of topics in the most bigoted manner
possible—individuals and groups in the culture fell into lockstep. Mabel
Jones West, 1920s leader of the women's auxiliary of the Ku Klux Klan, responded to the clarion call first, making very clear that Bourbon and Kluxer
had, in the tempests of the 1930s, drifted into lying down together.[28] West
summoned an emergency meeting of the Alabama Council of Women's
Democratic Clubs, of which she was president, and saw that the group
drafted a series of resolutions that echoed the Bourbon line and made clear

that the SCHW represented a severe cultural affront predicated on violation of race norms but extending to encompass the whole of southern society. The resolutions also made very clear that white Alabamians were holding the Roosevelt administration responsible for the "sinister attack" and "insult" to "Southern ideals and traditions" that had done "incalculable damage to the peace, welfare and progress of the South." "[L]eft-wing agitators . . . scheming left-wing politicians connected with the national administration and professional radical agitators" had been responsible for the assault, the women's groups resolved, as they specifically disowned one of their members for taking active part in the meeting. Because federal judge Louise Charlton had violated the most sacred of cultural tenets by enthusiastically participating in the inaugural SCHW, the women's group called for her resignation from their state executive committee; she obviously "no longer represents the people who placed her there."[29]

Once the anti–New Deal genie had been let out of the bottle, it was as if all of the pent-up southern Democratic frustration with Roosevelt's liberalism came flooding forth, especially from the Deep South's planting and industrial classes. It cannot be, nor is it being, argued that the Big Mule/Black Belt coalition worked in perfect concert or enjoyed unfettered unanimity on every issue. But it is an error of serious proportions to dismiss the power and influence of the Deep South's planter/industrial clique, especially on issues deemed central to their survival.[30] At this point in the New Deal, federal programs provided much-needed relief—even to large southern planters and businessmen who were, to some extent, feeling the crush of the Great Depression along with everyone else. But just as surely, the economic emergency that acted as discipline to keep large southern planting and commercial interests in the coalition would not be enough to retain an allegiance, however grudging and qualified, forever. In fact, the moment economic recovery was in sight, the federal government would once again be viewed with little more than suspicion, disdain, and outright hostility by planting and industrial interests that enjoyed running their megafarms and businesses as they saw fit without (as they saw it) the intrusive nose of the central government butting in.

To be sure, in 1938 the *Alabama Magazine* and Mabel Jones West still represented the far end of the neo-Bourbon and neo-Kluxer spectrum. But once they set the agenda for opposition to the Southern Conference as opposition to New Deal liberalism *itself,* disgruntled Democrats around Alabama needed no further encouragement. Former Birmingham mayor George B. Ward echoed the Democratic womens clubs' resolutions and added that he hoped Birmingham would never again play host to the SCHW—a wish that was requited. The Birmingham City Commission, comprised at this point by Big Mule representatives Jimmie Jones, Bull Connor, and Jimmy Morgan, called for HUAC to investigate the SCHW from top to bottom, looking for communist infiltration. Editorial opinion across the state reflected this mass outpouring of sentiment against the New Deal's liberal excesses. From the Black Belt, the *Selma Times-Journal* lamented the SCHW's advocacy of eliminating segregation and the poll tax and its approval of a federal anti-lynching law, a series of positions it termed "ill-advised." The *Montgomery Journal* was more forceful, denouncing the proposed making of the federal government a "policeman" with "federal bayonets" and the "scrap[ping] of every vestige of state rights in the regulation of internal affairs." Grover C. Hall of Old Grandma, the *Montgomery Advertiser*, expressed sorrow and re-gret at having initially supported the conference as something that could ameliorate regional ills and damned it as a "gratuitous insult" and "spit in the faces" of the southern people, both whites and moderate blacks. In fact, the conference had been a decided cultural affront, one that challenged the "folk-ways of our people" and the "way of life for both races" by "raising unpleasant extraneous issues" dealing with race relations. For Hall and other southerners of essentially conservative principles that were deeply rooted in the Social Darwinistic conventions of their age, New Deal liberalism was acceptable so long as the federal government provided relief checks and did not tamper with established social hierarchies. Such things were only "extraneous issues," and the tendencies of "fools and irresponsible radicals" to raise them could only "do more harm than good." Taken too far, Hall asserted, they could actually undo the "good work of moderating journals such, if we may say it, as The Advertiser."[31]

The response from Alabama's poorer sections was no better. Although New Deal programs such as the Tennessee Valley Authority (TVA) had done much to make North Alabama the most Democratic region in the state—and grateful inhabitants would return Democrats to Congress for decades—racially liberal events such as the SCHW meeting tore at the bonds between the region and the Democratic Party, bonds that would eventually come un-done. Instead of helping race relations, the meeting had actually hurt them, concluded the *Huntsville Times*. It was nothing more than a "collection of parlor pinks, left-wingers and social uplifters." The *Decatur Daily* agreed. The SCHW had been a worthless meeting of "crackpots." Perhaps the group considered itself to be liberal, the Morgan County journal mused, but not like anything approaching the Alabama definition of liberalism: "'Liberalism—

what sins are committed in thy name!'" The hill-country's *Tuscaloosa News* take on the meeting was perhaps the most telling for the future of the Democratic Party in Deep South states like Alabama:

> [A] dyed-in-the-wool New Dealer . . . Bibb Graves is not the only person who is shocked. . . . He is not the only Alabama man who, regarding himself as a New Dealer, is shocked and surprised by this revelation of what the REAL New Dealers—Eleanor Roosevelt, Aubrey Williams, and others of that stripe—are trying to do to the South. It is distressing that these people who are not forced to live in the South must destroy the harmony which it has taken us so many years to achieve . . . distressing that our peace and happiness must be sacrificed to these agitators who pose as socially-minded intellectuals . . . high-minded 'liberals' [yet are actually] . . . people on the federal payroll, living sumptuously off our taxes [coming] . . . down here among us to stir us to discord and strife. . . . [S]ome day [the SCHW will] be recognized as one of the most important events of its kind [because] . . . at last it opened the eyes of the South to the fact which the South had long refused to recognize. . . . [The SCHW] was not Democratic. It was New Deal, pure and simply, and the left-wing variety of the New Deal at that . . . [It was] a direct slap at the Democratic Party—the White Supremacy party as it has been constituted for years in the South—and an open revelation that the New Dealers are more concerned with the negro than with anybody else. . . . [They] do not see their folly. They do not realize they are in the process of transplanting Germany to the American South; they do not reckon what the white man of the South will do when his back has been pushed to the wall. . . . [It] was a valuable eye-opening shock . . . [but] it stank.[32]

As planned, the anti-SCHW animus quickly resonated with ordinary Alabamians whose racial sensibilities had been irretrievably offended. But like the elite and editorial version, their critique extended to a wholesale cultural denunciation of the group—its plans, origins, program, and any of its ideas—and the ritual summoning of the most sacred cultural pillars in defense. Key among these were religion and Reconstruction, but also a regional form of patriotism that clearly viewed the South as something separate and apart from the rest of the country. Southerners should now "wake up," an outraged Etowah County man advised in viewing the meeting. There has not been "a more dangerous meeting . . . of alien influences . . . *in our Southern country* in the past one hundred years" [emphasis mine]. "There should be a

week of prayer called to ask the Good Lord to again overshadow us with
that spirit which indwelled our forefathers of the [18]60s," agreed a Blount
County resident. Then Aubrey Williams and others of "that tribe [of] . . .
young Hitlers" and "nit wits" would be put on guard: "Such meetings gets
under we countrymen skin up in and around these diggins and . . . might
start something if they keep up." A Birminghamian, whose "blood is still
boiling," called the meeting "outrageous" and recommended that the Dies
Committee investigate immediately.[33] Perhaps more ominous for the future
of Democratic solidarity was the complaint of an Alabama schoolteacher
who found her New Deal allegiance shaken to the core by the racial and
"anti-patriotic" apostasy of the SCHW meeting: "I would like to be a liberal
but I begin to believe that the damn fool liberals will not let me do so."[34]

While Red-baited conference attendees such as Montgomery liberal
Virginia Durr thought the whole communist charge was a diversion from
"the real issues" of economic opportunity and "absolutely insane," Republicans sensed a crack in Alabama's culture wall and dove in.[35] B. Lonnie
Noonjin—an ambitious North Alabama businessman, real-estate operator,
and former University of Alabama and professional baseball star—hit on the
tried and true morality, patriotism, and southern culture themes to bash the
New Deal. He deplored the SCHW as a "very ominous" development that
made "real Southerners shudder" and denounced the New Deal as an "orgy"
and a departure from "sanity." "[T]he loss in moral values . . . Americanism
and patriotism," Noonjin informed the people of Alabama, "far outweighs
the benefits." The New Deal was no mere partisan difference of opinion. Its
designs were now clear. The South itself had been "sold out" by the Democratic program.[36] Of course, deviation from the accepted course of white supremacy was central to the treachery. Sensing, perhaps for the first time, that
Republicans were gaining traction on the white supremacy issue, Alabama
Democrats complained bitterly that the segregation issue had come up so
forcefully at the SCHW to hurt their party because J. D. Brown, publicity
agent for the state GOP, had "influenced" Bull Connor into appearing with
a riot squad to enforce the Jim Crow ordinance and tried to sell the *Chicago
Tribune* a story that the conference was dominated by communists.[37]

In a number of southern histories, the SCHW is cited as the high tide of
regional reform, accompanied by a roster of liberal attendees, and pretty
much left at that.[38] But in reality the SCHW marked instead the "softness"
of much of Alabama's variant of New Deal liberalism. Its aftermath makes
clear just how incredibly fragile and vulnerable to dissolution much of southern liberalism actually was. Before the ink had even dried on the SCHW's

resolutions, many Alabama New Dealers realized that they had made a terrible mistake. Southern economic liberals knew that as long as they paid ritual homage to the god of white supremacy, they could indulge their progressive tendencies on other issues. But so powerful were the regional conventions on that subject—and so hopelessly interwound with the mainstays of the culture itself (patriotic and religious)—that stepping over the color line could only incur the wrath of an electorate that would shut its ears to a progressive message on economics or anything else. This is the reason Lister Hill and John Sparkman tred so carefully, and sometimes so maddeningly, on race questions their whole careers. While observation of the cultural bounds of racial decorum did extend the life of economic liberals in the Deep South and the progress that they made on that front, their periodic gratification of the gods' hunger for at least rhetorical racial sacrifice also lent sustenance to the whole cultural belief system behind it. And it did so in a way that contributed to their own demise once the economic and the racial had been completely fused in the South by opportunistic conservatives. Paying ritual tribute to white supremacy, even if done for the noble reason of preserving the viability of economic liberalism, also led to the monster growing so large and so strong that eventually it could not be controlled—by anyone.

Even before the SCHW was effectively Red-baited, economic liberals who had attended the meeting ran from the group as if it were a house on fire. And, indeed, in Alabama it was. The anti–poll tax, anti–Jim Crow, and antilynching themes taken up by the conference alienated even southerners understood to be liberals who did not have to run for elective office. The *Raleigh News and Observer* spoke for many moderates and liberals around the region by pointing out that the conference began "in tragic mistake when action was taken which resulted in placing emphasis upon the one thing certain angrily to divide the South."[39] Notoriously reticent in the face of controversy, Bibb Graves announced loudly that he was "profoundly shocked" at what had transpired at the Birmingham meeting and was "shocked and surprised" at the course the conference had taken. Luther Patrick promptly resigned from the conference steering committee and said he had not had the "slightest knowledge" of the background or goals of some conference attendees. Lister Hill fled the scene of the crime, resolving to have nothing more to do with the heretics. John H. Bankhead wired former Klan maven Mabel Jones West, dutifully getting his resentment of the proceedings on record. F. D. Patterson, president of Tuskegee Institute, earned large bonus points with scandalized white Alabamians when he condemned the proceedings as the unproductive work of insurrectionaries from afar. New Deal columnist

John Temple Graves, who attended the meeting and expressed high hopes for it beforehand, immediately denounced the affair and its goals.[40] Congressman Joseph Starnes, a New Deal supporter from North Alabama and a member of the Dies Committee, filed a report on the SCHW as communist-inspired that helped persuade the HUAC to send a subcommittee to Birmingham to dig into the group and its members further. Starnes also agreed to speak to Mabel Jones West's Alabama Council of Women's Democratic Clubs organizational meeting for a new women's club that promised to devote itself specifically to "promoting American principles in Alabama, damning and downing un-American activities."[41] Of course, HUAC did not require much encouragement. The committee operated under the reactionary chairmanship of Texas congressman Martin Dies Jr., an earlier opponent of aliens and international bankers who had graduated to target Reds and, soon, New Dealers, whom he took for being the dupes of communists. "Stalin baited his hook with a 'progressive' worm," Dies declared, and the New Deal "suckers swallowed bait, hook, line, and sinker."[42]

Sentiment such as that of Joe Starnes corresponded with similar intransigence in Congress when issues were raised that challenged the southern dogma on race. Confronting the contemporaneous Wagner-Costigan federal antilynching bill, Alabama's two senators, both prominent attendees at the SCHW, locked arms and toed the regional line. John H. Bankhead said he resented the "visionary, shallow thinkers" and "self-handpicked would-be racial uplifters" who had demonstrated so little understanding of "fundamental Southern conditions." Just before his appointment to the U.S. Supreme Court, where he would make history by pushing the high court to the left on civil liberties and civil rights, Hugo Black's behavior testified to the power of electoral shackles in the Deep South. Just a year before the SCHW meeting, Black opposed the antilynching measure as a scheme that would somehow erode labor rights.[43]

As dramatic as any other reaction to the SCHW was that of George Huddleston—Alabama congressman, friend to labor, and a politician perennially described as a liberal New Dealer.[44] Yet Huddleston's behavior after the conference (which he attended) and his career as a whole make clear the softness that formed much of the core of New Deal liberalism in places like Alabama. It was a liberalism that did not extend to race. It was also a liberalism that embraced—and in some cases merely tolerated—the New Deal as a temporary stopgap measure to deal with an unprecedented emergency. It was a political bent that actually could be quite conservative, that relished a return to pre-depression days and a relationship between state and central government marked most notably by a pro-business laissez-faire. Like Bibb Graves, Luther Patrick, Lister Hill, John Bankhead—and even journalist John Temple Graves and black college president F. D. Patterson—U.S. congressman George Huddleston could not get away from the SCHW fast enough after its final gavel. Those Alabamians who stayed with the conference and its resolutions and successor educational fund—Aubrey Williams, the Durrs, William Mitch—were the exceptions. They were imported northerners foreign to Deep South cultural traditions, or the most exotic of native southerners regarded by the bulk of Alabamians to be as alien as they were exceptional.

Actually, George Huddleston's racial conservatism was nothing new. As early as 1912, he had made the mistake of publicly defending the race in the most paternalistic of terms yet had felt his hand stung by the hard slap of his home state's social conventions. "We have the negro here with us," the young Birmingham alderman had said in a speech to the Alabama Bar Association. "[W]e cannot kill him, we cannot deport him, we have got to make him a citizen." "The right of suffrage should be extended regardless of race and sex," Huddleston recommended in sounding not unlike the foremost scions of Black-Belt privilege at the state's 1901 constitutional convention. Yet a mere decade after the codification, the postdisfranchisement color line had stiffened considerably. Huddleston found himself confronted with his comments a year later when he announced for the vacant congressional seat of the venerable Oscar W. Underwood. A rival for the open seat informed the good people of Birmingham that the young alderman had publicly recommended the "kinky-headed Sambo and thick-lipped Dinah to vote and each to count as much as your vote, or yours, or yours." Shaken, Huddleston did, in the words of his grandson, "What politicians have always done: backtracked, claimed he was quoted out of context, changed the subject." He even said the bar association's stenographer had taken down his 1912 speech inaccurately. But he never made the same mistake again. In a 1929 speech to the Birmingham Women's Democratic Club, Huddleston went far in his defense of white supremacy, telling the women that "we battle against social equality between the races and for the purity of the blood that flows in our veins. The real issue is whether the people of the South shall be degraded mongrels of mixed and polluted blood." Two years later the congressman rose up out of his chair and "nearly hit the ceiling," remembered a female American Civil Liberties Union envoy who asked Huddleston, as a leading liberal friend of labor, to represent the accused "Scottsboro Boys." "I don't care whether they are innocent or guilty," Huddleston yelled at the startled woman. "They were found riding on the same freight car with two white women, and that's enough for me."[45]

What is interesting is just how temporary support was for the New Deal for southern liberals the stripe of George Huddleston. In 1933, the Alabama congressman supported the First Hundred Days of relief action by the Roosevelt administration, earning a personal note of thanks from FDR's top lieutenant, Postmaster General Jim Farley. Yet before the year was out, Huddleston was hinting at the conservative conviction that there was a tie between relief and un-American behavior, telling the Birmingham Real Estate Board that Roosevelt's recovery plans were "steps toward collectivism." The open break came a mere two years later. "My grandfather voted for the TVA," George Packer remembered, "but he never said a good word about it." For his grandfather and the people he represented, Washington became "something alien . . . a burden on them, a threat to freedom and custom." In 1935, Huddleston opposed the Social Security Act on the grounds of states' rights. A year later he found himself opposed for reelection by the Roosevelt administration, John L. Lewis, William Mitch, and upstart Alabama Democrat Luther Patrick. During the 1936 campaign, Huddleston called Indiana native Mitch a "carpetbagger" and stood by while a well-known supporter race-baited and Red-baited the union leader for consorting with black United Mine Workers organizer Walter Jones. "I am opposed to centralization of authority in Washington, and . . . the robbery of our states," Huddleston told his Alabama constituents. Then, carried away by the moment, Huddleston claimed a Confederate heritage for his father that existed only in his imagination: "My father fought for the rights of these states to live their lives, and to be free from a central autocracy in Washington, or any Summer resort. . . . I would bare my thin and ancient breast to die for these principles."[46] Instead of baring his breast at a set of neo-Confederate ramparts, Huddleston did the next best thing: In an impromptu election-eve restaurant encounter, he brained his opponent over the head with a ketchup bottle.

For Huddleston and other southerners who supported the early Roosevelt years, their break with the New Deal version of liberalism occurred because, they believed, liberalism had left them—not because they had left liberalism. The rhetoric and the sentiment would be repeated decades later as hundreds of thousands of anti–civil rights white southerners would leave the Democratic Party, claiming the same thing. "Men have called me a liberal, and I was glad to be called that," Huddleston told his colleagues in the U.S. House midway through the decade. "I have called myself a 'Democrat,' an old-fashioned, southern, Jeffersonian Democrat. I claimed that when I first came to the House. I claim that today. It is not my fault if . . . principles which at one time were considered liberal should now be considered conservative." "My principles and myself remain unchanged," he claimed; "it is the defini-tion of 'liberalism' which has been changed . . . [and] I am unable to accom-pany [it] . . . to the extremes of radicalism and that variety of 'liberalism'—spurious and false liberalism—the 'liberalism' of Mussolini and of Stalin and of Hitler."[47] In 1940 the former Alabama congressman went whole hog and supported Republican Wendell Wilkie for the presidency against FDR. In 1948, he joined the Dixiecrats. As Huddleston's grandson perceptively under-stood, the southern liberal allegiance to New Deal liberalism was the ephem-eral product of the calamity and cataclysm of the Great Depression. It was inherently temporary and contained within it the seeds of its own destruc-tion. As George Packer perceptively put it, "By 1948 the South's brief love affair with the federal government was over. Depression had begun the affair, and war had sustained it beyond its natural end. . . . Race became the lever with which conservatives pried the South out of the New Deal coalition, and they did it in the name of Americanism."[48]

The SCHW itself held on for ten years, eventually devolving into the Southern Conference Education Fund under James Dombrowski, which continued to do work on the voting rights and civil rights fronts but at a more modest level. There was some activity on voting rights during the de-pression decade, but almost all of it was disappointing. From 1932 to 1942, despite the best efforts of Black Belt African Americans led by Macon County's Charles Gomillion, only 100 blacks joined Alabama's voter rolls. Between 1939 and 1942, black Birmingham attorney Arthur D. Shores filed suit three times for the NAACP against the Jefferson County Board of Vot-ing Registrars. Malcolm and Pauline Dobbs, white radicals and local SCHW leaders, bravely led the African Americans to the steps of the Jefferson County Courthouse to register. But each time the board circumvented the suit simply by registering the individual plaintiff. In Mobile, state Demo-cratic powerhouse Gessner T. McCorvey buried the hatchet with rival state chairman John D. McQueen long enough to cooperate in cracking down on black voting and the "disgraceful and nauseating scenes" of large numbers of African-American voters being "bought up like so many sheep."[49]

Central to the successful resistance against black incursion on voting was a nearly perfectly solid front presented by the forces of planter and industri-alist conservatism. As early as 1933, McCorvey had insinuated himself in the middle of a Mobile cotton mill strike principally because he feared that the

oratory of labor "agitators" would stir blacks up against the white populace in
South Alabama and would spill over into areas not specifically concerned
with industrial relations. Bourbons decried any attempt at increasing black
voter rolls as part of a more generalized antidemocratic impulse among
southern conservatives. They professed enmity toward loosening ballot restrictions because, in their view, the vote already extends to "the gutter and
the cesspool. It blankets the mob. Every so-and-so a king!"[50] Increasingly,
Alabama Democrats found fault with the New Deal liberalism of FDR for
stimulating black efforts to register. Roosevelt had already invited the "conservative regime" out of the Democratic Party, they complained. Now he was
intent on wrecking it completely by appealing to the "Negro vote of the
North" as opposed to "anything South of the Mason-Dixon line."[51] To resist
the stirrings of blacks and progressive whites on this score, the Bourbons
relied on Reconstruction and Red-baiting. A black Birmingham communist
complained that everyone involved in the area's Right-to-Vote Club, even
nonradicals, were subject to Red-baiting: "Here's the communists. This here's
a communist outfit'" was the generic charge leveled at the group. Other conservative Democrats invoked the memory of the 1860s to work its magic:
"Who would have expected the carpet-bagger to spring to life after two
generations of merited oblivion within the Democratic Party and at the
bidding of a nominal Democratic President?" a leading conservative organ
asked. Gratification of the president's desire to enfranchise "vast numbers of
Negroes" who were attracted to his "economic philosophy and his political
strategy" would be to court a Reconstruction "tragedy [that] would be unthinkable [and] . . . wreck and destroy the Democratic Party. . . . The mind
staggers at the prospect."[52]

The 1940 presidential campaign thus provided more avenues for expression of disgust with the New Deal than the election four years prior. For one,
Franklin Roosevelt was seeking an unprecedented third term as president.
For the Bourbon press, the novelty opened up his campaign to unfavor-
able comparisons with the "rubber-stamp" elections of "Il Duce" and "Der
Fuehrer."[53] Opponents of the New Deal had also had four more years in
which to gestate their resistance to the growing liberal drift of the Democratic Party. Still, the Republican Party was not yet a viable possibility in the
South; a switch in partisan allegiance could not realistically be expected to
occur overnight. But the defeat of the GOP ticket in Alabama should not be
mistaken for a reason to disregard growing southern white discontent with
New Deal liberalism and the Democratic Party.

Southern Republicans by and large favored Ohio senator Robert H. Taft,

"Mr. Republican," for his severe anti–New Deal rhetoric. In Alabama, Taft supporters lined up behind B. Lonnie Noonjin while Claude O. Vardaman led a younger, urban Republican wing that favored New Yorker Thomas Dewey. When the Republican schism at the national convention led to the surprise nomination of Wendell Wilkie, Alabama Republican leader Oliver Day Street counseled the progressive Republican not to dare mention black rights or the antilynching bill in the South. "The so-called 'Negro question'" Street explained, "has more lives than the proverbial cat." If Wilkie had to mention race, he should stick simply to saying innocuous things about "justice" for blacks and do nothing to aggravate the scintillating "prejudices of the Civil War and the Negro," which would, in any event, be marshaled against any Republican candidacy in Alabama.[54]

While conservative Democratic opposition to the New Deal in 1936 had led only to a postelection gathering of dissident forces, the 1940 election actually saw the independent elector movement rear its head in the South. The dream recalled another Wormley House bargain of 1877, when southern bloc intransigence would throw a presidential election into the House of Representatives where Dixie could win regional concessions. Mississippi and Texas dissenters chose the unpledged elector route, while some South Carolina Democrats supported the favorite son candidacy of Virginia's Harry F. Byrd. Other disgruntled forces in South Carolina and Texas backed Republican Wendell Wilkie as the only "real Democrat" in the race, yet many southerners were turned off by his internationalism and relative progressivism.[55] While the separate elector movement floundered in the 1940 election, attracting only negligible support, it was, like the 1936 gathering of anti–New Deal forces, an important starting point—one that presaged a powerful rump movement, centered in the South, that loomed on the horizon for the Democratic Party.

Alabama flirted with the independent elector movement and actually organized several Wilkie Democratic Clubs before the fledgling insurgency was snuffed out by the powerful state Democratic Party. Conservative planter and business interests led the anti-FDR movement. Leading coal operator Charles F. DeBardeleben took out large advertisements damning Roosevelt's liberalism and New Deal "manipulat[ion]" and pushed Republican Wilkie's candidacy in the interest of "the 'American Way' . . . to keep America free" and for "truly loyal workers."[56] Hubert Baughn chimed in for Wilkie by pointing out that the "New Deal dictatorship" of the "Raw Deal" had made an abomination out of the Democratic Party in the eyes of "lifelong Southern Democrats."[57] But perhaps the most far-reaching dissent was voiced in

an open letter by Walker County small businessman and lifelong Democrat Robert H. Carr. "I am boiling over," Carr wrote. "I resent . . . the . . .
usurpation by Roosevelt . . . [of] the Democratic Party . . . so much that . . .
[m]y Democratic vote goes for Wilkie." The Democratic Party in Alabama
"resents the surrender of the party to one man," Carr declared in echoing the
melding of racial and social conservatism with free-market economics; one
man whose "gilded theories . . . passion for a totalitarian government with
himself as Fuehrer . . . his New Deal on bitterness and ill-will . . . [and] his
Fifth Column of hatred toward industry and business . . . [is] dangerous,
subversive and unnecessary, . . . symptom[atic] of [an] incurable urge to
meddle . . . [and] is making a sorry thing of the Democratic Party."[58]

The unhappy Alabama oligarchs tried to take full advantage of hurt
feelings in the state when Franklin Roosevelt passed over House speaker
William Bankhead for the second spot on the 1940 Democratic ticket. While
Bankhead and his brother in the U.S. Senate had made no secret of their
desire to see Will tapped for the vice-presidential spot, Roosevelt gave that
honor to Agriculture Secretary Henry A. Wallace after Supreme Court justice William O. Douglas had turned it down. For the Bankheads it was the
final straw in their strained relationship with FDR. For white Alabamians it
was yet another subject over which to feel that the New Deal had deserted
whites for "radical and Negro elements . . . the darkey vote . . . [and] dusky
Democrats."[59] Alabama Democrats returned from the national convention in
Chicago voicing bitter resentment over the treatment of Bankhead and the
South. "We have been sold down the river," Brewton's Ed Leigh McMillan
said. "Such things as this lead to Hitlerism." Wiregass delegates Will Lee
and Robert Malone actually voted against a third term for Roosevelt at
Chicago. Both the Black Belt's *Selma Times-Journal* and the hillcountry's
Talladega Daily Home spoke ill of the Chicago proceedings. "My God!," ex-
claimed Birmingham attorney R. DuPont Thompson. "As a life-long Democrat I [ask] . . . Is this the democracy of the Fathers?" The state Democratic
Womens' Clubs, represented by Mabel Jones West and Democratic national
committeewoman Laura Sharp, publicly deplored the surrendering of the
national party to New Deal politicians.[60] Near Birmingham a number of
Democratic veterans including Henry R. Howze, O. G. "Pap" Gresham,
F. M. Jackson, and bakery magnate Willliam P. McGough joined the Wilkie
movement. Democratic Wilkie Clubs organized in Walker, Jefferson, and
Mobile counties as a "patriotic duty" under the leadership of Robert H. Carr,
R. DuPont Thompson, and insurance man Fred H. White, respectively.
"If the Democratic Party is to last in the South," a national Democratic

committeeman from Gainesville announced, "we will have to follow a different course from what we have been following in the last few years . . . letting
the Eastern Democrats dictate to us."[61]

But in 1940 the state Democratic Party was easily strong enough to snap
the whip of party discipline and compel obedience to the regular standard
regardless of Roosevelt's increasing distastefulness. Wiregrass committeeman Robert Malone, who had opposed FDR at Chicago, announced publicly that he would vote for the president in spite of "the threat of totalitarian
policies." E. C. "Bud" Boswell—a Wiregrass politico who had played a large
role in quelling the 1928 "bolt" and would render yeoman service to the continued disfranchisement of blacks and poor whites after World War II—led
the disciplinary movement for the regular Democratic Party. The militant
Alabama Magazine cried foul, the *Selma Times-Journal* advised that bolting
the Democratic Party of Roosevelt would satisfy a higher calling of putting country above party and patriotism above mere partisanship, and archconservative industrialists such as Charles DeBardeleben cursed the party
discipline as a "stench in the nostrils of millions of . . . patriotic . . . [and]
free Americans."[62] But the ground was not yet ready to nurture the independent seed to the extent of an immediate and wholesale GOP harvest—
mostly because the regular Democratic Party still owned the trump card of
white supremacy. That would come later. Gessner McCorvey, now state
Democratic chairman, spoke to the people over a statewide radio hookup and
urged them to resist the impulse to bolt just because the Roosevelt administration had done some unsavory things that were now "water over the dam."
Bolting was not to be thought about, McCorvey instructed the populace,
because the preservation of white supremacy still depended on Democratic
regularity. Alabama had gone Democratic since 1874 when George S. Houston, "that great Democratic leader," had led the "white men of Alabama . . .
to redeem our State from [the] Carpet-bag misrule of the Reconstruction
era." As a consequence, McCorvey concluded, "we were just brought up to
believe that it was not the proper thing for a Southern white man to vote the
Republican ticket." Responding to McCorvey's plucking of their racial and
Reconstruction chords, crowds of jeering plain folk booed, hooted down, and
pelted with eggs the pro-Wilkie "Caravan of Democracy" in at least eight
places across the state: Vernon and Prattville in central Alabama, the mining
town of Jasper in northwest Alabama, and the north Alabama hamlets of
Florence, Sheffield, Moulton, Russellville, and Haleyville.[63]

Although the most reactionary part of the Big Mule/Black Belt machine
was on the losing side in 1940, there is no question that its forces were pick-

ing up steam and moving toward their eventual rendezvous with Republicanism. Franklin Roosevelt's personal popularity, looming American involvement in World War II, lingering gratitude for the economic resuscitations of
the New Deal, and party loyalty and patronage prevented any serious rupture
in the 1940 South. But it was also clear that the growing racial and economic
liberalism of the Democratic Party under FDR was resulting in more and
more powerful and vocal enemies in the South—enemies who would eventually find a warm home in the conservative modern GOP. Given some time,
money, and a few more high-profile sectional grievances, a strong independent or even third-party challenge might even become a reality in the short
term. As the legendary political scientist V. O. Key Jr. noted, the greatest
asset of the southern Bourbons was their highly developed political skills.[64]
It was an acumen that tapped into the cultural fabric of the South to repeatedly turn their numerical minority into a ruling majority. Central in the
transformation was the ability of the privileged to define "southern" interests
as their interests, to make "cultural" survival synonymous with their survival
and even aggrandizement. To this end, the Bourbons shrilly derided the
"class warfare" and this "business baiting and setting class against class" that
was becoming so much a part of the new national Democratic Party under
the New Deal. Increasingly in their rhetoric, they tied together "social legislation and labor controversies," white supremacy and laissez-faire.[65] Yet for
maximum popular resonance, the critical component was racial. As the state's
leading big planter and industrialist mouthpiece put it:

> In seven years Roosevelt . . . has drawn to himself the city gang, the hood
> lum and the bum . . . New York negro[es] . . . [and] Jew[s]. . . . All right,
> Southerners, if that is the thing you like, then vote for your Roosevelt. . . .
> The Democratic Party has maintained in the South that good local gov
> ernment can best be furthered by limiting that Party's membership . . .
> to the white race. That right of selective association is within their consti
> tutional right [and is] . . . in the public interest. That practice is now
> doomed. It can not survive a third term, for Franklin Roosevelt . . . has
> committed himself to the false premise that selective association is illegal.
> . . . Franklin D. Roosevelt—sent Franklin D. Roosevelt Jr. to Chicago to
> be photographed arm in arm with negroes . . . sent Mrs. Roosevelt to dine
> with the Pullman porters [and] to invite . . . over 400 negro housewives to
> the White House for afternoon tea. . . . What chance has the frail bound
> ary of tradition when this dominant family demands that it be abolished

and the South is filled with Lister Hills . . . [and other] Benedict Arnolds in command . . . to rubber stamp his wishes; . . . [when] pinks and radicals [are] in high place and favor in Washington, [and] public and private morals have suffered the fate of the Supreme Court and the Democratic Party? . . . God pity the South for the failure of its Democratic leaders in the crisis.[66]

Notes

1. Forney Johnston, Alabama senator Oscar W. Underwood's chief lieutenant, placed the senator's name into presidential nomination with a sensational attack on the hooded order and the proposition of an official party plank against the KKK. The Alabama delegation, dominated by a Big Mule/Black Belt alliance of wealthy industrialists, bankers, and planters, favored adoption of the plank because, while they sympathized with the order's racist philosophy, they also saw the Klan as a political threat that had to be squelched. On this subject, see Glenn Feldman, *Politics, Society, and the Klan in Alabama, 1915–1949* (Tuscaloosa: University of Alabama Press, 1999), 71.

2. Quotations in George Brown Tindall, *The Emergence of the New South, 1913–1945* (Baton Rouge: Louisiana State University, 1967), 544 (first), 557 (second), 556 (third and fifth), 555 (fourth), 543 (sixth). Ickes himself had served as president of the Chicago chapter of the NAACP.

3. In January 1935, the U.S. Supreme Court struck down part of the NIRA in *Panama Refining Company v. Ryan*, 293 U.S. 388 (1935). On 27 May 1935 the Supremes struck down the NIRA completely in *Schecter Poultry Corp. v. United States*, 295 U.S. 495, 550 (1935). A year after its *Panama Refining* decision, the high court invalidated the AAA in *U.S. v. Butler*, 297 U.S. 1 (1936).

4. Tindall, *The Emergence of the New South*, 620 (Sumners quotation).

5. *Congressional Record*, 75th Cong., 1st sess., Appendix, 661 (Glass quotations), cited also in Tindall, *The Disruption of the Solid South* (Athens: University of Georgia Press, 1972), 33, and Tindall, *The Emergence of the New South*, 621, 622, 624 (Manifesto quotation). See also Tony Badger, "Southerners Who Refused to Sign the Southern Manifesto," *The Historical Journal* 42, no. 2 (1999):517–34.

6. Stetson Kennedy, *Southern Exposure* (New York: Doubleday, 1946), 2 (second quotation), 3 (first quotation); Tindall, *The Emergence of the New South*, 627 (also first quotation).

7. Kennedy, *Southern Exposure*, 4–5. See also James C. Cobb, *Industrialization and Southern Society, 1877–1984* (Lexington: University Press of Kentucky, 1984).

152

 Glenn Feldman

8. For the malformed nature of Alabama's tax structure, see Malcom Cook McMillan, *Constitutional Development in Alabama, 1798–1901: A Study in Politics, Sectionalism, and the Negro* (Chapel Hill: University of North Carolina Press, 1955; reprint, Charlotte: Spartanburg Reprint Co., 1978); Bailey Thompson, ed., *A Century of Controversy: Constitutional Reform in Alabama* (Tuscaloosa: University of Alabama Press, 2002); Kyle Whitmire, "Who Would Want the Job Anyway?" *Birmingham Weekly*, 14–21 November 2002, 8.

9. Kennedy, *Southern Exposure*, 2–12, 7 (first quotation), 11 (second quotation).

10. Ibid., 4 (first quotation); Tindall, *The Emergence of the New South*, 637 (Foreman quotation), 641 (Pepper quotation), 626 (Roosevelt quotations). The impression was widespread. "It is fast becoming the opinion of all civilized people," a Brooklyn, New York, resident wrote, that Alabama is "a region where barbaric feudalism still exists." Charles Eckstat to Bibb Graves, 29 August 1935 (quoted), box SG 12165, folder 2, Alabama Governors Papers, Bibb Graves Papers, Alabama Department of Archives and History (ADAH), Montgomery.

11. Major Squirm column, *Alabama Magazine*, 1 May 1939, 15; Tindall, *The Emergence of the New South*, 624, 627 (George quotation), 629 (Smith quotation).

12. Tindall, *The Emergence of the New South*, 630 (first quotation), 633 (second quotation).

13. Virginia Durr oral interview by John Egerton, 6 February 1991, 9–10, Southern Oral History Project:4007, A-337, Southern Historical Collection (SHC), University of North Carolina at Chapel Hill; William Warren Rogers, Robert David Ward, Leah Rawls Atkins, and Wayne Flynt, *Alabama: The History of a Deep South State* (Tuscaloosa: University of Alabama Press, 1994), 502 (Connor quotation); Glenn Feldman, *From Demagogue to Dixiecrat: Horace Wilkinson and the Politics of Race* (Lanham, Md.: University Press of America, 1995), 109; Tindall, *The Emergence of the New South*, 636–37; *Alabama Magazine*, 5 December 1938, 5. See also Thomas A. Krueger, *And Promises to Keep: The Southern Conference for Human Welfare, 1938–1948* (Nashville: Vanderbilt University Press, 1967), and Linda Reed, *Simple Decency & Common Sense: The Southern Conference Movement, 1938–1963* (Bloomington: Indiana University Press, 1991). On the background of conference attendees such as Rob Hall and on the fact that one in five delegates were black, see Patricia Sullivan, *Days of Hope: Race and Democracy in the New Deal Era* (Chapel Hill: University of North Carolina Press, 1996), 98–101, and Sullivan, ed., *Freedom Writer: Virginia Foster Durr, Letters from the Civil Rights Years* (New York: Routledge, 2003).

14. On Gelders's background, see Sullivan, *Days of Hope*, 97. See also Tindall, *The Emergence of the New South*, 637, 638 (quoted), 639.

15. *Alabama Magazine*, 28 November 1938, 18 (first quotation), 3 (second quotation).

16. Ibid., 5 December 1938, 14 (first quotation), 28 November 1938, 3 (second and third quotations).

17. Ibid., editorial, 5 December 1938, 3–4 (quotations).

18. This phrase is ubiquitous in the parlance of southern whites, increasingly so as threats to traditional race relations grew throughout the twentieth century. See, for example, Fred D. Oakley, Potts Camp, Mississippi, to Eleanor Roosevelt, 5 March 1944 (quoted), folder 190.1, Eleanor Roosevelt Papers, Franklin Delano Roosevelt Library, Hyde Park, New York.

19. Charles G. Dobbins, "Alabama Governors and Editors, 1930–1955: A Memoir," *Alabama Review* 29 (April 1976):154 (quoted). An overly sanguine Dobbins also said in 1976 that "no longer is that true." A realization of the intertwined cultural tenets that supported racial discrimination in the South drove the Fellowship of Southern Churchmen who believed that the South's social conservatism was "rooted in its religious conservatism and that there can be little or no alteration of social conditions until the basic religious pattern has been radically and fundamentally changed." Quotation in Tindall, *The Emergence of the New South,* 635.

20. *Birmingham Post,* 21 June 1934 (Vardaman quotation), and *Birmingham News,* 28 August 1938 (Short quotation), both in the news clipping file: Political Parties—Republican—Birmingham and Jefferson County, Tutwiler Collection of Southern History (TCSH), Birmingham Public Library, Birmingham.

21. C. G. Snead to B. M. Miller, 31 March 1933 (quoted), in box SG 19947, folder 12, Alabama Governors Papers, Benjamin Meek Miller Papers, Alabama Department of Archives and History (ADAH).

22. Gould Beech, oral interview by John Egerton, Magnolia Springs, Alabama, 9 August 1990, 25 (first quotation), Southern Oral History Project:4007, A-342, Southern Historical Collection; *Alabama,* 28 November 1938, 18 (second quotation).

23. Radio address of Gessner T. McCorvey, SDEC chair, 14 September 1940, 1, 2, 5 (first quotation), LPR 99, box 81, folder 12, box 69, folder 14, both in State Democratic Executive Committee (SDEC) Records, ADAH.

24. Gould Beech interview, 7–8; *Alabama Magazine* charged that Williams was committed to "revolution and property communism"; see issue of 28 November 1938, 18 (quoted). Williams warranted this designation in the eyes of the reactionary publication because, as publisher of the *Southern Farmer* with Gould Beech as editor, the Alabama duo pushed racial and economic liberalism during the 1930s. Marshall Field and James P. Warburg bankrolled their newspaper. See Gould Beech interview, 7–8. Liberal thought such as this was exceedingly rare in Alabama yet it did emerge, occasionally, especially on economic issues. For examples, see Troy Whitaker, Gadsden, to the editor, *Alabama Magazine,* 14 December 1936, 15, and C. A. Thaxton to the editor, ibid., 19 April 1937, 15.

25. Nell Irvin Painter, *The Narrative of Hosea Hudson: His Life and Times as a Negro Communist in the South* (Cambridge: Harvard University Press, 1979), 141 (first quotation), 323 (second quotation).

26. *Alabama Magazine,* editorial, 28 November 1938, 3 (first quotation), 5 December 1938, 3–5, 14 (all other quotations).

27. Major Squirm column, ibid., 12 December 1938, 15 (quotation).

28. Ibid., 21 November 1938, 4. In the midst of its bigoted denunciations of the SCHW, the Bourbon organ still insisted on emphasizing its low opinion of the KKK. See, for example, Major Squirm column, 5 December 1938, 14.

29. George Londa to Mr. Bliven, 27 November 1938, Virginia Durr Papers, ADAH; *Alabama Magazine,* 5 December 1938, 6 (quotations).

30. Those interested in the nature, character, and power of the South's planting and industrial elite and their very real influence in politics and the economy should consult several basic texts as a starting point: V. O. Key Jr., *Southern Politics in State and Nation* (New York: Alfred Knopf, 1949; reprint, 1984); C. Vann Woodward, *Origins of the New South, 1877–1913* (Baton Rouge: Louisiana State University Press, 1951); and McMillan, *Constitutional Development in Alabama.*

31. *Selma Times-Journal, Montgomery Journal,* and *Montgomery Advertiser* editorials reprinted in and quoted from *Alabama Magazine,* 5 December 1938, 10–12.

32. *Huntsville Times, Decatur Daily,* and *Tuscaloosa News* editorials reprinted in and quoted from *Alabama Magazine,* ibid., 10–14.

33. Leroy Gossett, Gadsden, (Etowah County) to ed., *Alabama Magazine,* 12, 26 December 1938, both on 4 (first quotation); W. P. Gordon, Oneonta (Blount County) to ed., *Alabama Magazine,* 12 December 1938, 4 (second quotation); S. A. Riley, Birmingham, to ed., *Alabama Magazine,* 26 December 1938, 4 (third quotation). The Dies Committee refers, of course, to the House Un-American Activities Committee chaired by conservative Texas Democrat Martin H. Dies Jr.

34. In an index of just how popular the sobriquet *liberal* was during the period, the editor of the archconservative *Alabama Magazine* agreed with the sentiment of the disenchanted liberal educator: "Same here." See *Alabama Magazine,* 5 December 1938, 11 (quoted).

35. Virginia Durr oral interview by John Egerton, 6 February 1991, 3, 11, 30 (quotation), 31, SHC.

36. Noonjin was born and raised on an Etowah County farm and later moved into Gadsden where he had businesses. See *Alabama Magazine,* 26 December 1938, 6 (Noonjin quotations).

37. George Londa to Mr. Bliven, 27 November 1938 (quotation) in Virginia Durr Papers, ADAH.

38. See Wayne Flynt's section in Rogers et al., *Alabama,* 496–97; *Alabama Maga-*

zine, 26 December 1938; Tindall, *The Emergence of the New South,* 636–39. I have made the same error in earlier works. See Feldman, *From Demagogue to Dixiecrat,* 109, 121, 139, and *Politics, Society, and the Klan in Alabama,* 274. For a fuller exposition on the SCHW and its successor, the Southern Conference Educational Fund under James Dombrowski, see Sullivan, *Days of Hope,* and Reed, *Simple Decency & Common Sense.*

39. *Raleigh News and Observer,* 26 November 1938, quoted in Tindall, *The Emergence of the New South,* 637.

40. *Alabama Magazine,* 5 December 1938, 5 (Bibb Graves quotation and F. P. Patterson characterization), 7 (Bankhead response), 15 (Patrick quotation). A similar Bibb Graves quote about being "surprised and shocked" was reported on p. 12 of the same issue. Editorials reprinted from the *Selma Times-Journal* (10) and the *Tuscaloosa News* (13) also singled out F. D. Patterson for praise for exhibiting a proper African-American response. On John Temple Graves and F. D. Patterson, see Durr interview, 6 February 1991, 18–19, 23, SHC. Gould Beech also remembered the mass exodus after the meeting; see Beech, interview by John Egerton, 20–21. See also Sullivan, *Days of Hope,* 100. UNC Press director W. T. Couch also backed off later from much of the racial sentiment expressed at the meeting. He felt compelled to write an apologetic publisher's introduction, arguing against the sudden abolition of segregation, for Rayford W. Logan's edited collection of essays from leading black minds titled *What the Negro Wants* (Chapel Hill: University of North Carolina Press, 1944). In other places Couch was even more aggressive in his defense of Jim Crow. See Kennedy, *Southern Exposure,* 335–40.

41. Starnes was from Guntersville in Marshall County. See *Alabama Magazine,* 5 December 1938, 7, 10 (quotation).

42. Tindall, *The Emergence of the New South,* 625 (Dies quotation).

43. *Alabama Magazine,* 5 December 1938, 7 (Bankhead quotations); Tindall, *The Emergence of the New South,* 552.

44. See, for example, Wayne Flynt's characterization of Huddleston in Rogers et al., *Alabama,* 494, 501.

45. George Packer, *Blood of the Liberals* (New York: Simon and Schuster, 2000), 54–55 (first quotation), 56 (second and third quotations), 57 (fourth and fifth quotations).

46. Ibid., 114 (first quotation), 116 (second quotation), 124 (third and fourth quotations).

47. *Congressional Record* quoted ibid., 121.

48. Packer, *Blood of the Liberals,* 126, 178, 180. The quotation is from pp. 177 and 179, and it goes on: "Class politics, played so surely by the charismatic Roosevelt, wooed the South from its old hostility to central authority and obscured the forces that were

beginning to divide the Democratic Party. But once Roosevelt was dead and the war over . . . opponents of the New Deal saw their opportunity to turn the region against Washington by singing the old, sure song of race along with the new song of Communism." In an earlier, poignant passage on p. 120, Packer writes that "One can almost point to those weeks in Washington . . . [i]n the summer of 1935 . . . as the moment when liberalism, reaching the peak of its New Deal heyday, lost its connection to something vital from the past. . . . [T]o the harm of both, liberalism and populism, the braintruster with his briefcase and the one-gallused dirt farmer, parted ways."

49. Charles B. Gomillion oral interview by Hardy T. Frye, 2, interview #19, Hardy T. Frye Oral History Collection, Auburn University Archives (AU), Auburn, Alabama; Robert J. Norrell, "Caste in Steel: Jim Crow Careers in Birmingham, Alabama," *Journal of American History* 73 (December 1986):669–94, esp. 680; Gessner T. McCorvey to John D. McQueen, 24 April 1935 (quotation), 26 April 1935, both in box 64, folder 12, and Frank Boykin to John D. McQueen, 22 January 1935, box 64, folder 1, State Democratic Executive Committee (SDEC) Records, ADAH. On Pauline and Malcolm Dobbs, see Sullivan, *Days of Hope,* 205–6, 215, 216.

50. Henry H. Smith to B. M. Miller, 3 November 1933 (quotation attributed to McCorvey), box SG 19950, folder: Strike Situation, Mobile 1933, Alabama Governors Papers, Benjamin Meek Miller Papers, ADAH; *Alabama Magazine,* 28 March 1938, 3 (second quotation).

51. *Alabama Magazine,* 1 May 1939, 3 (first quotation), 28 August 1939, 15 (second quotation).

52. Painter, *The Narrative of Hosea Hudson,* 260, 266 (first quotation); *Alabama Magazine,* 14 November 1938, 3 (second quotation).

53. *Alabama Magazine,* 14 November 1938, 3 (quotation).

54. O. D. Street to Wendell Wilkie, 30 July 1940 (quotation), box 10, folder: Republican Political Correspondence, Oliver Day Street Papers, ADAH. Wilkie won only Winston County in Alabama, as FDR cruised to victory with a 200,000-plus vote margin. See Sledge, "The Alabama Republican Party, 1865–1978," (Ph.D. diss., Auburn University, 1998), 127–29.

55. Tindall, *The Disruption of the Solid South,* 34 (quotation); Wayne Greenhaw, *Elephants in the Cottonfields: Ronald Reagan and the New Republican South* (New York: Macmillan, 1982), 50.

56. Sample DeBardeleben-Alabama Fuel and Iron Company advertisements on behalf of Wilkie appeared in *Alabama Magazine,* 22 July 1940, 4 (first quotation), 11 November 1940, 6 (second and third quotations).

57. Ibid., 15 July 1940, 3 (second and fourth quotations), 22 July 1940, 3 (third quotation), 5 (first quotation).

58. Carr letter reprinted in its entirety, ibid., 22 July 1940, 5–7 (quoted).

59. Ibid., 29 July 1940, 5 (first quotation); Major Squirm column, ibid., 4 November 1940, 15 (second and third quotations).

60. Ibid., 29 July 1940, 5 (McMillan quotation), 6 (Thompson quotation), 7–10.

61. See ibid., 5 August 1940, 6, 7 (first quotation), 12 August 1940, 5 (second quotation). In Mobile, George H. Denniston, a leader of the Alabama State League of Young Democrats, resigned his post and announced his support of the Republican Wilkie. See ibid., 19 August 1940, 5–6. A Mobile native singled out the NLRB as evidence of the New Deal's "communistic employees" in concluding that the Democratic Party has been "taken over by foreign philosophies just as France has been taken over by her enemies." See L. W. Mabry, Mobile, to ed., ibid., 4 November 1940, 14 (quoted).

62. Robert H. Malone, Dothan, to ed., ibid., 4 November 1940, 14 (quoted). Mrs. A. Y. Malone of Dothan served as a Democratic National Committeewoman. See also ibid., 14 November 1938, 15; 19 August 1940, 4 (DeBardeleben quotation), 5–7; 4 November 1940, 8; 11 November 1940, 15. Birmingham's Reverend A. J. Dailey appeared as a featured speaker in the Wilkie caravan.

63. Radio address delivered by Gessner T. McCorvey, SDEC chair, 14 September 1940, 1, 2, 5 (quoted), LPR 99, box 81, folder 12, SDEC Records, ADAH. National Democratic committeeman Marion Rushton as well as Governor Frank Dixon assisted McCorvey in holding the regular Democratic line in 1940. See *Alabama Magazine*, 11 November 1940, 6. For the attacks on the caravan, see ibid., 4 November 1940, 8.

64. V. O. Key Jr., *Southern Politics in State and Nation* (1949; reprint, Knoxville: University of Tennessee Press, 1984), 5–6.

65. *Alabama Magazine*, 11 November 1940, 3 (second and third quotations), 5 (first quotation).

66. Ibid., editorial, 4 November 1940, 3 (quoted). While our historical interpretations have not always overlapped precisely, the author wishes to express his profound and public gratitude to Wayne Flynt for the exceptional example he has provided of intellectual curiosity, Reformist passion, and boundless support and charity of purpose.

7

"Wallaceism is an insidious and treacherous type of disease"

The 1970 Alabama Gubernatorial Election and the "Wallace Freeze" on Alabama Politics

Gordon E. Harvey

The 1970 Democratic gubernatorial primary election in Alabama is widely considered the nastiest in state history. That election saw George Wallace use the divisive and destructive politics of race to defeat Albert Brewer, who had assumed the governorship in 1968 after Wallace's wife, Lurleen, succumbed to cancer in the middle of her term. After a relatively clean primary, Brewer outpolled Wallace 42 to 41 percent with a lead of almost 8,000 votes, although both fell short of the necessary 50 percent needed to secure the nomination. Brewer received virtually all the black vote while splitting the white vote with Wallace. In the runoff Wallace used race to destroy Brewer's chances at winning, dashing any hopes that the state would move past the political intransigence that prevented it from addressing serious problems such as illiteracy and poverty. As Alabama's political nadir, the 1970 election offers an excellent example of the destructiveness of race in politics. One of the last skirmishes in the struggle for the direction of Alabama's Democratic Party, the race was the last best chance for the state to enter the new politically moderate, post–Civil Rights era in the South. The election also dashed a slowly growing impetus for reform begun by the moderate Brewer during his short tenure. In short, the 1970 election brought Alabamians to a crossroads at which they faced a choice to pursue the state's past or its future.[1]

Although in 1970 it failed to offer a candidate in the gubernatorial election, the state Republican Party had enjoyed limited growth in the early 1960s. For Alabama's nascent Republican Party, 1962 represented a coming out of sorts. The results of that year's elections revealed cracks in the foundation of the state's long dominant Democratic Party. That year George

Wallace defeated the liberal James E. "Big Jim" Folsom and the moderate Ryan deGraffenreid to win the Democratic nomination for governor, a victory that assured him the governor's chair. In that same election all of Alabama's incumbent congressmen won reelection, but Republicans were finally competitive as Tandy Little became the first Republican elected from Montgomery to the state legislature since Reconstruction. Although more Republicans lost than won in statewide elections, their few victories were notable and their losses were more competitive than ever, not only in Alabama but across the region as well.[2]

Not all of Alabama's Democratic incumbents had it easy that year. Lister Hill, the state's senior U.S. senator, serving since 1938, faced the most serious challenge of his political career. Hill had sponsored such important legislation as the Rural Telephone Act, the Rural Housing Act, the Vocational Education Act, and the National Defense Education Act and was father of the National Institutes of Health, the Hospital and Health Center Construction Act (Hill-Burton Act of 1946). But in 1962 he barely survived a Republican challenge to his seat. Hill had long been associated with the New Deal and had succeeded in bringing to his impoverished state dozens of important government services and millions of federal dollars. He and his fellow Alabama congressmen were so closely associated with New Deal liberalism that in 1947 *The Nation* judged Alabama, then under Governor Big Jim Folsom, the most liberal state in the nation. Liberal Alabama congressmen such as Hill, Carl Elliott, Bob Jones, Albert Rains, and Kenneth Roberts were successful as long as race was not an issue. All this changed in the wake of the 1948 presidential election, which saw Dixie's Democrats split from the national party over Harry Truman's civil rights positions. Those politicians who had once sidestepped race as an issue in their service to the state were haunted by it and hunted for it. Remaining loyal to the national Democratic Party ensured that they could continue to funnel millions of much-needed federal dollars to the state, but race soon became a millstone around their necks.[3]

An embittered Hill never recovered from his narrow 1962 victory; he retired six years later (replaced by Wallace associate Jim Allen) and remained baffled by what he perceived as ungrateful Alabama voters clouded by the politics of race. His slim margin of victory over Republican Jim Martin, a Gadsden businessman, by 50.9 percent to 49.1 percent, a mere 6,803 votes, proved an ominous sign for the future of the state's Democratic loyalists. Martin had traveled the state quoting his hero Barry Goldwater, criticizing Hill's loyalty to the party of John Kennedy and calling for "a return to the spirit of '61—1861."[4] Although Hill had consistently voted against civil rights legislation, the *Dothan Eagle* concluded that Hill had "lost touch with the people back home." George Wallace's home county of Barbour voted over-whelmingly for Martin while electing Wallace and every other Democrat on the ballot, leaving no doubts that the political landscape in Alabama had changed.[5]

The Hill-Martin contest led many in the state to proclaim the arrival of a two-party system. But signs of competition had existed since 1948, when the Democratic Party splintered into state's rights and loyalist factions. The split was reflected in Alabama politics and within the state's Democratic Party in an increasing sense after 1948 and erupted further by 1962.[6] Fac-tionalism within the state's Democratic Party caused state party leaders, called "old line Democrats" by the *Montgomery Advertiser*, great concern. One member of the state Democratic Executive Committee expressed his greatest fear in a fit of extreme prescience: "Alabama might go Republican all the way in 1964." To prevent the state's presidential electors from bolting and voting for third-party candidates, as all eleven had in 1948 and six of eleven had in 1960, the committee debated, but declined, to require them to vote for the national nominee. But such a measure had little chance without Wallace's unlikely support. Earlier in the year he had expressed his desire that the state's Democrats disassociate themselves totally from the national party, later rendered a moot point when 69.5 percent of Alabama voters backed Republican Barry Goldwater for president in 1964.[7]

In 1962, national party loyalists, such as state party executive commit-tee chairman Judge Roy Mayhall, controlled the state executive committee, while George Wallace, no friend to national Democrats, controlled the gov-ernor's office. Powerful and popular with voters, Wallace obviously held the upper hand, but Mayhall was determined to keep "old liners" in control. Dis-turbed by Wallace's defiant campaign language regarding the federal govern-ment and integration, Mayhall publicly and privately urged Wallace to pre-serve law and order when responding to school integration. He also rallied loyalists to fight Wallace's power in the statehouse. In a speech before the Young Men's Business Club of Birmingham shortly after the 1962 general election, Mayhall called for "calm, restrained leadership" and for Wallace to obey federal court orders regarding integration. This broadside against Wal-lace resulted in Mayhall's vilification by Wallace supporters. Mayhall was a former Wallace supporter himself and had been a key supporter of Wallace's victory in his native Walker County. But since then, as the *Montgomery Ad-*

vertiser reported, Mayhall had taken to "crying havoc over Wallace's politics." The two severely disagreed on the future of the state party. Wallace urged a break, while Mayhall called for loyalty to the national party in good times and bad. In the months after the 1948 Dixiecrat revolt, Mayhall had been the man assigned to bring back into the fold those who had bolted. And he now opposed Wallace's plans to break with Kennedy in 1964: "To lash out at the Kennedys because you are disturbed about integration makes about as much sense as kicking a tree because you've run your car into it." The *Montgomery Advertiser* agreed in part with Mayhall about Democratic loyalty for the 1964 election, calling it "hillbilly cawn" to push the third party route in order to deny Kennedy Alabama's support. Alabama Democrats were fractured not only by their disagreements over national party loyalty but also geographically, with a northern wing (Birmingham and northbound—industrial and hill country) less interested in race and a southern wing (the southern two-thirds of the state, which comprised the black belt and wiregrass) dominated by Wallace and the politics of race.[8] Most of Alabama's more liberal congressmen and moderate state politicians (including Brewer) hailed from the northern region of the state, with the exception of Hill, who came from Montgomery during the less racially dominated New Deal years. In this early 1960s battle for control of the party, the victory was Wallace's as he repositioned the state party in a move from loyalty to defiance.[9]

Alabama Republicans in 1963 looked optimistically to the future. In Georgia, Republicans broke the Democratic hold on the state senate and elected two of their own to that body. Alabama Republicans had effectively challenged such "liberals" as Lister Hill, drawing the attention of the nation. Even the state's leading Democrats predicted quick Republican growth. But all became moot as George Wallace instituted what journalist and historian Jack Bass called the "Wallace freeze" on Alabama politics.[10] In challenging the national Democratic Party for being too liberal while holding high the banner of segregation and conservatism, Wallace removed from political play every issue with which Republicans had made their successful gains against Hill. Alabama Republicans found their quiver empty. In 1966, Lurleen Wallace, running for governor in place of her husband who was constitutionally prohibited from consecutive terms, soundly defeated Jim Martin 63.4 percent to 31 percent. The Wallace name's multilevel appeal to Alabama voters, who were at once afraid of liberals, militants, and foreigners, prevented the further growth of the state's Republican Party while also forestalling in Alabama until 1982 the biracial coalition-building that had taken place in other southern state Democratic organizations in the late 1960s. Alabama's Democrats remained under the spell of Wallace and his cult of personality long after the rest of the South adjusted and moved away from Jim Crow politics.[11]

Into this maelstrom walked Albert Brewer. The only person in Alabama history to hold the offices of speaker of the house, lieutenant governor, and governor in succession, Brewer was a symbol to many of the promise of the New South, a foreshadowing of what the state could become after the Wallace era. But he soon became a victim in the war for control of the Democratic Party and a possible barrier to Wallace's presidential aspirations. Wallace based his presidential aspirations on a class warfare theme with muted, and sometimes not so muted, calls for law and order and control of "undesirables" and "militants." Supporting him were thousands of disaffected whites from around the nation who heeded his calls to stand up against a federal government obsessed with foreign aid that ignored the working class and to fight for law and order and help end the chaos created by "militants." The rise of the civil rights movement and the growth in numbers of black voters, which dramatically transformed the Democratic Party, fueled Wallace's popularity among whites, contributing to the rise of the "angry white male," while contributing to Brewer's electoral strength among blacks.[12]

By the mid-1960s, the system of segregation and disfranchisement that had dominated the region was falling apart. The 1964 Civil Rights Act and the Voting Rights Act of 1965 sounded the death knell for black political repression in the region.[13] By 1967, African-American voter registration skyrocketed in the South, growing 72.6 percent, with huge gains coming in Mississippi and Alabama. This increase contributed to the rise of racially moderate southern politicians as 52.1 percent of eligible blacks in the South were registered to vote by 1967. In 1965 Alabama, fewer than 93,000 blacks were registered to vote; by 1967 that figure had more than doubled to 248,432.[14] The impact of the 1965 Voting Rights Act was no greater at any time than in the elections of 1970. Throughout the South, well-educated, racially moderate, and reform-minded southern politicians won gubernatorial elections against segregationist opponents. Educated, young, and progressive, they represented a new style of leadership in the South.[15]

Albert Brewer fit this mold. Like many Alabama politicians, he owed much of his political success to his association with Wallace. Like Wallace, he entered the legislature during Big Jim Folsom's administration and supported many of Folsom's measures. Later handpicked by Wallace to be speaker of the house in 1963, Brewer enjoyed Wallace's support when he ran for lieutenant governor in 1966. As speaker, Brewer joined with Wallace, and

virtually all the state legislature, to formally protest federal school desegregation guidelines, and he was not above railing at federal judges about the
speed of court-ordered desegregation. Before becoming governor, Brewer remained relatively quiet on the issue. That he chafed at Federal District Judge
Frank M. Johnson's court orders for desegregation was not simply an outright defense of segregation. Brewer at heart was a gradualist, and he wanted
integration to take place at a slower pace than federal courts had ordered.
This notion was rooted in his fear that fast and forced integration would
exacerbate and accelerate white flight, contributing to a rapid erosion of the
tax base for public schools and preventing meaningful and peaceful integration from occurring. If desegregation did not proceed at a calmer pace than
the courts allowed, Brewer argued, there may be few public schools left to
integrate. His argument fell on deaf ears as federal courts had lost patience
with recalcitrance and delays of any sort from his predecessor in the governor's office.[16]

Prohibited from succeeding himself, in 1966 George Wallace ran his wife
Lurleen for governor. In that same election Brewer won the office of lieutenant governor with the Wallace stamp of approval. Lurleen's term was short-
ened when she succumbed to cancer, and Brewer assumed the governorship
in May 1968. Most people welcomed the new governor, who, at forty-three,
was the youngest in state history and in the nation at the time. His association with the Wallaces and his broad-based popularity with legislators from
rural and urban areas ensured, if not success, then at least a lengthy honey-
moon.[17]

Brewer's Wallace connection quickly became a problem. Observers inside
and outside the state speculated on whether the new governor could be his
own man. He was different from Wallace, they observed. Less inclined to rail
at federal authorities and more apt to push reform and a rational approach,
he risked much if he took too progressive a course. The *Montgomery Inde-*
pendent concluded that Brewer and Wallace were "firmly lashed together by
their past." Each had to walk a fine line. To the *Independent,* their mutual goal
appeared to be "to achieve separation without looking foolishly inconsistent.
If Brewer was sufficiently competent to be selected as Wallace's speaker of
the house and to mastermind the legislative destiny of many Wallace programs, how does he suddenly become a blackguard? Likewise, if Wallace is
the great man that Brewer often described him to be, earning Brewer's complete fidelity in the process, it won't be easy for Brewer now to rip the hide
off Wallace's back."[18] If he wanted to be governor once more, Wallace had to
dispel the growing sentiment among some of his own supporters that Brewer

had done a good job as governor. And Brewer had to attack the man to whom many of his own supporters were attached, either politically or emotionally. "Brewer does not hanker for a confrontation with Wallace," wrote the *Atlanta Journal*, but was "itching to be his own man."[19]

During 33 months as governor, Brewer established his autonomy by stopping kickbacks to agents in the statehouse, providing state employees with a modest raise, and establishing by executive order Alabama's first code of ethics. And in 1969, he implemented one of the most sweeping educational reform packages in state history, adding more than $100 million to public education over a two-year period while revising the way the state funded education. Brewer was the first governor since Big Jim Folsom to attempt a sincere, albeit failed, effort to reform the state's archaic and unfair constitution of 1901. Brewer tried to chart a middle course with regard to school integration, which he did not oppose. Instead he sought to integrate at a slower pace than that desired by federal courts—whose patience had worn thin from Wallace's past shenanigans—to prevent the sort of massive pubic school exodus of whites that had begun in earnest in Alabama and throughout the South. Brewer exhibited his racial moderation by appointing African Americans to positions on the newly created Alabama Commission on Higher Education, Alabama Education Study Commission, Constitutional Revision Commission, and Law Enforcement Planning Commission. By most accounts, the youthful governor brought a new attitude to Dexter Avenue, one that shifted the focus of state government from recalcitrance and intransigence to responsiveness and reform. To reporters, he stood in remarkable contrast to the defiant, brooding Wallace. One veteran legislative reporter remarked that with Wallace, "you ask him if it is going to rain and you get a fifteen minute speech on the federal judiciary."[20] Easygoing, open, with a sharp but good-natured wit, Brewer, to the *Anniston Star*, was an "entirely different man . . . working at the enterprises of peace with deep and sincere purpose." He struck such an optimistic chord with the *Montgomery Advertiser* that its editors endorsed him for governor two years before the election.[21]

Brewer began his campaign in October 1969, one of the earliest starts in state history, with the simple goal of producing as much public support as possible in an effort to dissuade Wallace from mounting a challenge. To that end, Brewer courted Wallace supporters throughout the year. Wallace hinted toward running as early as June 1969 by having an old friend, newspaperman Grover Hall, float trial balloons in his paper that hinted at a Wallace candidacy. Once, while Brewer was out of the state, Wallace called on legislative leaders, stoked the flames of federal court defiance, and promised he could do better "than some of these sissy folks have done."[22] Throughout 1969 each man campaigned without mentioning the other, at which the *Montgomery Advertiser* remarked, "If the backdoor campaign of Alabama continues its present pace, both Governor Albert Brewer and George Wallace will be going to the polls disavowing any intention of running against each other."[23]

Brewer secured endorsements from Winton "Red" Blount II, Alabama Republican and Nixon postmaster general, as well as Vice President Spiro T. Agnew. Newspapers reported that the GOP planned to support Brewer financially and "in any way possible without becoming publicly identified with him." The *Montgomery Advertiser* cautioned that "a GOP kiss in this state could be deadly," a caveat echoed by national political commentators Rowland Evans and Robert Novak. Such a strategy, they posited, might play right into Wallace's hands and "wrap around Brewer's neck what Wallace will call an unholy coalition of the Republican and Democratic national parties, militant blacks and country club millionaires, the White House and Alabama liberals."[24] The paper lamented the situation: "While much of the South seems to be heading toward a viable Republican party, Alabama is still in a limbo lovingly created and nurtured by Wallace. And yet, it is the rusting, dilapidated machinery of one-party domination which Wallace will use, presumably, if he does make his bid to oust Albert the Pretender from the House of Wallace next year."[25]

President Richard Nixon had long considered Wallace a threat to his presidency, especially after the 1968 presidential election, in which Wallace polled almost 10 million votes, the highest total of all third-party candidates up to that time. The 1970 contest offered Nixon an opportunity to perhaps impair any Wallace hopes for another run at the presidency in 1972, for the candidate who failed to win office in his own state surely could not win a national election. Even though Nixon had been unimpressed with Brewer after a 1969 meeting, he still funneled $400,000 to the Brewer campaign.[26]

"As we enter the decade of the seventies," Brewer predicted in an early 1970 Birmingham speech, "Alabama stands on the threshold of [its] greatest era." Promising to be a progressive governor, Brewer ran on his record— "full-time hard work"—a less than oblique reference to Wallace's constant absence from Alabama during his national campaigns.[27] The *Birmingham News* concluded that under any other circumstances, Brewer might be considered a "shoo-in." Still, that no one could predict with any certainty the outcome of the race was a testament to how strong Brewer had become politically. A February 1970 poll gave Brewer a commanding lead of 58 to 42 percent, seemingly confirming the conventional wisdom of the day.[28]

Newspaper and organizational endorsements revealed the geographic and demographic fracture in Alabama politics. Brewer received endorsements from the state's larger urban newspapers: the *Birmingham News, Anniston Star, Montgomery Advertiser, Mobile Register, Decatur Daily, Alabama Journal,* and *Huntsville Times.* Wallace received endorsements from newspapers in rural areas such as Andalusia, Dothan, Greensboro, Sumiton, and Centreville. While Brewer received the organizational endorsement of the AFL–CIO, Wallace was supported by many of that group's rank-and-file. The *Atlanta Journal* pleaded condescendingly for Alabama to do the right thing: "For Alabama's sake, for the South's sake, how nice it would be if the people of our neighboring state recognized that in Brewer they have had a governor more interested in Alabama than catapulting himself into national politics."[29] Even the Alabama League of Municipalities, with a long tradition of political neutrality, came "within an eyelash" of endorsing Brewer.[30]

Brewer spent a great deal of time in Jefferson County. With more than 270,000 registered voters, Jefferson County was vital to Brewer's campaign. Between March 23 and May 5, Brewer appeared there thirty times, promising to be a "full-time governor" and offering a "record of solid accomplishment that no wild promises can outdo. I will never make you ashamed you voted for Albert Brewer as your governor." The state was at a crossroads, he declared, "you're going to have to decide if we go forward or backward, we can't stand still. We deserve better than we've had it in the past."[31]

Wallace's campaign focused on relief for Alabamians from the federal courts, the federal government, and "militants." Even though Wallace promised a "bold and imaginary" legislative program, crowds at Wallace rallies generally came alive only when he promised that he would force Washington to "give us back our schools." "Every time a scalawag judge buses a student," Wallace stated, "he does so in violation of the law." He pledged to audiences that "I'll look 'em straight in the eye and tell 'em Alabama's all right, always has been all right, and we're right and you're wrong." Wallace's favorite gimmick, which illustrated well the fracture within the state Democratic Party, was to look under a prop table or cot and discover with mock surprise all his political enemies: "Well what do I have here, there's all the Humphrey-Muskie Democrats of Alabama, all of them right under there, and there's the chairman of the Democratic Executive Committee, and there's some militants, and I do declare, . . . there's some of the large newspapers in Alabama . . . and a special interest . . . well politics makes strange bedfellows, but the folks in bed with our movement are the people of Alabama."[32]

Wallace also reached an unsurprising level of nastiness. He promised voters he would make the governor's mansion alcohol-free, even though it had been so since the teetotaling Brewer became governor. Several pastors praised Wallace's antialcohol pledge while also endorsing Wallace's close relationship with the Almighty. Pastor Jesse Gann of Luverne's First Baptist Church urged his fellow pastors to support "one of the finest Christian men I have ever known." A vote for Wallace, wrote Gann, was a vote "for the highest good of all our people."[33]

Wallace operatives circulated doctored photos showing Brewer standing with controversial Black Muslim leader Elijah Muhammad and with boxer Cassius Clay. They were intended to further sully Brewer's name and link him with a recent attempt by black Muslims to establish a commune in Alabama and with controversy surrounding the possibility of a Clay fight in the state. The Wallace campaign's implication was clear: Brewer was the candidate of blacks, militants, and worst of all, at least to Wallace supporters, black militants. The original photos, from Brewer's campaign literature, showed him with country singer Johnny Cash.[34]

In an exercise reminiscent of the McCarthy era and an example of the extent of Wallace's political control over the state, Wallace campaign staff members collected data about Brewer supporters and disloyal Wallace supporters for future reprisals. Wallace loyalists sent to the campaign staff lists of Brewer supporters in their counties and collected data on people in each county who supported Brewer, or "openly fought" Wallace, during the campaign. Sage Lyons wrote Wallace to tattle on State Senator E. O. Eddins, who supported Brewer even though he had pledged fealty to Wallace. One Wallace campaign worker from Colbert and Lauderdale counties wrote Wallace to be watchful of disloyalty: "I don't want to see anyone who fought you try to come in the back door and get on your team. You will be surprised to know the elected officials, both county and municipal, who tried to defeat you. We know who they are and will give you their names."[35]

For all the attacks against him and his supporters, Brewer followed the advice of campaign advisers to remain out of the campaign gutter and conduct a clean campaign. He refused to match insults with Wallace and continued to stress that he would not be an absentee chief executive, alluding to Wallace's frequent out-of-state campaign trips, but rather a "full-time governor." Brewer dismissed rumors that he was catering to black voters, wanting to be the "black candidate," and scoffed at death threats against both him and his wife made in the later days of the campaign.[36]

The result of the primary was reported as far away as Jerusalem as Brewer shocked Wallace in a close contest, although both fell short of a majority required for outright victory. Brewer outpolled Wallace 42 percent to 41 percent, with a group of also-rans garnering the remainder, which prevented Brewer from an outright victory. A total of seven candidates, including former governor Big Jim Folsom, had entered the race. Segregationist and former Wallace speech writer Asa Carter—who called Brewer the state's "number one white nigger"—and millionaire businessman and perennial candidate Charles Woods stood out among the insignificant. Woods polled the most votes in the second tier group, 149,887, and forced the election into a runoff. It is likely that without Woods, Brewer would have defeated Wallace outright as both Woods and Brewer appealed to the same reform instincts in voters and to the same groups of voters. If anything, Brewer's slim lead at the end of the first primary proved the prophetess Jeanne Dixon partly correct: On a visit to Montgomery the day before the primary, she predicted a Brewer victory but failed to foresee a runoff.[37]

Brewer won only 29 counties to Wallace's 38, although Brewer outpolled Wallace by more than 8,000 votes. As expected, Brewer took most of North Alabama and the urban areas, except Dothan and Mobile. Wallace ran well in rural areas except for the black belt, in which blacks held a voting majority. Those counties went to Brewer, especially after he received the endorsement of John Cashin's black-oriented Alabama Democratic Conference. Brewer could also look to Alabama history as he went into the runoff: no candidate since 1914 had won a runoff after placing second in the primary.[38]

Among the millions taken aback by Brewer's strong showing, Richard Nixon saw an opportunity. Obsessed with Wallace for years, Nixon and his advisers saw the perfect opening to damage Wallace politically, if not drive him altogether out of national prominence. Before the first primary, Nixon forwarded $100,000 to the Brewer camp in a bumbling exchange of money between Brewer's press secretary Bob Ingram and Nixon operative Herbert Kalmbach. Now the administration funneled another $300,000 to the Brewer campaign. The Nixon money eventually comprised almost a third of Brewer's total campaign budget.[39]

But money would not be enough. Brewer had been warned that Wallace was no mere mortal. "With Wallace, you aren't up against flesh and blood," one person wrote the governor, "You are competing against witchcraft, hypnotism and the Devil." Wallace felt vulnerable and lingered on the verge of defeat since he first ran for governor in 1958. To compound his fears and feed his paranoia, several Wallace supporters suggested that he withdraw from the race to avoid an embarrassing defeat. Withdrawing might be considered the stately thing to do and could help remake Wallace's image into that of concerned statesman for the 1972 presidential campaign. In the first campaign, Wallace had portrayed himself as a defender of states' rights ideology and spokesman for the working man. He abandoned that strategy after his narrow defeat and resorted to familiar tactics to win the runoff. Wallace's brother Gerald explained that the campaign planned to "throw the niggers around his neck," while another aide explained that Wallace intended to "promise the moon and holler 'nigger.' "[40]

While Brewer hoped that Alabama was "past the point of putting class against class, race against race, and ethnic group against ethnic group," Wallace proved otherwise as thousands of leaflets turned up in the state's rural areas and working-class white sections of urban areas.[41] Leaving little to the imagination, one leaflet displayed a photograph of a white girl surrounded by a group of black boys and implored white voters to "WAKE UP ALABAMA! BLACKS VOW TO TAKE OVER ALABAMA." The Klan distributed flyers suggesting that Brewer's two young daughters had been impregnated by black men.[42] Another smear sheet asked, "Can only 23% of the white people and their Negro friends elect the next governor? Not if you vote for your own kind." Still other flyers falsely reported that if Brewer were elected, 100 white state employees and 50 white state troopers would lose their jobs to blacks. A Wallace radio ad asked white husbands if they wanted their wives pulled over at night by black state troopers.[43]

If the runoff campaign brought race-baiting to a new low, it brought thousands of new voters to the polls. Between May 5 and June 2, more than 30,000 people registered to vote, which guaranteed to exceed the record turnout of 1,019,680 set in the primary.[44] Many of the new voters, including whites from rural areas, lent their support to Wallace as he won the runoff with 51.5 percent of the vote with the largest turnout in Alabama political history: 1,085,783. The election, wrote Dan Carter, "became a referendum on Alabama voters' admiration for macho politicians and their fear of blacks."[45] It was no surprise that Brewer maintained his strong support from the black belt and urban areas with middle- to upper-middle-class voters. But he lost support in North Alabama, while Wallace succeeded in turning reform-minded Woods supporters to his column. Wallace picked up almost 140,000 votes to Brewer's gain of about 100,000. The only areas in which Brewer won a majority of the vote were large metro areas and the black belt.[46]

With his dream of winning his own term as governor shattered, Brewer found it hard to restrain his bitterness and disappointment. "This is the dirtiest race I've ever seen in my political life," he declared, "It was Nigger, Nigger, Nigger all over again." He had tried to sidestep the race issue, as he had deftly done throughout most of his political career, but Wallace would not let race go.[47]

Condolences flooded Brewer's office. Maine's Senator Edmund Muskie praised Brewer for being a strong, if lonely, voice of southern moderation. Black political leaders praised Brewer for his campaign. Birmingham's Louis Willie praised the "man who refused to stoop to appeals of bigotry and race hatred in order to win the governor's chair." Another of Birmingham's most prominent black businessmen, A. G. Gaston, echoed Willie's sympathies. Gaston expressed pride in the governor and his "greater service to the citizens of Alabama by your conduct and we shall be the future beneficiaries."[48] On election eve, Birmingham mayor George Seibels had written a heartfelt note to Brewer: "It is after midnight," wrote Seibels, "and within a few hours people (by the thousands) will be going to the polls in what I consider the most important election we've ever had in Alabama. You have played the game fairly and decently and you and all working with you are to be commended. Your foe (or his supporters) bring anything but credit to our beloved state."[49] One Alabama citizen did not mince words in explaining why Brewer lost: "the scum allways rises to the top."[50]

Perhaps the most notable condolence came from former Alabama congressman Carl Elliott. He had a distinguished career in the House of Representatives and was one of Alabama's few voices of racial moderation in the wake of *Brown v. Board* (1954). "Today has been a day of vicarious misery for me," Elliott wrote Brewer, "I felt for you as I saw the master of hate and racism unleash his vicious campaign against you." Elliott had seen his political career destroyed when he fought Wallace in the mid-1960s, a battle which destroyed him financially and politically. He had hoped for a better outcome for Brewer. "But, as I'm sure you know, by now, Wallaceism is an insidious and treacherous type of disease," he wrote, "It slips up on one, ensnares him, destroys him, and moves to the next victim." Elliott implored Brewer to not give up the fight. Alabamians, he told the young governor, "so much need a leader to appeal to their better, instead of their baser, instincts. You did that and I salute you for it."[51]

A touched Brewer assured the former congressman that had he to do it over, he would change nothing: "Only you know what a campaign with Wallace truly involves, and I share your thoughts that there is only one honorable way to run a campaign." Brewer assured Elliott that his hope for a "New Alabama" was not dead: "I remain confident that our state will one day realize all of the things that you and I have hoped for and worked for, you much more successfully than I. When that day comes, we can rejoice that we had a small part in realizing that dream."[52]

Alabama's chance to enter the new post–Civil Rights South died for a short time with Brewer's defeat. Indeed, every southern state except Alabama elected a New South governor after 1970. Alabama still has not. In an ironic turn, it took a tragic death to provide Alabama a New South governor in Albert Brewer. His racial moderation, his businessman's zeal for efficiency in government, and his concern as a parent for education reform made Brewer an early model of the New South governor that was to dominate the 1970s South. Paradoxically, Alabama may have had the region's first New South governor, even if it never elected one. Brewer's defeat at the hands of George Wallace dashed the hope for a New Alabama for which people such as Carl Elliott sacrificed their political and financial lives. The 1970 election also continued a disturbing, but not surprising, trend in Alabama politics: In each gubernatorial election between 1958 and 1970, Alabama voters voted for the more segregationist candidate.[53]

Wallace's second administration was not a rousing success. He spent more time out of the state than he spent in it and failed to address those pressing problems that had long plagued Alabama, namely education, poverty, and jobs. The power and influence with the legislature that he enjoyed in the early 1960s had all but disappeared following reapportionment of the state legislature in 1966, which saw a transfer of power from the black belt to urban areas, inaugurating a period of urban legislative power for which such areas had long clamored. The result was Wallace's inability in 1971 to pass general and education budgets through the legislature. He was forced eventually to rely on his friend Harry Brock of Birmingham Central Bank and Trust to provide a bailout for the state that year. Brewer had enjoyed a much better relationship with rural and urban blocs in the state legislature and was successful at reform in his short period in office. If, as Dan Carter posits, Wallace "laid the foundation for the conservative counterrevolution that reshaped American politics in the 1970s and 1980s," he did Alabama no favors in doing so. The state was arguably worse off after his years as governor than it was before them.[54]

"The Wallace freeze" on Alabama politics, as Jack Bass and Walter deVries described it, prevented the development of a true two-party system in Alabama and stalled the development of Democratic intraparty competition until the late 1970s, when the Wallace mystique was all that remained of a terribly ill and increasingly irrelevant governor. After its relative success of 1962, the Alabama Republican Party had to wait until 1980 to elect a senator—former Vietnam POW Jeremiah Denton, who served only one term—and to wait until 1986 to elect a governor in Guy Hunt, who won election only after an embarrassing episode of fratricidal infighting by the Democratic candidates during their primary. In 1978, lifelong Republican Fob James changed his party affiliation in order to win the governor's chair, which served not only as a bow to Wallace's influence on the political culture of the state but also a condemnation of the state's weak Republican Party. And it was not until 1982 that George Wallace, seeing the changing nature of the Alabama electorate, apologized to black voters and won their support in the 1982 election, in which he won one-third of the black vote and bested popular Republican and Montgomery mayor Emory Folmar 59.6 percent to 40.4 percent. The 1982 election ushered into the Alabama Democratic Party the biracialism that had existed in other southern states since the early 1970s. For a brief moment in 1970, paramount changes in southern politics, the legacy of the civil rights movement, and Albert Brewer's performance as governor almost thawed Wallace's freeze on Alabama politics. It came close to ushering the state, if not into full membership in the New South, then at least into a transitional period where candidates no longer had to lay sacrifices on the altar of race before addressing the state's most pressing social and economic problems.[55]

Notes

1. *Birmingham News*, 31 May 1970; Bob Ingram, *That's the Way I Saw It* (Montgomery: B & E Press, 1986), 5; V. O. Key, *Southern Politics in State and Nation*, new ed. (Knoxville: University of Tennessee Press, 1984), 37–41.

2. *Montgomery Advertiser*, 7, 8, 11 November, 16 December 1962; *Birmingham News*, 16 December 1962.

3. William Dean Barnard, "Southern Liberalism in Triumph and Frustration: Alabama Politics, 1946–1950" (Ph.D. diss., University of Virginia, 1971), 1–10, 17–24, 53–104, 129–32, 133–60, 210–24, 278–329; Virginia van der Veer Hamilton, *Lister Hill: Statesman from the South* (Chapel Hill: University of North Carolina Press, 1987), 75, 104–8, 110–30, 200–212, 291–92. For an excellent study on the end of the solid Democratic South, see Kari Frederickson, *The Dixiecrat Revolt and the End of the Solid South, 1932–1968* (Chapel Hill: University of North Carolina Press, 2001). Earl Black and Merle Black point out that southern Democrats were, by and large, able to in-

sulate themselves from Republican attacks by emphasizing their conservatism, but such was not possible in Alabama, because Wallace's influence was too great to be ignored and Hill and fellow Senator John Sparkman were too closely associated with the New Deal; see their *Rise of Southern Republicans* (Cambridge: Harvard University Press, 2002), 114–73.

4. Hill's reelection came with a great deal of help from North Alabama voters, who were more supportive of the national Democratic Party and of Hill's efforts to bring New Deal federal money to the state. See *Montgomery Advertiser,* 4 December 1962. The Martin quote is from Numan V. Bartley and Hugh D. Graham, *Southern Politics and the Second Reconstruction* (Baltimore: Johns Hopkins University Press, 1975), 98–99.

5. In Barbour County, Martin outpolled Hill 1,311 to 1,091. See *Montgomery Advertiser,* 8 November 1962; Wayne Greenhaw, *Elephants in the Cottonfields: Ronald Reagan and the New Republican South* (New York: Macmillan, 1982), 55–57; Hamilton, *Lister Hill,* 210–24, 278–329; Black and Black, *The Rise of Southern Republicans,* 126–28; *Dothan Eagle,* 11 November 1962.

6. Some Alabama Democrats felt confident in the future of their party's rule over the state. Martin's near victory, according to Democrat Ed Reid, was a "flash in the pan deal"; see *Montgomery Advertiser,* 11 November 1962.

7. Ibid.; Alexander P. Lamis, *Southern Politics in the 1990s* (Baton Rouge: Louisiana State University Press, 1999), 19.

8. Earl Black found that in Alabama those areas with a high black population were areas that consistently supported militant segregationist candidates. Those counties with a lower black population tended not to support such candidates. See Earl Black, *Southern Governors and Civil Rights: Racial Segregation as a Campaign Issue in the Second Reconstruction* (Cambridge: Harvard University Press, 1976), 52–58.

9. *Montgomery Advertiser,* 9, 18 December 1962; Alexander Lamis, *The Two-Party South,* 2d expanded ed. (New York: Oxford University Press, 1990), 4–5, 76–92.

10. Jack Bass and Walter Devries, *The Transformation of Southern Politics: Social Change and Political Consequence Since 1945* (New York: New American Library, 1977), 57–86. The two Georgia Republican victories came in Muscogee and Fulton counties; see *Montgomery Advertiser,* 7 November 1962.

11. Lamis, *The Two-Party South,* 76–92; Bass and DeVries, *The Transformation of Southern Politics,* 57–86.

12. After 1970 and especially into the 1980s, a candidate need only spark the imagination of voters to play what many call the "race card." Years of warning against federal intervention in the South's racial traditions had conditioned voters to listen for certain words. In Wallace's case, he warned against myriad and unnamed "outside agitators," "bureaucrats," and "militants." But all knew of whom he spoke—he did

not need to actually identify the target. Politicians' use of this racial code only improved over time. On the changing nature of southern politics and the use of racial code, see the following: Carter, *The Politics of Rage* (New York: Simon & Schuster, 1995), 324–70; Carl Elliott and Michael D'Orso, *The Cost of Courage* (New York: Doubleday, 1992); Merle Black, "Racial Composition of Congressional Districts and Support for Federal Voting Rights in the American South," *Social Science Quarterly* 59 (December 1978):435–50; James M. Glaser, *Race, Campaign Politics, and the Realignment in the South* (New Haven: Yale University Press, 1996); Numan Bartley, *The Rise of Massive Resistance: Race and Politics in the South in the 1950s* (Baton Rouge: Louisiana State University Press, 1969); Bartley and Graham, *Southern Politics and the Second Reconstruction*; Richard Pride, *The Political Use of Racial Narratives: School Desegregation in Mobile, Alabama, 1954–1997* (Urbana: University of Illinois Press, 2002); Frederickson, *The Dixiecrat Revolt*; Morgan Kousser, *Colorblind Injustice: Minority Voting Rights and the Undoing of the Second Reconstruction* (Chapel Hill: University of North Carolina Press, 1999); William Warren Rogers, Robert David Ward, Leah Rawls Atkins, and Wayne Flynt, *Alabama: The History of a Deep South State* (Tuscaloosa: University of Alabama Press, 1994), 566–88; Anne Permaloff and Carl Grafton, *Political Power in Alabama: The More Things Change . . .* (Athens: University of Georgia Press, 1995), 300–306; Lamis, *Southern Politics in the 1990s*, 20.

13. Bartley and Graham, *Southern Politics and the Second Reconstruction*, 18–19, 184–90; Key, *Southern Politics in State and Nation*; Richard L. Ergstrom, "Black Politics and the Voting Rights Act, 1965–1982," in James F. Lea, ed., *Contemporary Southern Politics* (Baton Rouge: Louisiana State University Press, 1988), 83–106; Earl Black and Merle Black, *Politics and Society in the South* (Cambridge: Harvard University Press, 1987), 99.

14. Ergstrom, "Black Politics and the Voting Rights Act," 83–106; Larry Sabato, "New South Governors and the Governorship," in Lea, ed., *Contemporary Southern Politics*, 194–213; Lamis, *The Two-Party South*, 4–5.

15. Sabato, "New South Governors and the Governorship."

16. See *Alabama Journal*, 8 January 1963; Jack Bass, *Taming the Storm: The Life and Times of Judge Frank M. Johnson, Jr. and the South's Fight over Civil Rights* (New York: Anchor Books, 1993), 212–25; Gordon E. Harvey, "Albert P. Brewer, 1968–1971," in Samuel L. Webb and Margaret E. Armbrester, eds., *Alabama Governors: A Political History of the State* (Tuscaloosa: University of Alabama Press, 2001), 235–38.

17. *Montgomery Advertiser*, 16 August, 9, 10 October 1968; *Opelika Daily News*, 10 October 1968; *Alabama Journal*, 4 September 1968.

18. *Montgomery Independent*, 5 March 1970; Permaloff and Grafton, *Political Power in Alabama*, 269–73.

19. *Alabama Journal,* 20 February 1969; *Franklin County (Ala.) Times,* 20 February 1969.

20. *Montgomery Advertiser,* 5 July 1970. For an excellent study of the many failed constitutional reform efforts in Alabama, see Bailey Thompson, ed., *A Century of Controversy: Constitutional Reform in Alabama* (Tuscaloosa: University of Alabama Press, 2002).

21. For a more thorough discussion of education and integration in the Brewer administration, see Gordon E. Harvey, *A Question of Justice: New South Governors and Education, 1968–1976* (Tuscaloosa: University of Alabama Press, 2002). For other elements of Brewer's administration, see chap. 7 of Jeffrey Frederick's excellent dissertation, "Command and Control: George Wallace, Governor of Alabama, 1963–1972" (Ph.D. diss., Auburn University, 2003); Harvey, "Albert P. Brewer"; *Anniston Star,* 31 March 1969; *Birmingham Post-Herald,* 1 January 1969; *Alabama Journal,* 12 March 1969; *Birmingham News,* 19 February 1970; Permaloff and Grafton, *Political Power in Alabama,* 292–93; *Montgomery Advertiser,* 6 August 1968.

22. *Mobile Register,* 26 October 1969; Carter, *The Politics of Rage,* 383; Francis Hare to Brewer, 16 May 1969, Brewer to Francis Hare, 19 May 1969, both in Albert Brewer Personal Papers, Box 19, Alabama Department of Archives and History (ADAH), Montgomery, hereafter cited as Brewer Papers.

23. *Montgomery Advertiser,* 11 December 1969; *Alabama Journal,* 10 December 1969; *Mobile Register,* 26 October 1969; Carter, *The Politics of Rage,* 383; Hare to Brewer, 16 May 1969, Brewer to Hare, 19 May 1969, Brewer Papers.

24. *Houston Post,* 14 December 1969.

25. *Austin (Tex.) American,* 30 December 1969; *Montgomery Advertiser,* 14 December 1969.

26. The story of the $400,000 in Nixon money is best told by Bob Ingram in his hilarious accounting from *That's the Way I Saw It,* 16–22. In an interview with Dan Carter, Harry Dent intimates that Nixon also gave money to the Wallace campaign as a way of hedging his support on the chance that Wallace won the election: Carter interview with Dent, Columbia, S.C., 20 July 1988, in the Dan Carter materials on *The Politics of Rage,* Special Collections, Woodruff Library, Emory University; Carter, *The Politics of Rage,* 328, 384, 504; *Montgomery Advertiser,* 9 January 1970; Permaloff and Grafton, *Political Power in Alabama,* 293–95.

27. The Brewer campaign had conducted a poll shortly before he announced that showed him with a lead over Wallace. Though the results were kept secret, Brewer commented that he was "well satisfied" with the results (*Birmingham News,* 12 February 1970). Brewer's announcement for governor, 10 February 1970, Birmingham, Alabama Governors Papers, Albert Brewer, Speeches, SG 12678, Reel 3; Brewer cam-

paign speech, 16 March 1970, Decatur, Brewer Papers, Box 12; *Montgomery Advertiser,* 11 February 1970; *Birmingham News,* 11 February, 16 March 1970.

28. Bob Ingram writes that the Brewer campaign's own poll numbers had Brewer ahead of Wallace by 18 points as late as April 1. See Ingram, *That's The Way I Saw It,* 12; *Birmingham News,* 11, 12 February 1970; *Alabama Journal,* 26 February 1970.

29. Quoted in *Montgomery Advertiser,* 24 April 1970. Jeffrey J. Frederick notes that a Brewer campaign internal poll gave the governor a 19 percent lead over Wallace in January 1970; see Frederick, "Command and Control."

30. Brewer and Wallace endorsements are listed in the *Birmingham News,* 29 March 1970; see also endorsements in the *Montgomery Advertiser,* 5 April 1970; *Anniston Star,* 19 April 1970; *Birmingham Post-Herald,* 21 April 1970; *Tuscaloosa News,* 6 April 1970; *Geneva Reaper,* 2 April 1970; Brewer press release, 8 April 1970, Brewer Papers, Box 44; *Birmingham News,* 22 March, 8 April 1970; *Montgomery Advertiser,* 3 May 1970; Permaloff and Grafton, *Political Power in Alabama,* 295–96.

31. *Birmingham News,* 24 March, 29 April, 2 May 1970; *Montgomery Advertiser,* 1–3 May 1970; *Charlotte (N.C.) Observer,* 26 April 1970; see also various 1970 Brewer campaign itineraries, Brewer Papers, Boxes 53, 55.

32. Quote from Dan Carter's notes from WSFA-TV Montgomery footage of the 1970 campaign, in Dan Carter materials on *The Politics of Rage; Montgomery Advertiser,* 1 May 1970; *Birmingham News,* 4 April 1970.

33. Brewer's greatest vice seemed to be his consumption at times of up to a dozen Coca-Colas a day. See *Alabama Journal,* 29 April 1970; Pastor Jesse Gann to "Brother Pastors," 26 March 1970, Brewer Papers, Box 49.

34. Brewer campaign newspaper, "The Brewer Journal," in Public Information Subject File, Albert Brewer Administration Papers, SG, 7039, ADAH, Montgomery, hereafter cited as Brewer Administration Papers; "Hale County Supporters for Brewer," n.d. (ca. 1970); Sage Lyons to George Wallace, 8 June 1970, Lee Williams to Wallace, 20 July 1970, Leonard Beard to Wallace, 15 July 1970, all in George C. Wallace Papers, LPR 124, Box 30, Folder 5, ADAH, Montgomery, hereafter cited as Wallace Papers.

35. *Montgomery Advertiser,* 22, 23 April 1970; *Alabama Journal,* 22 April 1970; Permaloff and Grafton, *Political Power in Alabama,* 296–97; Brewer campaign newspaper, "The Brewer Journal," in Public Information Subject File, Brewer Administration Papers.

36. The *Montgomery Advertiser* also credited Woods with preventing Brewer from winning an outright victory. See issues of 4, 6, 7 May 1970; Dan Carter's notes on WSFA-TV Montgomery footage of the 1970 campaign in his notes on *Politics of Rage; Birmingham Post-Herald,* 2 June 1970; Carter, *The Politics of Rage,* 393.

37. Permaloff and Grafton, *Political Power in Alabama,* 296–98; Carter, *The Poli-*

tics of Rage, 391–92; *Montgomery Advertiser,* 7 May 1970; Frederick, "Command and Control."

38. Carter, *The Politics of Rage,* 388–89, 392–93; Ingram, *That's the Way I Saw It,* 16–22.

39. Quotes from Carter, *The Politics of Rage,* 392; Reuben T. McKinley to Brewer, 12 April 1970, Brewer Papers, Box 48; *Montgomery Advertiser,* 8 May 1970.

40. If Brewer ran a restrained and vague campaign before the runoff, he, and Wallace, let the promises flow freely in the runoff. Brewer pledged tax cuts of $17.6 million, including a decrease in automobile tag taxes. He also promised to exempt pharmaceuticals from state sales taxes. Wallace promised voters he would abolish the state sales tax on groceries, as well as decrease utility taxes while increasing homestead exemptions for senior citizens. See *Montgomery Advertiser,* 7–9 May 1970.

41. Carter, *The Politics of Rage,* 392–93; Permaloff and Grafton, *Political Power in Alabama,* 296–98; *Montgomery Advertiser,* 14 May 1970. The 26 July 1970 edition of the Sunday newspaper magazine *Parade* actually published a letter that asked about Brewer's daughters, alleging that they had relationships with black men; a copy of the magazine is in Brewer Papers, Box 50.

42. Ibid.

43. Anti-Brewer flyers, Brewer Papers, Boxes 7, 8, 48–49; Permaloff and Grafton, *Political Power in Alabama,* 297; *Alabama Journal,* 27 May 1970; Carter, *The Politics of Rage,* 393.

44. Brewer to Mrs. Arthur Brewer (no relation), 25 May 1970, Brewer Administration Papers, SG 22637; *Birmingham News,* 31 May 1970; *Montgomery Advertiser,* 14 May 1970. State officials estimated that almost 1.5 million voters actually turned out in May, but many left without voting because of frustration with extremely long lines at polling places. See *Birmingham Post-Herald,* 2 June 1970; *Montgomery Advertiser,* 8, 13 May 1970; Numan V. Bartley and Hugh D. Graham, *Southern Primaries and Elections: County and Precinct Data, 1950–1972* (Baton Rouge: Louisiana State University Press, 1978), 21–22; Alabama Secretary of State, *Gubernatorial Election Results: 1946–1998* (Montgomery, 1998), 25.

45. Carter, *The Politics of Rage,* 394–95; *Gubernatorial Election Results,* 25.

46. Carter, *The Politics of Rage,* 394–95; *Birmingham Post-Herald,* 4 June 1970. See also "Tabulation of Democratic Primary Election, June 2, 1970," in Brewer Administration Papers, SG 22658; Frederick, "Command and Control."

47. *Birmingham News,* 3 June 1970; *Birmingham Post-Herald,* 4 June 1970.

48. Sen. Edmund Muskie to Brewer, 23 June 1970, Brewer Papers, Box 52; Louis J. Willie to Brewer, 4 June 1970, and A. G. Gaston to Brewer, 5 June 1970, both in Brewer Papers, Box 50.

49. George Seibels to Brewer, 2 June 1970, Brewer Papers, Box 50.

50. C.R.M. to Brewer, 3 June 1970, ibid.

51. Carl Elliott to Brewer, 3 June 1970, Brewer Papers, Box 25.

52. Brewer to Carl Elliott, 30 June 1970, ibid.

53. *Birmingham Post-Herald,* 22 September 1970; *Montgomery Advertiser,* 4 June 1970; Rogers et al., *Alabama,* 570–84. In 1998, following an endorsement of Winton Blount by Birmingham mayor Richard Arrington, Fob James supporters distributed flyers which asked many of the same questions asked by Wallace flyers about Brewer relative to black support for Blount. The implication was the same: Blount, like Brewer, was the candidate of the blacks, especially the Arrington political machine in Birmingham, long criticized and vilified by white conservatives. See *Mobile Register,* 5 July 1998; *Atlanta Journal-Constitution,* 1 July 1998. For more on New South governors John West, Albert Brewer, and Reubin Askew and their efforts at education reform, see Harvey, *A Question of Justice,* Sabato, "New South Governors and the Governorship," and Earl Black, *Southern Governors and Civil Rights,* 52.

54. Bass and DeVries, *The Transformation of Southern Politics,* 57–86; Carter, *The Politics of Rage,* 12; Black and Black, *The Rise of Southern Republicans,* 149–51, 217–18. For Wallace's post-1970 problems, see Jeff Frederick, "Command and Control." Bob Ingram asserts that Brewer's 1978 failure was owing in part to his "bad loser" image that grew from Brewer's comments after the 1970 election—that it was the nastiest ever (*That's The Way I Saw It,* 14–15, 21).

55. Lamis, *Southern Politics in the 1990s,* 22–23; Bass and DeVries, *The Transformation of Southern Politics,* 57–86; Carter, *The Politics of Rage,* 12; Earl Black, *Southern Governors and Civil Rights,* 52–58; Black and Black, *The Rise of Southern Republicans,* 149–51, 217–18.

8

Divide and Conquer

Interest Groups and Political Culture in Alabama, 1929–1971

Jeff Frederick

In his monumental study of poverty in Alabama, *Poor but Proud,* Wayne Flynt artfully yet methodically challenges a thousand stereotypes about poor whites. Far from being toothless rednecks content to spit tobacco, swill rot-gut, and blast racoons with Granddaddy's 12-gauge, the poor whites Flynt described had dignified lives characterized by devotion to family, worshiping a God who offered hope for a brighter future, and coping daily with frenetic changes in a rapidly developing market economy. These folks were hardy stock, not hapless victims, and they could think on their feet, even if some had rarely darkened the doors of a schoolhouse. As opposed to living a life of self-inflicted humiliation and presumed inferiority, Flynt's Alabamians "created a subculture that had meaning to them, that survived various homogenizing influences, and one that they often considered superior to the culture of their economic 'betters.'"[1]

Throughout the twentieth century, these poor whites and the similarly impoverished black citizens found few voices that dared to challenge the state's deficient education system, overturn the Black Belt–Big Mule coalition that delineated the hierarchical political landscape, or demand a more inclusive economy. To be sure, mavericks like Julia Tutwiler, Aubrey Williams, Gould Beech, and Jim Folsom, along with a handful of well-intentioned union leaders and activist Christians, made some ripples in the otherwise placid waters of the status quo. Yet these voices were largely powerless to alter a political culture created by powerful interest groups and embraced by the voting populace for cultural, economic, and political reasons. Even when reform-minded progressives proved skillful enough to get elected, they stood little chance of enacting their agendas. Depending on the decade and the issue, swimming upstream against entrenched pressure groups and their presuppositions about political economy could get one branded a liberal, socialist, communist, outside agitator, or nigger-lover. And striking workers and other dissidents were likely to lose their jobs and maybe even their lives.[2]

The elites and interest groups that constructed this stultified system knew exactly what they were doing and proceeded with ruthless precision, even as they baldly stated their intentions: disfranchisement of blacks and poor whites. Having weathered Reconstruction and survived what historian Lawrence Goodwyn called "the Populist Moment," the Heart of Dixie's industrial elite and planter remnant conspired to lock in place a system that muted future threats. The state's 1901 constitution created a compounding annual poll tax of $1.50, a literacy test, property and residency requirements designed to hamstring tenants, and an ambiguous good character litmus test. The poll tax was particularly punitive since many small farmers had already devolved into sharecropping and had little disposable income for voting. Within 20 years, a cumulative poll tax of $30 represented over 20 percent of the annual income for many folk. Any one of these provisions was enough to disfranchise many of the poor; together, they instantly sliced the pool of potential voters by over 200,000. Further indication of elite intentions was evinced by their chicanery during the ratification vote on the new governing document. If the final vote is to be believed, 12 black belt counties, overwhelmingly African-American in population, voted 32,224 to 5,471 to ratify the very document that was certain to disfranchise them. At least 10 counties cast more votes than they had adult males over the age of twenty-one. Six decades later, many poor and black Alabamians were still locked out of the political process and needed federal intervention to get back on voter rolls.[3]

The 1901 constitution did more than just restrict suffrage; it created a system of governance under which interest groups prevented progressive ideas from even being considered. Legal scholars J. Michael Allen and Jamison W. Hinds have concluded that the document "teems with special exemptions and privileges granted to particular cities, counties, industries, and interest groups." Economic elites slashed property taxes, set maximum city and county tax rates, and set limits on tax indebtedness. Power to make even the most pedestrian changes was left to the state legislature. The lack of home rule reduced most legislative sessions to a blizzard of local bills while rendering city and county commissions impotent on many matters. The result is a purposefully inefficient state government, a regressive tax system that makes the poor pay disproportionally for middling state services, a thick layer of economic and political protection for interest groups, and a landscape where interest groups have no fear of local elections since only legislators in Montgomery have the ability to make significant change. For most of the twentieth century, a legislative session meant lobbyists on the floors of both houses, interest group leaders selecting legislative committee assignments, routine killing of bills that met with their disapproval, and shameless exchanging of campaign funds and gifts. Alabama's weak Corrupt Practices Act of 1915 offered few strictures on campaigns or pressure groups, and major ethics laws were kept off the books until the late 1960s.[4]

This is not to suggest that interest groups are by nature un-American, antidemocratic, or even antirepublican. Political scientist Robert Dahl, among others, has suggested that such groups are actually an asset to the democratic process. Thus, when the Alabama Highway Improvement Association lobbied in 1920 for better roads under the slogan "Get Alabama out of the Mud," it was clear that their desire to build more roads melded nicely with the need for farmers to get crops to market and for citizens to travel safely. Pattie Ruffner Jacobs and the Alabama Equal Suffrage Association fought to gain the franchise for women—the state never ratified the Nineteenth Amendment—but few today would argue that her case had no merit. When the League of Municipalities formed in 1926 to represent the overlooked interests of Alabama's growing towns and urban centers, it provided a voice for many municipalities at a time when apportionment and legislative clout clearly favored rural counties. When circuit judge George Wallace lobbied the legislature on behalf of the Alabama Tuberculosis Association for increased per diem for the afflicted, it was a noble endeavor to help the helpless, including at least one Wallace family member.[5]

Yet a close examination of Alabama history reveals that the state's interest groups have too often taken shortsighted positions which have stunted economic development and remain far too powerful in their ability to forestall or weaken reform efforts. "They have run the state forever," former lieutenant governor Jere Beasley noted; "they run it now and they ran it then." Politically, interest groups have created a culture where fiscal and social conservatism predominate in Montgomery and the federal government is kept at arm's length. Alabamians are more tolerant of progressive representation, at least on economic matters, by their congressional delegation but still recoil in horror with the idea of federal accountability or "social engineering." Federal money is welcomed in the state as long as it does not include federal meddling.[6]

Interest groups are not the only factor in the development of this political culture. The state's political culture has been shaped by many recurring themes germinated in the Old South: fiscal conservatism, frontier cultural folkways about independence and self-reliance, a zeal for southern rights styled by Dixon Hall Lewis and William Lowndes Yancey, and the powerful role of personality. Yet interest groups emerged triumphant in the twentieth century, controlling Montgomery and creating a centrifugal force whereby nearly all legislative matters were subject to their whim. And with poverty and disfranchisement the norm for many white and black Alabamians prior to 1965, interest group influence was nearly impossible to counteract. As political scientists Peter Aranson and Peter Ordeshook have demonstrated, pressure groups have many advantages that individual citizens do not enjoy: complex communication strategies, access to decision-makers, expertise in monitoring both individual votes and macro trends, and influence in obtaining group membership compliance. As a result, they note, "the officeholder would always prefer to transact with leaders of organized groups rather than with individual citizens."[7]

Beyond winning in the marketplace of ideas against interest groups, individual Alabamians were often powerless to exert much regulation. Political scientist David Martin has demonstrated that Alabama has some 40 state boards that regulate the practices of various trades. The preponderance of board members come from the very professions they are charged with monitoring. And tax exemptions wrangled by some interest groups total as much as two-thirds of the annual budget. Political scientist Clive Thomas has dubbed Alabama one of nine states where interest groups are dominant, not complementary or subordinate, forces. "Politics is just dirty," Hilton Watson, a longtime lobbyist for the Alabama Forest Association, summarized; "I still contend that if the people of Alabama knew what went on at the capitol they would rise up in arms."[8]

Traditionally, agricultural interest groups have wielded the most power in state politics. The Alabama Cooperative Extension Service (ACES), based at Auburn University, created a system of political influence that took root in Montgomery and spread throughout every county in the state. In addition to disseminating scientific techniques for improved crop yields and livestock production, county agents became focal points for dispersing political ideology. "The county agent," Hilton Watson wrote, "was one of the key men in the county and usually if somebody was running for office they sought out that support." ACES offered programming for farmers of all socioeconomic classes, including blacks, but was heavily involved with large landowners. Those with extensive holdings were more educated, more receptive to scientific and experimental ideas, and less dependent on annual harvests for subsistence. The "poor but proud" were often unwilling to risk a reduced yield in the event that the ACES agent was wrong—in the midst of numerous good ideas, ACES recommended the planting of kudzu as a pasture crop—and this group was less of a priority for political reasons anyway. In a 1949 speech, Aubrey Williams, president of the radical Alabama Farmers Union, claimed that "few [small] farmers even see a county agent, much less have a service visit from one."[9] Though their political clout was already substantial, ACES was a driving force in the birth and growth of the Alabama Farm Bureau. Extension director L. N. Duncan organized the first meeting, which took place on the campus of Alabama Polytechnic Institute (API), later renamed Auburn University. Originally designed to be a haven for cooperative buying, the Farm Bureau eventually grew into a massive organization whose political leverage exceeded even that of ACES. Within only a few years of the Farm Bureau's genesis, local merchants were upset at ACES because county agents had been directing farmers to buy seed, fertilizer, and supplies from the Farm Bureau. One agent, John Blake, was taking so much heat from "friends-turned-to-enemies" that he wrote Director Luther N. Duncan for an official policy: "should we recommend Farm Bureau feeds to the exclusion of all other commercial feeds?" Duncan left little doubt, declaring he was "proud of the enemies we have made." In addition to rerouting purchasing to the Farm Bureau, agents were expected to lead membership drives in their districts. Some county agents found the shilling distasteful and time-consuming. "I should be delighted," a Butler County agent named Brockway declared, "to be relieved of my responsibility of Farm Bureau."[10]

Organizational leadership changes illustrate the roles that ACES played within API and the relationship between the Farm Bureau and ACES. When Brandon Knapp left the Auburn presidency, and with an aborted presidential triumvirate failing, API tapped Duncan to lead the state's land-grant college. Forty-four percent of Duncan's annual salary was allocated directly from ACES and Agricultural Experiment Station funds. Despite his promotion, Duncan continued to head ACES for two more years. When he finally resigned the directorship, he recommended P. O. Davis, a Farm Bureau publicity advisor since its inception, to succeed him. Davis became such an integral hub in the wheel of Alabama politics that governors came to him for policy decisions. "Will you have somebody to draw up the type of appeal that you think I should make," Governor Frank Dixon wrote to Davis about state farm policy during the World War II era. Davis and his staff prepared a press release for Dixon replete with a woeful jeremiad for the plight of Alabama farmers, including the forceful rejoinder that "nothing should get in the way of farmers."[11]

The political machinations of ACES and the Farm Bureau led to some bitter battles when progressives threatened. Unable to shake the conservative political influence of big ticket agriculture, Governor Jim Folsom tried to weaken it by packing the Auburn board in a direct challenge to ACES's power. In an executive session meeting of the API trustees, Folsom friend Gould Beech, editor of the progressive *Southern Farmer*, leveled four charges at ACES, including "constant interference and manipulation in the internal affairs of the Farm Bureau Federation" and "engaging in political activities." A resolution was offered deriding ACES for its comprehensive campaign to thwart an income tax amendment submitted for a popular vote in 1945. Such a position, Folsom's forces on the board contended, was particularly an anathema because "only one farmer out of twenty could have profited in any way whatever from the position taken by the extension service." Piling on the criticism, Folsom elicited a memorandum from education superintendent Austin Meadows asserting that ACES "has not cooperated wholeheartedly" on certain unnamed school policies. Contacts in the U.S. Department of Agriculture suggested that Alabama's farm production had fallen in recent years, adding credibility to accepted notions that ACES rarely helped the small farmer or sharecropper. In a subsequent meeting, Davis denied nearly all the charges but pled ignorance on the political involvement, claiming that no firm policy existed that prevented such activities.[12]

Most of Folsom's evidence about the poor performance of ACES on farm issues was circumstantial, and while ACES lost some legislative clout with the diversification of the state's economy, the Farm Bureau only grew stronger. At its peak, the Alabama organization was the fourth largest in the country. Rival interest groups knew the Farm Bureau was the most powerful institution in state government. "They have more money to spend," Watson summarized, "than most of them do and they represented a segment of the population. . . . It was sort of like motherhood. You just didn't fight agriculture. They could put two or three hundred people in the capitol any day that they wanted to display to the legislators that we don't want their bill."[13]

More often than not, the simple mention that the Farm Bureau had a position on a bill caused legislators to run for cover. "In the heat of the debate," author Harold Stanley quotes an unnamed state senator concerning a piece of legislation, "I slipped and said, half facetiously, that I knew the Farm

Bureau was fighting me on this. And damned if two or three who had stood with me until then didn't switch over and vote with the Farm Bureau." The bureau could put together a mass mailing to a legislator straddling the fence on a bill quicker than lesser organizations could make a telephone call. Unfortunately for the vast lot of poor farmers, it rarely represented their interests. The cost of membership prevented many small landowners and nearly all tenants from joining. The bureau's lobbying power, combined with its indifference to poor white farmers, cemented a status quo in which many of the poor could not afford to vote, were therefore unelectable, and had the smallest of voices in state government.[14]

Nothing motivated the major agricultural pressure groups to band together like the fear of increasing the ad valorem tax. Even when neighboring states like Georgia, Florida, and Tennessee were making substantial investments to their educational infrastructure, agricultural interest groups wore Alabama's distinction of the lowest property tax rates in the country like a badge of honor. The Alabama Cattlemen's Association decried a world where money-grubbing, tax-crazed liberals wanted to "lower the earnings of farm people . . . and give it to other favored political groups." The Forestry Association lobbied for years to get their land assessed on a formula of gross capitalization in order to lower their rates. Eventually Joe Graham, executive vice president of the Alabama Forest Products Association, convinced the legislature to exempt growing timber from any ad valorem taxes at all. "The amazing part," a colleague wrote in congratulations, "is that you only had two votes against the bill in the house and two votes against it in the senate." Even when legislative committees were authorized to investigate the state's antiquated ad valorem assessment procedures, the Farm Bureau and Forestry Association packed the study group with rural solons. The Farm Bureau and its partners easily beat back tax reform efforts in virtually every decade from 1929 to 1971. In the end, rural interests succeeded in modifying the ad valorem system to a classification arrangement where farm and timber owners, no matter how large, paid the lowest rates on the scale.[15]

Tax rates for many landowners bordered on the absurd. Those producers who had less than 160 acres were completely exempt from ad valorem taxes. In 1969, the state's 21 million acres of forest land yielded an average of 16 cents per acre in property taxes. A typical property assessment valued timber land at between $20 and $40 per acre. Even so, forest acreage sold at an average of $250. Beyond taxes, most rural interest groups opposed increases in unemployment compensation and the minimum wage and were not shy about letting Senators Lister Hill and John Sparkman know their feelings.

Into the twenty-first century, Alabama could still lay claim to the lowest tax rates and one of the highest poverty rates in the country.[16]

Even George Wallace, arguably the most popular and powerful figure in Alabama's political history, had little interest in bucking the state's agricultural power structure. In 1971, when Alabama faced both a federal mandate to rewrite its unconstitutional ad valorem system as well as internal pressure from state lawsuits, Wallace chose to back the Farm Bureau's classification plan rather than fight for a more equitable system. The governor appeared in so many commercials that some young Alabamians began referring to him as the "Farm Bureau Man," unaware that he had another job as the state's chief executive. Agricultural groups such as the Alabama Poultry Industry Association welcomed Wallace's assistance. "We are hopeful the legislature will follow Governor Wallace's recommendation," an association press release appealed, "that an equitable classification ad valorem tax bill be passed. Any unfair taxation on agriculture could result in many farmers being forced to leave their farms and move to the already crowded cities." Eventually, Wallace challenged Alabama's utility interest groups, particularly the Alabama Power Company, but he never confronted the Farm Bureau or Forestry Association even though he had the power and skill to do so.[17]

In the midst of protecting a regressive tax system, the Farm Bureau diversified its interests enough to turn its insurance division, Alfa, into a cash cow. Ed Lowder, an influential Farm Bureau leader, broadened his personal holdings until he became a leading real estate and banking tycoon in Alabama. Lowder's son Bobby completed the agricultural power tradition in the state by becoming a powerful trustee on the Auburn University board. Committed to a myopic vision of how a land-grant university should operate, Lowder has been roundly criticized in many quarters for micromanaging the university, using his political connections to load the Board of Trustees with pawns, and devoting an inordinate amount of resources to the school's athletic teams. By the turn of the twenty-first century, Lowder had reshaped the board until nearly every member was either on the board of his own company, Colonial Bank, or had loans with it.[18]

The most devastating effect of interest group power was the construction of a closed political culture in Alabama. Flexing their muscle through lobbying, campaign involvement, and the occasional use of graft, interest groups oversaw the legislative process like a Roman emperor whose thumb provided the verdict of life or death. But this power was cemented further with the acquiescence of the state's conservative churches. While some social justice advocates like L. L. Gwaltney preached about a society where political and

economic institutions should be constructed for brotherhood and cooperation, they were usually paddling upstream. "We want a state where there will
be no slums," Gwaltney wrote in 1937, "a state that sees and has compassion
for its humblest citizen. . . . The unemployed do not want charity any more
than the rest of us. They want work that can provide for their loved ones,
just as the rest of us do." For every Gwaltney, Alabama produced several
William F. Prices. A Selma pastor, Price warned of "communistic agencies
and enterprises" that were plotting to corrupt both church and state. The
result of such staunchly conservative influences, Flynt suggests, was to trans-
form some social service efforts into agencies that ignored "lynching, racial
and economic injustice, soaring infant mortality rates, poor public schools,
warfare between labor and management, and pervasive poverty."[19]

While it is true that most white Baptist pastors supported Franklin Roosevelt and the New Deal, most were unwilling, just the same, to use their
pulpits to demand changes from Montgomery. Not coincidently, many Alabama politicians claimed to be practicing Baptists or Methodists, the state's
dominant Protestant denominations. W. M. Beck, speaker of the Alabama
House of Representatives, recoiled in horror when his denomination's journal, *Alabama Baptist*, included an advertisement for the liberal *Southern
Farmer*. Turning to the right, throughout the 1950s and 1960s the *Alabama
Baptist* articulated positions against federal aid for education and Hill-Burton
funding for hospitals. Baptist minister Henry Lyon, the self-described "High
Priest of Segregation," played a prominent role on state textbook committees,
earning nominations from Governor George Wallace and Governor Lurleen
Wallace. Some evangelicals, such as Albert Brewer, used their faith to push
for major reforms. Even so, they often found themselves out of step with
rank-and-file members of rural churches who were conditioned to question
social change as an unnecessary evil.[20]

From 1929 to 1971, the combination of powerful interest groups and social
agencies that frowned on reform led to a distinctive political culture at the
capitol: white supremacy, rural power, minimal investment in education or
high-skill industry, and a quest to keep property taxes as low as possible
within a broadly regressive tax structure. White supremacy and rural power
were southern phenomena and were present in smaller doses elsewhere
across the country. And while other Deep South states tried to keep taxes
and services low while recruiting low-wage industry, Alabama had no peer in
its ability to keep state government frozen in time. It was almost as if elites
and middle classes banded together every few weeks or so to remind Montgomery to spend as little of their money as possible.

Newcomers to the state found it curious that property taxes were so low while the sales tax was so high. "We have lived in over half a dozen states," Louis Galt wrote to Governor George Wallace, "and never found a sales tax so high. Now we hear that Alabama has so much money that you do not need federal funds for the public schools. . . . Are the schools of the state so good that you do not need any improvements?" In 1962, Wallace campaigned against any increase in the sales tax, noting its regressive effects on poor folk. When a Wilcox County legislator modified an administration bill to replace corporate income tax and insurance premium tax increases with a one-cent sales tax hike, Brewer, the governor's speaker of the house, assumed Wallace would want the bill killed to honor his campaign commitment. Wallace had no interest in facing down interest groups and signed the sales tax bill. "I'll just get out there and yell nigger," Brewer recalled the governor quipping, "or whatever and they will never give it a thought."[21]

Grassroots protest movements were launched with some regularity based on class, union membership, religion, and ideology. Almost without exception, they failed. The white primary, the poll tax, and extralegal violence closed off political access. Crop liens, subsistence wages, weak unions, and company scrip made economic improvement for workers next to impossible. In 1960, more than one in three Alabamians had a per capita income of less than $1,500. As late as 1970, one in four Alabamians was still living in federally defined poverty. If elites failed to control the poor through political and economic means, the broad brushes of race, gender, and fear of communism could be applied with devastating results. Negro-loving, communist sympathizers with no appreciation for the proper place of women, after all, stood little chance of gaining converts in a place like Alabama where the severity of those charges were impressed on young minds by their parents, grandparents, and ministers. Even Senator Lister Hill, hardly a racial progressive, was accused of being a "nigger lover" in his campaign against Jim Simpson, an attorney and state senator who was ardently opposed to unions. Historian Robert J. Norrell summarized the cavalcade of factors that prevented Birmingham, arguably the South's most industrialized city, from forming an effective working-class coalition across racial lines: "Too many unionists could not vote; internal divisions dissipated too much of labor's clout; whites became too consumed with race; politicians too frequently betrayed their labor supporters; in the end, too much power was arrayed against a weakened and divided working class."[22]

Ironically, while the political culture hardened in Montgomery, Alabama's congressional delegation was earning a reputation for economic liberalism. In the throes of the Great Depression, Alabamians turned to New Deal supporters again and again in congressional elections. Lister Hill was instrumental in the passing of important New Deal legislation, including the Tennessee Valley Authority, the Hill-Burton Act, and later the G.I. Bill of Rights. Hugo Black championed the Fair Labor Standards Act and later became a prominent Supreme Court justice. John Sparkman assisted the Roosevelt administration on TVA, rural electrification, and farm legislation. John Bankhead II sponsored the Farm Tenancy Act of 1937, which allowed 20,000 tenant farmers to get loans for the purchase of their own land. Whether Hill and the rest were part of some neo-Whig resurgence as Gordon Harvey and others have suggested is problematic, but the Alabama delegation did mobilize the power of the federal government to dump resources into the state.[23]

Though most Alabamians welcomed the New Deal dollars, business elites, particularly Birmingham's industrial tycoons, vehemently opposed the New Deal. In addition to financing campaigns to unseat the New Dealers, Birmingham's barons printed *Alabama: The News Magazine of the Deep South*, an antiunion weekly designed to point out the subversive nature of government handouts. Try as they might, the Big Mules were largely unable to shake the popular image of Roosevelt in Alabama, nor the belief that politicians in Washington should be allowed to operate differently than politicians in Montgomery. After all, the coffers in Washington were filled with the dollars of 48 states. And if Alabama was to receive a bit more than an equal share, who were Alabamians to quibble?[24]

Despite their popularity, New Deal relief efforts were too little, too late for many in Alabama, and even then a disproportionate amount of resources was directed to urban areas. As much as anything, Flynt concludes, Roosevelt's alphabet soup brought "a ray of hope for the future, a bit less fear of their bosses, a little more control of their own lives, and a bit of pride in themselves." Decades later, the country music group *Alabama* demonstrated the power of memory in a state where front porch swings still squeak, mamas and grandmas still take pride in their cornbread, and daddys and granddaddys still know a thing or two about calling up a wild turkey: "We were so poor that we couldn't tell, cotton was short and the weeds were tall. But Mr. Roosevelt's gonna save us all."[25]

This bifurcated political culture—fiscal conservatism in Montgomery, economic progressivism in Washington—might have survived had a torrent of activism and resistance not been unleashed with the 1954 *Brown vs. Board of Education* decision. Even as white Alabamians welcomed Hill, and Black, and Sparkman, and Carl Elliot and others providing capital, they expected

steadfast protection of segregation and white supremacy. For Alabama's political elites, race, just like special interest hegemony, had been a settled issue
since the ratification of the 1901 constitution. But after *Brown*, economic
progressives were no longer trustworthy; their liberalism might extend to
social engineering, a taboo laced with presuppositions about intelligence,
sexual license, and political corruption and reinforced daily in the state's cultural institutions. Lister Hill nearly lost his senate seat to Jim Martin in 1962.
Martin, a Republican, previously thought to be an endangered species in the
state, swept into Congress two years later with four of his Grand Old Party
colleagues. Carl Elliot, who wrote the 1957 National Defense Education Act,
was turned out of office, and the state's Democratic Party, previously led by
those sympathetic to the national party, was seized by leaders who considered
John Kennedy, Robert Kennedy, and Lyndon Johnson to be treasonous.[26]

More than anything or anyone, George Wallace presided over the destruction of the economic progressivism component of Alabama's political
culture. After Wallace took office in January 1963, the state's congressional
delegation was never as cohesive, as effective in gathering influence and resources or as economically progressive. Over the course of a political generation, the governor depicted every federal action as either a usurpation of state
power, a sociological experiment in race-mixing, or a calculated personal attack on the good people of Alabama and the South. And Wallace cast these
latest federal incursions against the context of Reconstruction, something
mill workers and small farmers and mechanics had heard about at the dinner
table, at the office water cooler, in the local tavern, and in the pews of their
churches for nearly a century. Thus George Wallace, hateful and extremist to
many outside of the state, seemed perfectly reasonable to many white Alabamians because his bleatings about a second Reconstruction were in perfect concert with powerful memories that had been constructed in a binary
society. Whether these memories were more mythology than history was
largely irrelevant; for many, perception is scarcely different from reality when
the stakes seem so high.

Wallaceism in all its forms never challenged the prevailing culture in
Montgomery. Teachers' salaries increased, a bounty of low-wage industry re-
located to the state, and a network of junior colleges popped up. Yet nothing
was ever done to make an Alabama education at least as good as elsewhere
in the South, and the regressive tax code was left alone, free to strangle the
social mobility of another generation of poor Alabamians. Interest groups
continued to be the arbiter of what the legislature and the governor could
accomplish. Like a virus run amok, the political culture in Montgomery

seemed to infect every new generation of public servants. "I think most of the legislators," Hilton Watson recalled, "really are sincere about going up there, doing a good job in helping their county. But they get contaminated after they are there a lot. And they see that the task is almost impossible. That's probably what disgusts some of them and causes them to give up."[27]

While this seems tragic enough, the destruction of the state's formerly favorable relationship with Washington had effects that can never be fully documented. Instead of seeking capital, seed money, and economic development, Alabama fought tooth and nail over every federal mandate for civil rights compliance, adequate mental health facilities, humane prisons, and pollution control. In a speech on 4 July 1964, Wallace lashed out at civil rights, the people who favored them, and the federal government. The Civil Rights Act of 1964 was a "fraud, a sham, and a hoax . . . an act of tyranny. It is the assassin's knife stuck in the back of liberty. . . . With this assassin's knife and a blackjack in the hand of the federal force-cult, the left-wing liberals will try to force us back into bondage." The law's proponents were "left-wing radical apologists," "vultures of the liberal left-wing press," "pinknik social engineers in Washington," and "communist front organizations with high sounding names." The federal judiciary, hell-bent on enforcing the law, was "the greatest single threat to individual freedom and liberty in the United States today." The ultimate intent of the laws was to "destroy the rights of private property, to destroy the freedom and liberty of you and me . . . where there are no property rights, there are no human rights." Wallace unequivocally asserted that neither he nor his state would enforce the law.[28]

For over a decade, Wallace used the bully pulpit of the governor's office and thousands of campaign rostrums across the state, region, and nation to usher in what historian Dan Carter has called a "transformation in American politics." Wallace, and the generation of local and state officials he inspired, blasted the South's two historical villains, African-Americans and the federal government, until integration was as difficult as possible and the state was scorned by the Kennedy, Johnson, and Nixon administrations. When federal legislation softened voter registration restrictions and eliminated the poll tax, thousands of first-time, white Alabama voters and a few black ones, conditioned by their love for Wallace, chose to back their favorite son.[29]

From 1929 to 1971, Alabama's undereducated, impoverished, and vulnerable citizens—Wayne Flynt's people—were poorly served by a political culture that prevented reform, imbued interest groups with near-veto power, and eventually used race to extirpate a fruitful relationship between the state and the federal government. No lower-class whites and no blacks had the education, the money, or the political access to change the system. But by 1971, urban reapportionment wrested power away from the black belt planter remnant. Federal voting initiatives granted the franchise to thousands of Alabamians who had previously been too poor or too black to vote. Issues of overt racial politics, though far from over, were waning. At that point, poor Alabamians ceased to be passive victims of the political elites that told them that low property taxes, high sales taxes, and a hierarchical political economy were more important than good schools, decent jobs, and hope for a better future. At that point, poor Alabamians had enough political access to strip away some of the vestiges of interest group domination that made life in the state more difficult than it had to be. Yet they did not.[30]

Perhaps political cultures become so ingrained that change requires a seminal event, like *Brown,* to alter the foundation. More ominously, perhaps ordinary Alabamians have developed an Orwellian ethos that some are more equal than others: no major educational revenue enhancements have been passed since 1971; no significant tax reforms have become law; efforts at constitutional reform have been swept aside. Maybe, as Flynt suggests, the poor, historically, have been too skeptical of reformers and too individualistic to organize. Pessimists suggest that a culture that distrusts the federal government and expects little from state government has no foundation from which to demand better services.[31]

But such negativity strips the poor of the dignity and resolve that Flynt has documented so poetically. And if southern history teaches anything, it is that even the most entrenched political, economic, and social institutions can be changed. Yet until the "poor but proud" reclaim some ownership of the political culture in Alabama, interest group power seems unlikely to wane.

Notes

1. Wayne Flynt, *Poor but Proud: Alabama's Poor Whites* (Tuscaloosa: University of Alabama Press, 1989) ix–xiii, 333–62.

2. Ibid., 264–77.

3. Center for Business and Economic Research, University of Alabama, *Alabama Business and Economic Indicators* 68, no. 12 (December 1999):1–4; Flynt, *Poor but Proud,* 91; Lawrence Goodwyn, *The Populist Moment: A Short History of the Agrarian Revolt in America* (Oxford: Oxford University Press, 1978), 271–322; Wayne Flynt, "Alabama's Shame: The Historical Origins of the 1901 Constitution," *Alabama Law Review* 53, no. 1 (Fall 2001): 1–8 (www.law.ua.edu/lawreview). For more on Alabama's constitutional history, see Malcolm Cook McMillan, *Constitutional Development in*

Alabama, 1798–1901: A Study in Politics, the Negro, and Sectionalism (Chapel Hill: University of North Carolina Press, 1955).

4. J. Michael Allen III and Jamison W. Hinds, "Alabama Constitutional Reform," *Alabama Law Review* 53, no. 1 (Fall 2001) (www.law.ua.edu/lawreview); Flynt, "Alabama's Shame," 3–5; David L. Martin, "Alabama: Personalities and Factionalism," in *Interest Group Politics in the Southern States*, ed. Ronald J. Hrebenar and Clive S. Thomas (Tuscaloosa: University of Alabama Press, 1992), 251, 267.

5. Robert Dahl, *Dilemmas of Pluralist Democracy* (New Haven: Yale University Press, 1982), 66–67, 74, 188; "Get Alabama out of the Mud," 1920 brochure of the Alabama Highway Improvement Association, Alabama Associations Collection, LPR 136, Alabama Department of Archives and History (hereafter ADAH), Montgomery; "Prospectus of the Alabama League of Municipalities," ibid.; interview, Albert Brewer, 14 August 2001, Birmingham.

6. Interview, Jere Beasley, 24 July 2001, Montgomery.

7. Peter H. Aranson and Peter C. Ordeshook, "Public Interest, Private Interest, and the Democratic Polity," in *The Democratic State*, ed. Roger Benjamin and Stephen L. Elkin (Lawrence: University of Kansas Press, 1985), 118–31.

8. Martin, "Alabama: Personalities and Factionalism," 252–54; Clive S. Thomas, "Change, Transition, and Growth in Southern Interest Group Politics," in *Interest Group Politics in the Southern States*, ed. Hrebenar and Thomas, 342–43; transcript of oral history interview of Hilton Watson, recorded by Dwayne Cox, July 24, 1992, Auburn University Archives and Special Collections, Auburn, Alabama.

9. Watson, interview; letter from P. O. Davis to L. N. Duncan, 1 September 1930, Records of the Alabama Cooperative Extension Service (hereafter ACES), RG 71, Box 7, Auburn University Archives and Special Collections; Minutes of the Monthly Conference of the ACES Overhead Staff, 7 December 1929, ibid.; unidentified Alabama newspaper clipping, [1930 or 1931], ibid.; Flynt, *Poor but Proud*, 351.

10. Dwayne Cox, "Luther N. Duncan, the Extension Service, and the Farm Bureau, 1921–1932," *Alabama Review* 51, no. 3 (July 1998):185; letter from John Blake to L. N. Duncan, 1 December 1930, and letter from L. N. Duncan to John Blake, 2 December 1930, Records of the ACES, RG 71, Box 6; Minutes of the Monthly Conference of the ACES Overhead Staff, 2 November 1929, ibid., Box 7; Minutes of the Executive Committee of the Alabama Farm Bureau, 14 January 1932, ibid., Box 10.

11. Minutes of the Board of Trustees Meeting of Auburn Polytechnic Institute (hereafter API), 1 March 1937, RG AU521, Auburn University Archives and Special Collections; biographic sketch of Posey Oliver Davis, undated, Records of the ACES, RG 71, Box 7; letter from Governor Frank Dixon to P. O. Davis, 6 October 1942, ibid., Box 82; "Suggested Press Release of Governor Frank Dixon," undated,

ibid.; Cox, "Luther N. Duncan, the Extension Service, and the Farm Bureau," 184–97.

12. Minutes of the Meeting of the Board of Trustees of API, 27 February, 17 March 1947, RG AU521, Auburn University Archives and Special Collections; "Statement of Basic Failure of the API Extension Service," Executive Session, 27 February 1947, ibid.; memorandum from Austin Meadows to James Folsom, undated, ibid.; Minutes of the Meeting of the Board of Trustees of API, 17 March 1947, ibid.

13. Martin, "Alabama: Personalities and Factionalism," 288; "Alabama Farm Bureau History," www.fb.com/alfb/history.htm; interview, Watson.

14. Harold Stanley, *Senate vs. Governor, Alabama 1971: Referents for Opposition in a One-Party Legislature* (Tuscaloosa: University of Alabama Press, 1975), 63–74; Flynt, *Poor but Proud*, 275, 297.

15. "Statement of Policy Resolutions of the Alabama Cattleman's Associations 1952 Annual Meeting," Resolution One, Alabama Associations Collection, LPR 136, ADAH; "A Plan for Sound Ad Valorem Taxation," November 1966, Alabama Forestry Association Papers (hereafter AFAP), RG 678, ACC 83–7–23, Auburn University Archives and Special Collections; "Legislation Affecting Alabama's Forests and Forest Industries," Eighth Auburn Forestry Forum, 11–12 June 1969, ibid.; letter from William H. Stimpson to Joe Graham, 11 August 1967, Box 3, ibid.; *Mobile Press-Register*, 18 December 1966.

16. Carl A. Newport, "Forest Taxation Laws: A Summary by States," undated study by the *Journal of Forestry*, AFAP; "Alabama's Ad Valorem Taxation Problem," draft of speech by Representative Sid McDonald, undated, AFAP; letters from Joe Graham to John Sparkman and from Joe Graham to Lister Hill, 2 August 1966, ibid.; letter from the W. J. Word Lumber Company to John Sparkman, 18 May 1966, ibid.; "2001 Historical Poverty Tables," U.S. Census Bureau, www.census.gov/hhes/poverty/histpov/hstpov19.html.

17. Statement of Martha A. Hornbeak to the Senate Interim Committee, 28 October 1971, Administrative Files of Governor George C. Wallace, SG22709, ADAH; "Press Release of the Alabama Poultry Industry Association," undated, SG22675, ibid.; "petition to Intervene before the Public Service Commission," 5 March 1971, SG22669, ibid.; speech of George Wallace to the Legislative Interim Committee on Utility Rates and Procedures, undated, SG22669, ibid.; letter from George C. Wallace to Attorney General John Mitchell, 20 August 1971, SG22669, ibid.; Jeff Frederick, "Command and Control: George C. Wallace, Governor of Alabama, 1963–1972" (Ph.D. diss., Auburn University, 2003), 564–70.

18. Martin, "Alabama: Personalities and Factionalism," 258; Wayne Flynt, unpublished draft of manuscript of *Alabama in the Twentieth Century*, 321–22; *The Plainsman*, 27 September, 6 December 2001, 17 January, 25 July 2002.

19. Wayne Flynt, *Alabama Baptists: Southern Baptists in the Heart of Dixie* (Tuscaloosa: University of Alabama Press, 1998) 373–90.

20. Ibid., 393–98, 445–46, 486–93; Frederick, "Command and Control," 449–508. For more on Albert Brewer's education reforms, see Gordon Harvey, *A Question of Justice* (Tuscaloosa: University of Alabama Press, 2002).

21. Letter from Louise Galt to George Wallace, 18 August 1966, Administrative Files of Governor George C. Wallace, SG22416, ADAH; interview, Brewer.

22. Flynt, *Poor but Proud*, 244–77, 358; Bruce Nelson, "Organized Labor and the Struggle for Black Equality in Mobile During World War II," *Journal of American History* 80, no. 3 (December 1993):984; Robert J. Norrell, "Labor at the Ballot Box: Alabama Politics from the New Deal to the Dixiecrat Movement," *Journal of Southern History* 75, no. 2 (May 1991):202.

23. Norell, "Labor at the Ballot Box," 211–223; Gordon Harvey, "Lister Hill, 'Godfather of Maxwell Field': A Case Study in Southern Economic Development," *Alabama Review* 53, no. 1 (January 2000):3–29.

24. Norrell, ibid., 215–19.

25. Flynt, *Poor but Proud*, 332; Alabama, *Song of the South*, Southern Star Album, song written by Bob McDill, 1999.

26. Frederick, "Command and Control," 172–88.

27. Ibid., 83–92, 591–96; interview, Watson.

28. "The Civil Rights Movement," speech of George Wallace in Atlanta, Georgia," 4 July 1964, Essential Documents in American History, 1492–Present, pt. 1, item number 9709120870; Frederick, "Command and Control," 128–29.

29. Dan T. Carter, *The Politics of Rage: George Wallace, the Origins of the New Conservatism, and the Transformation of American Politics* (New York: Simon and Schuster, 1995); Frederick, "Command and Control," 231–42, 507.

30. I have specifically chosen the years from 1929 to 1971 to be the subject of this essay. The year 1929 marked the beginning of the Great Depression for many Alabamians, and the decade of the 1930s witnessed important developments in the growth of corporate farming, mechanization, and additional clout for agricultural interest groups. After 1971, a new wave of important interest group battles took shape. Beginning late in 1971, the Alabama Education Association became much stronger as the Wallace administration mobilized the heretofore weak teachers' lobby by threatening retirement and other funds. Wallace's failed ploy energized the AEA and turned its leader, Paul Hubbert, into an important power broker for the next three decades. The years after 1971 were also the context for an increasingly bitter fight between Wallace and the public utilities.

31. Flynt, *Poor but Proud*, 362.

9

The Scholar as Activist

Dewayne Key

Pontotoc, Mississippi, was not a place I had visited, or even heard of, prior to becoming acquainted with Wayne Flynt. Its relative obscurity and small, southern, country-town character made it like a thousand others scattered throughout the Deep South. But only from such a place as Pontotoc, and many small towns in between, could there emerge an activist-scholar such as Wayne Flynt. His perspective on the history of the region and its social issues, and his search for some measure of justice for the poor, set him apart from other academics that I have known.

Growing up in a small town and a small world gave Flynt the experience and authority for his most important work, *Poor but Proud*, a history of Alabama's poor whites. Only through experience could one derive the proper appreciation for, and give sufficient attention to, the details that make the book a critical celebration of the state's forgotten people. As a descendant of poor Homer Flynt, Wayne gained both a cultural and familial connection to the people about whom he wrote, which allows readers who hail from more fortunate origins to come away with a similar empathy for the plight of the state's poor. Those of us who grew up poor in Alabama came away from this book with our lives enriched, our emotions stirred to tears, and our hearts at peace with the satisfaction that our story had finally been told in a powerful, honest way. Flynt's intimate familiarity with the history and the continuing plight of Alabama's poor led him to a life of social activism.

Perhaps a year after *Poor but Proud* was published, I first heard of Dr. Flynt through a lengthy essay by Howell Raines, published in the *New York Times Magazine*. The article, "Alabama Bound," ran on 3 June 1990, and it explained the awkward, backward way in which Alabama government operates. Raines quoted Dr. Flynt on several aspects of Alabama's antiquated constitution, inequitable tax system, unfair method of governing, and conservative voting habits, including an ominous Flynt warning to Alabama legislators in that year: "God will judge us, as will history."

Just one month earlier I had been member of the Alabama Coalition for Equity (ACE), a group of mostly poor rural school systems that filed a school funding lawsuit alleging that the way the state funded public schools was unfair and unconstitutional. We were encouraged that Raines had given national attention to Alabama's absurdities and fascinated to find an academic who not only had understood our claims but had the fortitude to say aloud what most people in Alabama public life had declined to acknowledge, much less to address. It was both refreshing and heartening to this small group of school superintendents (about 10 percent of the state's total number of local school chiefs, primarily from small, obscure systems) to have someone speak out against the state's outrageous shortcomings in matters of public policy. We in the coalition had come to realize that litigation was the only hope for a solution to the pervasive problems that plagued public education. We were excited to find an eager advocate and ally in Wayne Flynt. We continue to appreciate the fact that, more than fifteen years later, his voice has not wavered and he continues to address our state, its shortcomings, its unrealized potential, and particularly its maltreatment of its poor citizens.

Apart from his books and interviews, Flynt spoke out to identify flaws and shortcomings in our state government. This is an honorable act in itself, but to actively advocate change and remediation is genuinely courageous. His advocacy on behalf of Alabama's poor, oppressed, and disadvantaged, and his indignation at their treatment by our own state government through outrageous public policy, has been the trait that has set him apart from others in academia. Finding fault is easy. Advocating for change in the face of rejection and hostility is not.

Constitutional reform has been a particularly important issue to Flynt, since many of the state's ills can be traced back to the state's 1901 constitution. Helping to initiate and perpetuate Alabama Citizens for Constitutional Reform was Flynt's most notable endeavor, and his efforts to educate and inform audiences across the state on this issue have been tireless and productive. Coupled with the efforts of other reform-minded public servants, his endeavors have resulted in a far broader public understanding of the dire need for a new constitution. In this respect, his research informs his service to the public. In his many books on Alabama history, Flynt has documented the roots of the state's ills, many of which emanate from the archaic state constitution that centralized power in Montgomery and denied localities the power to rule themselves.

One of Flynt's most significant social contributions has come in his attempts to awaken the conscience of established religion. An ordained Baptist minister who has vowed to go to his grave a Baptist, Flynt's religious beliefs and convictions have made it easier for some churches to accept his academic approach to the state's problems and his moralistic calls for reform. In this sense, he has succeeded in appealing to their faith, which has significantly broadened the acceptance of his message within Alabama's mainstream churches. Specifically, Flynt has tweaked the conscience of white churches to embrace the cause of racial reconciliation.

Thus it came as little surprise to me when the Flynts' church, Auburn First Baptist Church, took a leading part in advocating tax reform and the church's role in reforming the state one town at a time. In 2000, Flynt and Dr. Gerald Johnson, a political scientist, persuaded their congregation to approve a donation to the Auburn city schools of an amount equal to the property taxes the church would have paid the city if it were not exempt. Although $4,662 was by no means a windfall for the school system, the symbolic act was priceless. Flynt then challenged every congregation of every faith in the state to donate their exempted property taxes to their local school system. Several other Baptist churches followed suit, and, thanks in large measure to this particular brand of theology-based advocacy, a number of other prominent denominations accepted the challenge to become actively involved in tax and constitutional reform. Several of these churches publicly supported a failed 2003 tax reform initiative.

In introducing resolutions before the Alabama Baptist Convention for other Baptist churches to donate their property tax savings to their local education systems and for Alabama's Baptist churches to support a lottery for education reform, Flynt implored his fellow Baptists to action, and he may have reached as broad an audience as he has at any time. Although his resolutions eventually fell to defeat, Flynt's logic was compelling and his theology was difficult to refute. For those in the audience wearing wrist bands engraved with "WWJD" (What Would Jesus Do?), his simple message of loving one's brother, regardless of income, race, or social status, struck a chord. His most nearly incontrovertible challenges have been given to those Christians who oppose tax reform that would give relief to the poor and tax increases that would aid programs for the poor, yet who claim to advocate Jesus' compassion for the poor.

Whereas progressive-minded Alabamians have been encouraged by Dr.

Flynt's activism, not everyone has responded positively or eagerly embraced his pronouncements on public issues. Some have asserted that his policy suggestions, although supported by his research, amount to merely one man's opinion. His attacks on powerful lobbying groups such as ALFA—the Alabama Farmers Federation, a powerful insurance lobby—and even his own university's board of trustees have been met with harsh criticism. Some opponents suggested that he be removed from university service and that he did not deserve his Distinguished University Professorship at Auburn.

But perhaps no other cause is closer to Flynt's heart than the plight of the South's poor. As a long-standing member of the board of directors of the Alabama Poverty Project, he has been in a position to be hands-on in helping to mold public policy on behalf of the poor. Flynt commits a great deal of time and energy to this worthy cause, and his speeches across the state have served to inform many people about the true state of affairs regarding Alabama's poor. His presentations to civic clubs, school leaders, business groups, and church groups have significantly raised awareness of the real poverty issues in our state.

I was privileged to meet Dr. Flynt through my own involvement in a public policy issue related to education. As early as 1986, while serving the first year of my eight-year tenure as superintendent of the Lawrence County, Alabama, school system, I became aware of the remarkably disparate educational opportunities of students in Alabama public schools. It became apparent right away that educational opportunity, student achievement, and a list of other key educational indicators correlated closely with wealth indices. While cause and effect were not necessarily indicated by the data, one thing was certainly clear: In school systems where greater wealth existed, per-pupil expenditures were much higher. As much as a twofold disparity in per-pupil expenditure existed between the highest spending and the lowest spending school systems. So if the state was responsible for the state school system, then it was also responsible for the wide disparity of opportunity brought on by the disparate expenditures.

The state funding "system" for its schools was a patchwork arrangement tied mainly to earned teacher units, driven primarily by "average daily attendance" in the state's 129 school systems. No reckoning was made of whether a system was in a prosperous or poor part of the state. Neither was account taken of whether a local school system had the ability or willingness to generate local revenue to supplement state funds. Consequently, school systems with high tax bases, because of either property wealth or commercial wealth, could generously contribute additional revenue to supplement the meager state allocation. School systems that were poor—primarily those in rural, underdeveloped counties—because of either low property wealth or very limited retail activity, could furnish only a paltry amount of revenue to supplement the state funds. Thus there were the "haves" and the "have-nots" among the various school systems. Perhaps the most grievous absurdity in the state's "system" of funding its schools was the fact that through certain "incentives," the state was actually furnishing more money per pupil to the more affluent systems than to the poorer. The state of Alabama spent significantly more dollars of state revenue (as distinct from local revenue) per pupil in affluent systems than in those less affluent, which amounted to as much as a 1.25 to 1.0 disparity. State money, coupled with the locally generated revenue in the more affluent systems, allowed those systems to spend sometimes twice as much per pupil in state and local money to educate their children than poorer systems.

Like Dr. Flynt, I was a farm boy, but I learned to cipher fairly well. I had a good general grasp of what was fair and what was unfair, and as superintendent of Lawrence County schools I had witnessed the problem firsthand. Alabama's funding scheme for its schools seemed really unfair. I found a number of school leaders mostly from poor systems who were very much in agreement with my contention. Plus, I found sympathetic friends in some leaders of the Alabama State Department of Education. In fact, state superintendent Dr. Wayne Teague openly supported our position. But what convinced us that we were doing the right thing was the vigorous opposition emanating from many affluent school systems and from the leaders in the state legislature.

Therefore, in 1990, we superintendents and school boards from some of the state's poorest school systems retained the services of a legal team headed by former Alabama chief justice C. C. "Bo" Torbert and Jim Speake to sue the state for some measure of relief or reform on behalf of our newly formed Alabama Coalition for Equity, aptly referred to as ACE. In May of that year we filed suit. Our contentions were primarily that the state had a responsibility to educate its schoolchildren, that its citizens had a constitutionally mandated, fundamental right to education, and that the present scheme of funding our schools was flawed and unfair.

In 1991, the court heard evidence on a pivotal constitutional question related to an amendment to Article XIV, Section 256 of the 1901 Alabama constitution, amendment 111.[1] We had contended in our suit that this amendment was unconstitutional in its removal of the responsibility for public education from state government. Adopted in 1956, Amendment 111 was a typical segregation amendment, not unlike those adopted in several states across the Deep South in the wake of the U.S. Supreme Court's 1954 *Brown v. Board of Education* decision. In August 1991, Circuit Court Judge Eugene Reese ruled that Amendment III was unconstitutional *ab initio* and struck it from the state constitution.[2]

As *ACE v. Governor Guy Hunt* and *Harper v. Governor Guy Hunt* (the companion suit filed several months later by the ACLU) unfolded, Dr. Flynt made himself readily available to all parties to assist, first with information, later with mediation. In March 1993, Judge Reese declared the state's education funding scheme unconstitutional and ordered that it be remedied. Political posturing and some chaos ensued, followed closely by appeals. Eventually the case was appealed to death. The partial remedies that occurred were far more than many people expected but far short of anything we plaintiffs would call genuinely fair.

When the court ruled on behalf of the plaintiffs in the spring of 1993, Reese and Alabama governor James E. Folsom Jr. appointed Flynt to the position of facilitator to work with both sides in deriving a solution to the funding problem. Flynt helped to establish a direction for a proposed remedy and to assist us (plaintiffs and defendants alike) in navigating the treacherous waters of Alabama politics as we set about to find a satisfactory resolution of the case. In October 1993, education reform advocates presented the legislature with the Alabama First plan, which combined increased taxes with strict accountability rules as a means of fulfilling the order of the court. Dr. Flynt was immensely helpful in facilitating compromise, seeking appropriate ways to address the needs of the poor, and providing information, both to us and to many others not directly involved in the case. Early in the process, he detected what turned out to be fatal flaws in the Alabama First legislative proposal and remedy plan. He discouraged the use of too much "outside" influence in the development of the proposal and accurately predicted the dramatic, vitriolic response of conservative groups to the tax provisions in the plan. He advised us to steer clear of those confrontations. However, there was no way he could steer the entire political mechanism clear of the onslaught of opposition that was perpetrated by the combination of conservative opponents and antitax mossbacks. The reform package failed to pass after losing the support of Alabama Education Association executive director Paul Hubbert, who, in the heat of a tight primary challenge to Governor Folsom, declared the reform too expensive. When an exasperated legislature passed a budget for the fiscal year 1994 with a single total as its only line item, it was the task of Dr. Flynt to mediate a final distribution of the budget.[3]

Wayne Flynt is an accomplished scholar and teacher—he taught one of my sons and helped guide him to graduate study in history—but he is much more. He is a spiritual man who is guided by timeless principles of compassion and fairness and justice and who has become a sort of modern prophet to his region and state. He is a patient man who perseveres as he pursues the acceptance and incorporation of these principles in the formation of public policy in this state.

Notes

1. Amendment III, Section 256 of the Alabama Constitution (1901): "It is the policy of the state of Alabama to foster and promote the education of its citizens in a manner and extent with its available resources, and the willingness and ability of the individual student, but nothing in the constitution shall be construed as creating or recognizing any right to education or training at public expense, nor as limiting the authority and duty of the legislature, in furthering or providing for education, to require or impose conditions or procedures deemed necessary to the preservation of peace and order."

2. Although Reese ruled the amendment unconstitutional, it remained part of the constitution unless the voters chose to remove it by constitutional amendment. See Order of 13 August 1991, *Ala. Coalition for Equity, Inc. v. Hunt*, No. CV–90–883 (Cir. Ct. Montgomery Co., Ala.); in 2004, a proposed amendment to remove Amendment III from the state constitution failed by 1,850 votes, 691,300 to 689,450 (Alabama Secretary of State, Official Election Results, 24 November 2004).

3. On 10 January 2002, the Alabama Supreme Court ruled that the Alabama Constitution did not provide equal protection under law for its citizens, and overturned Judge Reese's 1993 ruling.

IO

Evangelist for Constitutional Reform

Bailey Thomson

In the spring of 2002, the Journalism Department at the University of Alabama bestowed on Wayne Flynt its Clarence Cason Writing Award. Flynt joined a circle of former winners that included luminaries such as Edward O. Wilson, the biologist and Pulitzer Prize recipient, and Gay Talese, the renowned nonfiction writer.

The awards committee, on which I had the pleasure of serving, noted that Flynt combined a writer's sensibility with a scholar's curiosity and an activist's passion. Indeed, he came the closest of all the distinguished winners to embodying the spirit of the late Cason, whose 1935 book, *90 Degrees in the Shade,* became a minor classic among the southern Regionalist school. It was not enough for Flynt to tell the truth about Alabama's often tragic past and to tell it in such a manner that would engage and enlighten readers. He sought to inspire readers and listeners through his own example of engaged citizenship to redress these wrongs. In his remarks at the awards banquet, Flynt explained his motivation: "Why have I chosen in recent years to spend so much more time on the rubber chicken lecture circuit and so much less time in the solitary confines of an archive? Because how the particular kind of history I write affects public policy is really important to me. It is important for religious reasons that have to do with my conception of biblical justice. It has to do with regional issues, because I do not believe that only white Anglos can claim to be Southerners. And it has to do with what it means or once meant to be American: to act on behalf of the commonwealth, the entire community, not just one's own self-interest."

It is in this role as activist that I have come to know Wayne Flynt best, first as an editor observing his efforts to promote social justice and more recently in working alongside him to draw attention to Alabama's notoriously racist and reactionary 1901 constitution. As did Flynt, I trained to be a historian and found that the best stories came from my own state's attic. However, I drifted into newspaper work, only to return two decades later to my alma mater, where I now teach journalism in Cason's old department. Such a perspective encourages one to see the totality of Flynt's contribution. He achieves a balance between reflection and action, truth and justice, detachment and commitment. He is rare among scholars in that he actually makes news as well as interprets past events, leaving disinterest at the library's door when contemporary issues call him to battle. He is rare also in that he professes evangelical Christianity as a major motivation for his work, eschewing the scholar's typical reticence about such personal things.

I have too many memories of Flynt for a single article to contain. But there are two qualities about him that, for me, particularly illustrate his active life. One is his willingness to share what he knows and thinks with diverse groups. The other is his evangelist's zeal for attacking injustice, which I first observed during my years at the *Mobile Register.*

Flynt may be the most celebrated speaker of his generation in Alabama. Put him on a program, and one is virtually guaranteed an audience. He is equally popular among producers of television documentaries. In fact, a team at the University of Alabama devoted a film to his campaign for social justice. What is it about his rhetoric that draws listeners? What makes his messages compelling?

The word *authenticity* comes to mind. He does not command the center stage through his appearance. He has the gaunt look of his hill-country forebears, accentuated by his graying hair and searching eyes. His voice seldom varies in pitch or intensity. He does not pound the podium. Nor does he flash images upon a screen. Typically, he reads from yellow legal pages.

As if to defy further the speechmaker's art, Flynt draws his evidence and aphorisms from history. He shares the experiences of obscure people and places, weaving a common bond between then and now. His stories often dwell upon how events in the past affected ordinary citizens and continue to haunt their descendants. Some might complain that he is too harsh in his condemnation of the ruling classes' conduct, especially in their persistent refusal to share their wealth in order to educate the children of their workers and other common people. Yet in Flynt's view, all actors in history must stand accountable before the bar of justice, although particular circumstances separate one generation's experiences from those of another.

In his frequent talks about Alabama's 1901 constitution, for example, Flynt is merciless in excoriating the sins of large landowners and industrialists who wrote their selfish interests into the document and then imposed it on everyone else through electoral fraud. He traces much of the apathy and distrust that citizens often express toward their state government to the constitution's deliberate disfranchisement of blacks and poor whites. He delights in the theme that history has consequences not only in terms of what is done but also of what is left undone. From those to whom fate and birth have been generous, much will be expected from future historians. Flynt reserves his greatest scorn for the well-to-do who prefer to do very little about the state's serious problems, the people who are simply too busy to be bothered: "Well meaning and likable, vaguely aware that something is amiss, wishing that someone would do something to make it all better or right or go away or whatever, but they are too busy . . . to figure out what all the uproar is about."

Another disastrous consequence of the 1901 constitution was that it enshrined a regressive tax system that starved public education and other services that might help Alabamians climb out of poverty and be productive citizens. Many of Flynt's own family members grew up with poor or nonexistent schools. His father's brother, for example, had been in the third grade when hard times forced his school to close in 1932. The boy never returned to school, and illiteracy dogged him as an adult.

"My family is full of stories of people who had enormous ability but never really had much opportunity because of the educational system of the state," Flynt recalled in 1992. "One reason I feel so strongly about educational reform is because I see . . . the consequences of it in my own uncle." Better schools form part of a litany of reforms that he has championed over the last few years.

He shared that personal history with me as I interviewed him for a profile I later published in the *Mobile Register.* The newspaper had presented him with its "Alabamian of the Year" award in recognition of his advocacy for social justice. Like a modern-day Jeremiah, Flynt had traveled around the state, lamenting how failed leadership and selfish interests had left the state languishing at the bottom. He even testified on behalf of plaintiffs who demanded equal spending on students, no matter where they lived. The lawsuit, heard in a Montgomery courtroom in 1992, maintained that the state's funding treated poor school districts in an unconstitutional fashion. As the plaintiffs' last witness, Flynt declared that Alabama had never invested enough in its children, and ignorance and blasted lives were the bitter legacy of that stinginess. Moreover, he had the statistics to prove his point.

This mantle of itinerant preacher fit comfortably on Flynt's thin shoul-

ders. Despite the impressive weight of academic honors and titles accumu-
lated over his career, his first calling remained that of a Southern Baptist
minister. He was ordained in the summer of 1961, while working as a youth
minister at Park Memorial Baptist Church in Anniston, a congregation that
had nurtured and inspired him as a high school student. Three years earlier,
he had chosen Birmingham's Howard College—now Samford University—
because he wanted to attend a Southern Baptist school. So eager was he to
start college and so afraid of failure that he graduated from Anniston High
School on a Friday night and enrolled at Howard the following Monday.
     That fright kept Flynt going summers and winters, so that he finished
college with honors in three years, majoring in history and speech. He
paused long enough, however, to be president of the student body and southern coordinator among college students for Richard Nixon's unsuccessful
presidential campaign in 1960. Flynt's background accounted in part for his
anxiety and contributed later to his disillusionment toward the ministry.
     He was born in Pontotoc, Mississippi, in 1940 to parents who struggled to
gain a foothold in the middle class. His father sold biscuits, meat, and insurance, frequently moving the family around Alabama and Georgia. Young
Wayne attended a dozen schools before the Flynts landed in Anniston when
he was in the tenth grade. He remembers being a "terrible" student, angry
and undisciplined in his studies.
     A teacher named Janet Lefevre provided him an outlet in which to excel
when she introduced him to debate. "She convinced me I could in fact contribute something and that I could do whatever I wanted to do," he said.
Scholarships poured in during his senior year, and Flynt readied himself to
begin his ministerial studies.
     He already had a splendid model in B. Locke Davis, the thoughtful and
internationally minded pastor at his home church. Davis took a broad view of
the ministry and the church's need to address social issues. "It never occurred
to me there were a lot of small-minded and rather intolerant fundamentalist-
type Baptists floating around in the world who ultimately would dominate
the Southern Baptist Convention," Flynt said.
     As the young college student began preaching at churches, he suffered a
moral crisis. Earlier he had decided racial segregation was wrong: "I believed
at the time that ethically and morally there was no way to reconcile Christianity to segregation." But how could a young minister find a pulpit in Alabama to espouse such views? Veteran preachers who had dared to defy prevailing racial mores had lost their jobs. Moreover, Flynt saw no immediate
possibility for change in Alabama.

His answer was to flee with his wife, Dorothy Anne, to Florida State University and pursue a doctorate in southern history. While there, Flynt also broadened his concept of Christian calling: "I decided no matter what you do, it is a ministry, whether it's teach college students or manage a business or engage in medical practice." When he finished graduate school four years later, he and his wife returned to Birmingham, where he joined the faculty of Howard, and she continued to teach in the public schools. Just twenty-four, Flynt grew a mustache to add years to his appearance: "My students all looked older than I did."

In 1977, the Flynts moved to Auburn University, where he became head of its history department and eventually a distinguished research professor. Comfortable with his new settings, he began publishing important books about the South's poverty, politics, and religion. He and Dorothy Anne also settled into the community and raised their two sons, David and Sean.

Flynt saw a great story in the region's impoverished whites, despite their economic and social deprivation. Their plight reminded him of his own family members' struggles to survive in the mountains and hills of northeastern Alabama. He crowned his research with a book titled *Poor but Proud: Alabama's Poor Whites*. The book was at once scholarly and autobiographical. It won the coveted Lillian Smith Award for Non-Fiction in 1990.

Later, he turned to the history of southern evangelical Christians, coming full circle to his original interest in religion. He and Dorothy Anne spent three months in the Orient while he taught and did research in Hong Kong and China on missionaries from Alabama. This experience helped inspire *Alabama Baptists: Southern Baptists in the Heart of Dixie* in 1998.

Flynt's prodigious scholarship drew admiration from readers and reviewers. My first encounter with his work was when I reviewed his *Dixie's Forgotten People* in 1979. His insights informed my own editorials and columns at a time when my newspaper, the *Shreveport Journal,* had developed a keen interest in writing about the piney woods poverty of northwest Louisiana.

Not all scholars, however, agreed with Flynt's interpretation of poor whites. One critic, for example, once pulled me aside to complain that Flynt romanticized such people and overlooked how their bigotry and antitax sentiment had slowed the state's progress, right up until the modern era. "The reality is that it's this diabolical combination of the rich and the poor that keeps us in a hole," the critic said.

Flynt has trained his rhetorical guns upon the landholding and industrial interests, known first as the "Bourbons" and later as the "Big Mules." That emphasis is not unusual. Most historians agree that Alabama and other states

of the Deep South saw democracy drastically reduced during the reaction
that followed the Populists' revolt in the 1890s—a revolt, by the way, that
showed some promise of uniting farmers along class lines rather than continuing to divide them by race. Where Flynt differs from many of his colleagues, however, is that he uses such historical insights, along with statistics
on school spending, health care, and other important indicators, to help
audiences understand why certain wrongs persist in Alabama.

One admirer from those intense battles over spending on social services
was state representative Jimmy Holley, a Democrat from Coffee County.
Flynt's speeches about the plight of poor children in Alabama inspired him
to sponsor increased aid to dependent children. The Alabama Legislature
had not raised welfare payments since 1976, leaving a mother with two children to cope on $118 a month. Even Mississippi was more generous. With
Holley prodding them, legislators raised payments three years in a row, seeking to match the southeastern states' average level of aid.

Flynt confided in the interview that he would just as soon that someone
else carried this message to the public: "I wait in vain for the ministers of the
state to come out and say poverty is unjust. . . . I wait in vain for the academics to talk about education reform, especially the college academics, who ba-
sically see education reform as a war between K-12 and the colleges for the
pie—who gets the biggest slice." At the time, he was logging about 40,000
miles a year on his car. Only in his early fifties, these controversies already
had begun to age him. Yet for Flynt, the alternative to action was unacceptable. "Our option is to ignore the problems or let the courts solve them,
which is what we usually do in Alabama," he said. "I never thought the courts
gave us as good a solution as we could devise ourselves if we had the leadership and vision to act on these problems."

There is no choice, then, but to go forward and proclaim what one believes is the truth. Otherwise, Flynt has argued, one must accept a state that
ranks last or near last in virtually every category that measures quality of life.
One also must turn his head from unspeakable poverty, ignorance, and intol-
erance. He simply could not do it.

Yet he confessed to his audience during the Cason Award dinner that he
sometimes wearied of his activist role. Away from home and office, speaking to strangers and often parrying the thrusts of opponents, Flynt missed
the cloistered life of the academy, the solitude of the library, the small stakes
of faculty meetings. And he warned that the state's politics could be mean-
spirited: "If your feelings are easily hurt, better avoid it. Public policy enemies

in Alabama will do more than try to get you fired. They will lie about you, distort your position and spread gossip in order to destroy your credibility."

So why does he remain in the fray? Why has he given so much of his life and his energy to what many people might consider a hopeless cause of redeeming Alabama's historical sins? How does he tolerate the discouraging responses from cynics or the reluctance of so many people simply to become involved? I will venture an answer.

For all his jeremiads, Flynt has maintained over the years an unshakeable faith in democracy—that is, in the ability of citizens to make the right choices once they have been sufficiently informed of the truth. For that reason, he always returns telephone calls from reporters, accepts more speaking engagements than he really has time for, and pens biting commentaries for op-ed and editorial pages. Part of his reward is that, while some things remain the same, others have changed beyond recognition. For example, Flynt is delighted that newspapers such as the *Mobile Register* have gone from being bastions of the status quo to producing the best investigative journalism he has seen in his lifetime. He also detects a transformation among the state's top business leaders, many of whom now take a significant interest in addressing the state's problems. Finally, more good people are entering public life, either as volunteers or as elected officials.

To Flynt, such activity suggests a change in Alabama's public life. The past and the present finally are being reconciled in a way that has religious meaning for him. "If you are an evangelical Christian," he once told me, "you ought to be as concerned about this world as much as you are concerned about the world to come." Flynt's life has been his testimony to this commitment as well as a priceless gift to a state that often has shunned its prophets.

II

The Historian as Public Policy Activist

Dan T. Carter

In January 1980 I was beginning a Fulbright appointment to teach a seminar on southern history to a group of English schoolteachers attending night classes at the Polytechnic of Central London. Just before I left for my overseas flight, I had packed a copy of Wayne Flynt's *Dixie's Forgotten People: The South's Poor Whites*,[1] recently published in the Minorities in Modern America series. And in one of the first cold, dark days after I arrived, I read it through in one sitting.

At less than 200 pages, it was obviously a synthetic work, covering a broad time period and often little more than a gesture toward the complex stories that made up the history of a people who have been defamed, patronized, or simply ignored in regional and national history. But I responded immediately to the underlying voice of the author. There was deep sympathy for the struggles of those men and women he wrote about, but also a tough-minded vision that could only come from someone who had combined firsthand experience with a scholar's eye. This was not history written through rose-colored glasses.

A decade later, Wayne Flynt published *Poor but Proud: Alabama's Poor Whites*,[2] and here he more than fulfilled the promise of *Dixie's Forgotten People*. Twice the length of his first book on the South's poor whites and with a smaller stage, here he was able to blend his larger story with telling and often heartbreaking details drawn from oral history and folk culture as well as more traditional sources. It was not simply an effort to describe poor whites as a "class" or a "problem," but rather as a group of people who struggled to make sense out of their economically impoverished lives and to maintain a sense of their dignity in a larger culture that often treated them with contempt or derision. The great passion that drove Wayne Flynt came, in part, from his own identification with those struggles. It was, he said "the story of my ancestors and those of most white Alabamians now living in the relative affluence of the last years of the twentieth century." And it was written with a purpose: "to help us all remember where we came from and the price others paid for our journey" (xii).

I responded positively to *Poor but Proud* because of its contributions to our understanding of a neglected aspect of southern and American history, but I also recognized a point of view that I shared. I am well aware of the dozens of pithy epigrams that relegate the study of history to an act of self-delusion. As the radical historian and disillusioned former communist Joseph Freeman pointed out, "Everyone falsifies history even if it is only his own personal history. Sometimes the falsification is deliberate, sometimes unconscious; but always the past is altered to suit the needs of the present." Wayne Flynt has made a similar observation, observing that, in his interviews with those who sprang from the poor of Alabama, "I noticed how selective memory is, often editing out the worst episodes and remembering the good times" (xiii). Even historians—particularly those who care passionately about what they write— can seldom maintain a sense of complete objectivity, he noted.

Many of my students (and nonstudents for that matter) greet this frank acknowledgment of personal involvement with disillusionment. Few recognize the irony that historians are the last individuals to begin with the oft-stated claim of politicians and pundits that "history proves that . . ." because they understand that what we call history is our understanding—our belief—about the past. This does not mean that any scholar should accept the notion that "history" is simply a weapon to be used as a tool in a struggle for ideological dominance. We are professionally obligated to remain committed to the importance of careful historical research and documentation as well as balance and fairness. But it seems to me to be a mark of honesty to acknowledge that what drives most of us who study history is, in Flynt's words, a passionate belief that the "past is important to the present."

Like Wayne Flynt, I have always rejected the notion that historians should be bloodless chroniclers of the achievements (or follies) of mankind. I believe that the search for moral justice should lie at the heart of our civic culture, that one of the tasks of the historian—of any committed intellectual—is to scrutinize carefully and thoughtfully where we have failed to live up to the best values of our culture.

This is particularly true for historians who write about recent events and thus often deal with issues that affect public policy. As Flynt said in an op-ed piece in the *Birmingham News* of 24 March 2002, historical writing about such public policy issues is "important to me . . . for religious reasons that have to do with my conception of biblical justice." The regional context is equally important, he wrote, "because I do not believe that only white Anglos can claim to be Southerners." Above all, he said, that history speaks to "what it means or once meant to be American: to act on behalf of . . . the entire community, not just one's own self-interest."

In this same op-ed piece, Wayne Flynt reflected upon the fact that historians have played a disproportionately large role as public intellectuals in American life. Some serious students of history, he observed, have moved beyond words to direct political participation—Woodrow Wilson, George McGovern, and Newt Gingrich (to name just a few). More commonly, they have served as commentators, analysts, and advocates. George Bancroft, arguably the first American historian, was a fervent Democrat who wrote presidential speeches and served as an advisor to Andrew Jackson. Although sociologist/historian W. E. B. DuBois never had the ear of a president, at a time when African Americans were systematically segregated, he eloquently reminded Americans of the gap between their rhetorical commitment to equality and their practical embrace of discrimination. In the years that followed, William Dodd, Arthur Schlesinger, C. Vann Woodward, and John Hope Franklin were some of the many historians who wrote and spoke out in this tradition.

Wayne Flynt is far too modest to list himself in that group but—in reality—he has played an important role in bringing his own historical perspective to bear on some of the most important public policy issues of the American South and his native Alabama. Over the years, he has spoken to dozens of civic and community organizations; he has written op-ed pieces, and he has been a major participant in public advocacy groups—particularly those dealing with issues of education. If his ideas have not always carried the day, he has been able to raise questions and challenge conventional wisdom in a way that has enriched public life more than any academic figure in Alabama's modern history.

That influence is surprising. At least since the Civil War, a deep and pervasive anti-intellectualism has often shaped the thinking of white southerners who have equated serious thought with radical challenges to their moral, political, and racial values. As regional politicians have shown, one of the surest applause lines has been a sneering reference to academics or individuals who profess to respect the life of the mind. And for every J. William Fulbright, there have been dozens of George Wallace clones who found in "pseudo-intellectuals" the perfect scapegoat for fearful and frustrated follow-ers. As Wayne Flynt bluntly acknowledged in an interview in the mid-1990s, anti-intellectualism has long been rampant in Alabama, and many citizens are frankly hostile to higher education, fearful that exploring new ideas would require them to abandon their religious traditions and their commu-nity values.[3]

There are a number of reasons why I believe Flynt has been able to be effective despite the inherent suspicion of many people in his state. Sincerity, the news pundit Daniel Schorr once suggested, is essential for anyone in public life: "If you can fake it, you've got it made." Well, no one ever accused Wayne Flynt of faking his deep commitment to the well-being of the people of Alabama (or of his fellow human beings). Even when critics have dis-agreed, at least a fair number have listened respectfully because they recog-nize that lifelong commitment. He is not the first white southern liberal who has managed, by force of personality, to transcend the anti-intellectualism of the region. Dr. Frank Porter Graham, president of the University of North Carolina at Chapel Hill from 1930 to 1948, was one of the most liberal social activists in the region, and he held positions on race, social justice, and inter-national affairs that were often out of step with the people of his state. After his appointment to the United States Senate in 1948, he was, in fact, defeated two years later by a race-baiting opponent who convinced a little over half of the white voters of the state that Graham was a dangerous man because of his belief in racial justice. But for nearly 20 years, the people of North Caro-lina listened to and supported their beloved "Dr. Graham" because they were convinced that he acted selflessly and without self-interest even when they did not share his views.

The willingness to tolerate the gadfly has sometimes been put to the test in Flynt's case. Passionately, he has outlined the deficiencies in the state: the continuing level of poverty, the poor performance levels in primary, secon-dary, and higher education, and the myopic refusal of the state's citizens to finance support for the social investments necessary to lift Alabama from the bottom ranks in income, education, and public health. At one point in a guest newspaper editorial, he bluntly asked the people of his home state: "Do you want to live in a state as sorrily governed as this one? Do you believe that your children or grandchildren can put up with what you have come to accept as normal? Do you want science textbooks where the warning about evolu-tion contained in the insert contradicts the findings in the text? Do you want the most regressive tax system in the United States, where the prevalent phi-losophy is those who earn least should pay the highest percentage of their income in taxes and those who make the most should pay the smallest percentage?"

And there are not many college professors—tenured or not—who would so scathingly document the shortcomings of the chairman of his university board of trustees and his president. ("Whether because of his obsession with football—as some critics claim—or his determination to recast . . . [Auburn] according to his own inaccurate and myopic understanding of what a land grant university ought to be [board member Bobby] Lowder has used his political influence to pack the board with trustees beholden to him." The result, Flynt suggested, was an interim president who was an "extension of Bobby Lowder's ego and political power.")[4]

To some degree, Wayne Flynt has become a spokesperson for those Alabamians frustrated with the status quo. But I think, at a deeper level, he represents the figure of "Atticus Finch" extolled in Harper Lee's *To Kill a Mockingbird.* Even as individuals have acted selfishly and in ways clearly inconsistent with their avowed moral and religious beliefs, Flynt has acted as the conscience they secretly wanted—even when they ignored his admonitions.

Finally, I think that Wayne Flynt's combination of his deep roots in Alabama and his profound religious faith makes it difficult for critics to condemn him as an outsider (a convenient weapon used against critics of the region). He is hardly one to exploit that faith; he has been quick to expose the hypocrisy and shallowness of those who use religion to engage in varieties of what he called "public pandering." As he said in February 2000 when political candidates were jockeying to see who had the "deepest experience with Jesus," he retained a skeptical eye and recalled a piece of advice he had heard when he was a ministerial student at old Howard College (now Samford University): "Be wary of preachers whose sermons never stray far from the sins of adultery and fornication. They have illicit sex on the brain." It was advice with broader implications, he concluded.[5]

At the same time, anyone who reads his public statements or his scholarship can see the many ways that his religious faith has shaped his commitments. His outstanding account of the church that has been his lifelong home (*Alabama Baptists: Southern Baptists in the Heart of Dixie*)[6] reflects the careful balance of commitment and fair-mindedness that has marked his career. Unflinchingly, he shows the petty and often small-minded ways in which his fellow Baptists have acted. As one reviewer said, this was hardly "triumphalist denominational history."[7] But his deep empathy for the struggles of his fellow Baptists allows him to transcend the smugly censorious tone that has often marked the writing of historians when discussing religious faith in the Deep South. Above all, it reflects the hallmark of an individual who has never confused his own deep beliefs with certainty about specific public policy.

When he accepted the 2002 Clarence Cason Award for Nonfiction Writing, he talked about the thing that concerned him most: the fact that most voters were simply too unconcerned to debate or even to care about the pressing issues of the state. For them, he said, the appropriate epitaph was "from the 1920s for an earlier 'Lost Generation': 'Here were busy, godless people, their only monument a thousand miles of asphalt and a hundred lost golf balls.'"

Whatever happens in the future, it can be said that Wayne Flynt challenged their quiescence every step of the way. As a consequence, his career has been a remarkable blend of academic excellence and public service.

Notes

1. (Bloomington: Indiana University Press, 1979).
2. (Tuscaloosa: University of Alabama Press, 1989).
3. "The Future of Education: Interview with J. Wayne Flynt," *Auburn Horizon*, May–June 1996.
4. *Birmingham News*, 25 January 2004.
5. Ibid., 13 February 2000.
6. (Tuscaloosa: University of Alabama Press, 1998).
7. *Alabama Review* 53 (January 2000):73.

Contributors

Susan Youngblood Ashmore teaches history at Oxford College of Emory University. She has published a number of essays, including "Continuity and Change: George Brown Tindall and the Post-Reconstruction South," in *Reading Southern History: Essays on Interpreters and Interpretations,* edited by Glenn Feldman, and is revising her dissertation, a study of the War on Poverty and its links to civil rights, for publication.

Brooks Blevins, assistant professor of history and director of regional studies at Lyon College, holds a Ph.D. in history from Auburn University. He is the author of *Hill Folks: A History of Arkansas Ozarkers and Their Image* and *Cattle in the Cotton Fields: A History of Cattle Raising in Alabama.*

Dan T. Carter is Education Foundation Professor of History at the University of South Carolina. A former president of the Southern Historical Association, his many works include *Scottsboro: A Tragedy of the American South; When the War Was Over: The Failure of Self-Reconstruction in the South;* and *The Politics of Rage: George Wallace, the Origins of the New Conservativism, and the Transformation of American Politics.*

An associate professor at the Center for Labor Education and Research at the University of Alabama–Birmingham, **Glenn Feldman** has written and edited a number of books on southern history. These include *Politics, Society, and the Klan in Alabama, 1915–1949; The Disfranchisement Myth: Poor Whites and Suffrage Restriction in Alabama;* and *Reading Southern History: Essays on Interpreters and Interpretations* (editor).

Jeff Frederick is assistant professor of history at the University of North Carolina–Pembroke. The author of numerous essays and review, he is completing a study of George Wallace's terms as governor of Alabama.

Birmingham native **Gordon E. Harvey** is L. M. McKneely Professor of Humanities and associate professor of history at the University of Louisiana at Monroe, where he also directs the graduate program in history. He is the author of *A Question of Justice: New South Governors and Educational Reform, 1968–1976* and is working to complete a biography of Florida governor Reubin Askew.

DeWayne Key is the former superintendent of the Lawrence County (Alabama) school system and an outspoken advocate for school reform.

An active scholar of southern religious history, **Andrew M. Manis** teaches at Macon State College. He is the author of *Southern Civil Religions in Conflict: Black and White Baptists and Civil Rights, 1947–1957* and *A Fire You Can't Put Out: The Civil Rights Life of Birmingham's Reverend Fred Shuttlesworth.*

John Shelton Reed is William Rand Kenan Professor of Sociology Emeritus at the University of North Carolina–Chapel Hill. One of the foremost authorities on southern culture, he is the author of many titles, including *My Tears Spoiled My Aim and Other Reflections on Southern Culture; The Enduring South: Subcultural Persistence in Mass Society;* and *1001 Things Everyone Should Know About the South* (with Dale Volberg Reed).

Richard D. Starnes is associate professor of history at Western Carolina University and senior research associate at the Mountain Heritage Center. He is the author of *Creating the Land of the Sky: Tourism and Society in Western North Carolina* and editor of *Southern Journeys: Tourism, History, and Culture in the Modern South.*

The late **Bailey Thomson,** a longtime newspaper reporter and editor, was professor of journalism at the University of Alabama. He was honored to be a part of this collection, and his essay was among the last things he wrote prior to his untimely death in the fall of 2003. His last major work was *A Century of Controversy: Constitutional Reform in Alabama* (editor).

Index

Southern Christian Leadership Conference (SCLC), 51
Southern Committee to Uphold the Constitution, 100
Southern Conference Education Fund, 145
Southern Conference for Human Welfare (SCHW), 130, 136–139, 140–145; and Alabama newspaper reaction to, 138; and Communist involvement, 131–132; and November 1938 meeting, 131–132, 138; and opposition to, 132–133, 136; and voting rights, 132
Southern Farm Bureau, 130
Southern Historical Association (SHA), 1
Southern Manifesto, 128
Southern Sociological Congress (1913), 66
Sparkman, John, 33, 141
Stennis, John, 43, 45
Student Nonviolent Coordinating Committee (SNCC), 43
Sumners, Hatton, 128

Taft, Robert H., 146–147
Talmadge, Eugene, 93, 126, 131; and Franklin Roosevelt, 99; and "Georgia Answers Roosevelt," 100; and 1940 gubernatorial campaign, 101–102; and racist resistance, 99–102
Talmadge, Herman, 44
The Great Irony (of southern politics), 134
Thomas, Jesse O., 95
Thomas, Mac, 50
Thurmond, Strom, 43, 45
Toole, Glen, 97, 106
Toon, Thomas F., 78
Torbert, C. C. "Bo," 200
Toynbee, Arnold J., 9
Truman, Harry, 33, 38, 159
Tuskegee Institute, 43, 44
Tutwiler, Julia, 179

U.S. House Un-American Activities Committee (HUAC), 132, 138, 142

U.S. Senate Labor and Public Welfare Committee, 38

Vann, David, 51
Vardaman, Claude O., 134
Voices for Alabama's Children, 1
Voting Rights Act (1965), 26, 56; and black voting registration increases, 162

Wagner-Costigan Anti-Lynching Bill, 142
Wallace, George C., 30, 37, 47, 49, 50–55, 158, 166, 181, 186–187, 190, 212; and "Wallace Freeze" on Alabama politics, 161, 171; and busing, 166; and race-baiting, 169
Wallace, Lurleen, 158, 161, 163, 187
War on Poverty, x, 27, 29, 30, 31, 34, 35, 39, 44, 48, 49, 50, 51, 52, 56; and Area Redevelopment Act (ARA), 31; and Economic Opportunity Act, 26–65; and Manpower Development Training Act (MDTA), 31, 44; and Office of Economic Opportunity, (OEO), 27, 30, 45, 47, 48
Ward, George B., 137
Watkins, Ben, 97, 106
Watkins, Lillie Mae, 12
Watts Act (1903), 76
West, Mable Jones, 136–137, 141
White supremacy in the South, 133–134
Wilkie, Wendell, 145, 147
Wilkinson, Horace, 131
Williams, Aubrey, 135, 139–140, 143, 179, 183
Williams, Harrison, 42
Williams, Howard V., 96
Winship, Herring, 96
Woods, Charles, 168
Woodson, Carter G., 9
Woodward, C. Vann, vii, 56, 67
Wright, Son, 97

Yancey, William Lowndes, 182
Yarmolinsky, Adam, 44

Zimmerman, David, 15, 16